GROWING
Fruits & Nuts
IN THE SOUTH

GROWING *Fruits & Nuts* IN THE SOUTH

THE DEFINITIVE GUIDE

WILLIAM D. ADAMS & THOMAS R. LEROY

Photographs by William D. Adams

TAYLOR PUBLISHING COMPANY

DALLAS • TEXAS

THIS BOOK IS DEDICATED TO
OUR LOVING, PATIENT, AND SUPPORTIVE WIVES,
DEBBI ADAMS AND SANDY LEROY.

Printed on recycled paper

PUBLISHED BY
TAYLOR PUBLISHING COMPANY
1550 WEST MOCKINGBIRD LANE
DALLAS, TEXAS 75235

DESIGNED BY LURELLE CHEVERIE • ROCKPORT, MAINE

ILLUSTRATIONS BY DEBORAH J. JACKSON-JONES

LIBRARY OF CONGRESS CATALOGING-IN-PUBLICATION DATA

Adams, William D.
Growing fruits and nuts in the south : the definitive guide /
William D. Adams, Thomas R. LeRoy.
p. cm.
Includes index.
ISBN 0-87833-806-3 : $24.95
1. Fruit-culture—Southern States. 2. Nuts—Southern States.
I. Title.
SB355.A33 1992
634′.0976—dc20 92-14528
CIP

PRINTED IN THE UNITED STATES OF AMERICA

10 9 8 7 6 5 4 3 2 1

contents

FORTY-EIGHT PAGES OF PHOTOGRAPHS FOLLOW PAGE 74.

preface

This book is for the home gardener and small acreage producer who want to grow high-quality fruits and nuts. It is designed somewhat like a cookbook—homeowners and commercial producers will be able to follow it step by step to successfully produce any crop they want to grow.

Whatever the crop, we have placed a priority on the quality of the fruit or nut when describing its merits. No one can afford to plant varieties that rarely produce because they are susceptible to freezes or because they rot while being transported from the field to the roadside stand. But how many customers are going to return to a roadside stand or pick-your-own establishment that is less convenient than the grocery store if the fruit tastes no better than what has been shipped in? Not many. It's surprising that stores continue to stock some of this poor quality fruit. Surely much of it must get thrown out.

As we have endeavored to pursue these ideals, many people have helped. We are particularly indebted to the many southern fruit enthusiasts who have been testing varieties for many years and who were most willing to share their experiences. One of these enthusiasts, Dr. Leon Atlas, has planted hundreds of varieties in his own yard for his friends' enjoyment while keeping up with his busy internal medicine practice. Dr. Ethan Natelson and Dr. David Ulmer are also busy physicians who have contributed much to our knowledge of southern fruit production.

Extension fruit and pecan specialists have also been very generous with their knowledge. Dr. John Lipe, Extension Fruit Specialist in Fredericksburg, Texas, has reviewed sections of the text as has Robert (Skip) Richter, Extension Horticulture Agent in Montgomery County, Conroe, Texas. Bill Goff, Horticulturist-Pecans, Alabama Cooperative Extension Service, Auburn University, provided a great deal of information on pecans.

The late Ted Teddlie began helping the Harris County Extension Service as a Master Gardener volunteer. His enthusiasm for fruit crops led him to suggest the formation of the Gulf Coast Fruit Study Group and the development of our demonstration orchard. We sincerely appreciated the time that we had to work with Ted and know that he is missed by all who had the privilege to know him. We also want to thank Yvonne Gibbs, who has since assumed Ted's role in the Gulf Coast Fruit Study Group and is doing an excellent job.

Stephanie Gebhardt, our faithful associate at the Harris County Extension Center has been a great help. She not only takes a great interest in her work, but she also manages to keep us on track.

We would also like to thank the following for their contributions to the book:

Bill Rohde	Mrs. K.M. Anderson
Tom Collins	Dr. Loy Shreve
Dr. David Byrne	Doug Shores
Bill Isons	Ed Hiltpold
Dan Copeland	Jim Mallory
Albert Moorehead	John Panzarella
T.O. Warren	Neil Sperry

1 planning YOUR HOME orchard

The science and art of fruit culture can be an interesting and exciting hobby for almost everyone. From the apartment dweller's patio garden, with strawberry pots and dwarf fruit trees, to the expanses of a small family farm, fruits are truly for everyone.

Before starting your "orchard," whatever the size, there are a number of things you must consider. What kind of fruit do you like? What grows well in your area? How large do these plants get? What are these plants' pesticide requirements? All these questions and more should be considered before the first fruit tree goes in the ground.

Fruit trees last for years, so proper planning is essential to avoid mistakes that can be disappointing and time consuming. There is nothing worse than planting a tree and waiting five years just to find out that the tree won't bear fruit in your area. If you have already experienced this problem, Chapter 13 will show you many ways to correct such mistakes and grow new varieties without pulling up the plant and starting over.

Evaluating the Site

The first step in planning a home orchard is evaluating the site. Observe your home environment: Determine which areas are shady and which are sunny, which direction the prevailing winds blow, where the water drains, and what your soil is like.

Start by assessing your soil's drainage. Because drainage is so important to good fruit growth, it is a good idea to check your soil for internal drainage. Take a posthole digger and dig a hole 32 to 36 inches deep. This should be done when the soil is moist, but not immediately after a prolonged period of rainfall. Dry soil will not give you an accurate test. Fill the hole with water and watch to see how long it takes the water to drain. If the hole is dry in less than 6 hours the drainage is almost too good and all the fruits you grow will need irrigation. If the hole is dry in 12 to 24 hours, the soil drainage is excellent; if it is dry in 24 to 36 hours, it's considered adequate; and if it takes more than 36 hours to drain you will probably need raised beds for most of the fruits you want to grow.

Once you've assessed the internal drainage of the soil, you should have a soil test done to determine the pH (acidity or alkalinity) and the levels of available nutrients. Your local extension agent or nursery owner can help you with this. Most agricultural universities have a testing lab that will test growers' soil for a nominal fee. The information gained from a soil test can be invaluable in designing a fertilization program and in determining whether the addition of lime or sulfur is needed to adjust the soil pH.

Making a plot plan, like those used by landscapers, will help you organize your orchard. A plot plan is a scale drawing that notes the physical feature of your home site.

A good plot plan should include:

- all property lines
- foundation lines for home and other buildings
- any utility easements
- compass directions
- driveways and sidewalks
- gas lines, water lines, sewer or septic lines, and meter boxes
- overhead electrical lines
- existing tree and shrub locations
- wind directions (seasonal)
- water drainage patterns as well as low spots or areas where water stands
- sun and shade patterns
- different soil types

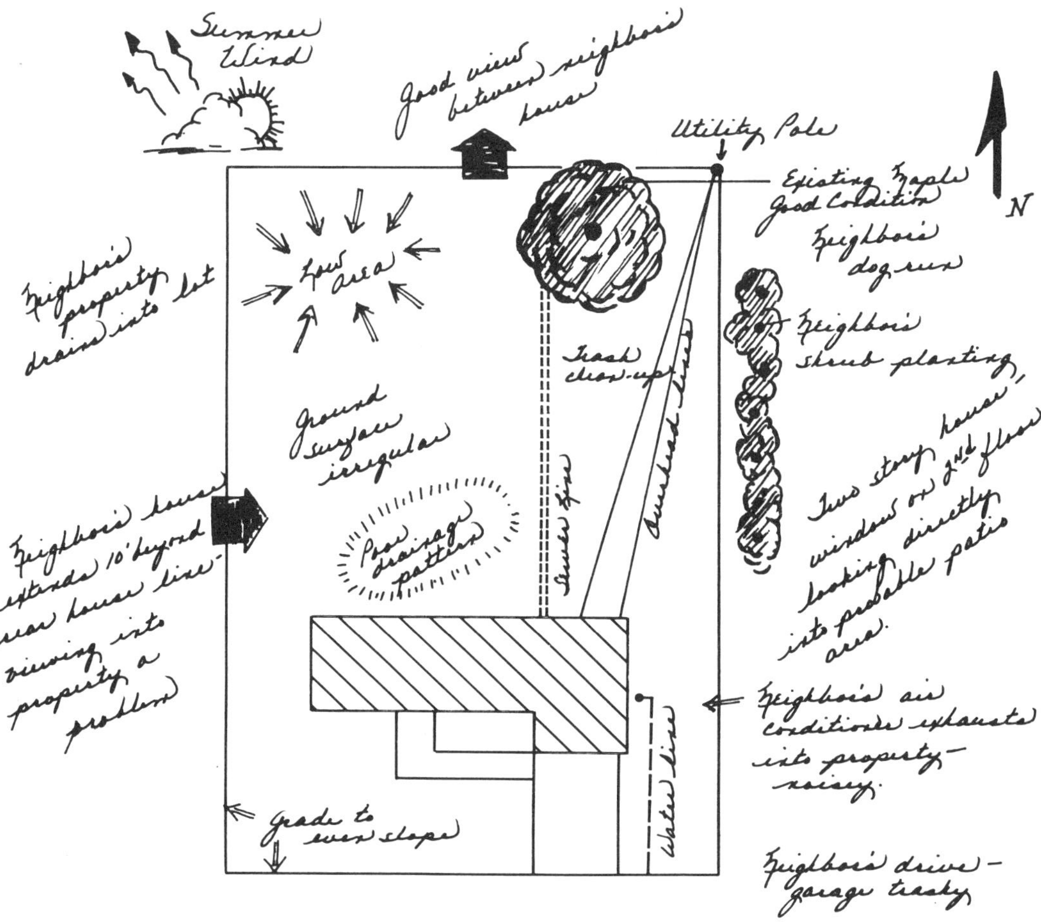

Taking the time to systematically evaluate your site will help you organize your plans for a home orchard and will eliminate the chance of costly mistakes that make gardening a chore instead of a pleasure.

Soil Preparation

I once had a knowledgeable gardener tell me it's better to put a 25-cent plant in a $2.00 hole than a $2.00 plant in a 25-cent hole. Soil is everything! Once you determine the drainage and nutrient levels (with a soil test), you're ready to make some decisions about the needs of the fruits you plan to grow.

Most fruits grow best in slightly acidic soils. Sulfur can be used to acidify an alkaline soil, and lime can be used to make acidic soil less acidic.

Sulfur Needed Per 100 Square Feet

pH CHANGE NEEDED	SANDY SOIL	LOAMY SOILS	CLAY SOILS
8.5 to 6.5	4.5 Pounds	5.5 Pounds	7.0 Pounds
8.0 to 6.5	2.5 Pounds	3.0 Pounds	4.5 Pounds
7.5 to 6.5	1 Pound	2.0 Pounds	2.25 Pounds
7.0 to 6.5	.25 Pound	.3 Pound	1.0 Pound

Lime-$CaCO_3$ Needed Per 100 Square Feet

pH CHANGE NEEDED	SANDY SOIL	LOAMY SOILS	CLAY SOILS
4.0 to 6.5	6.0 Pounds	16.0 Pounds	25 to 30 Pounds
4.5 to 6.5	5.0 Pounds	13.0 Pounds	20 to 25 Pounds
5.0 to 6.5	4.0 Pounds	10.5 Pounds	15 to 20 Pounds
5.5 to 6.5	2.75 Pounds	8.0 Pounds	12 to 15 Pounds

NOTE: DOLOMITIC LIME WITH MAGNESIUM MAY ALSO BE USED.

If it's necessary to use lime or sulfur, it should be incorporated as deeply as possible. Fall is an excellent time to apply these products because it takes time to react with the soil and elicit the needed change. (Use a finely ground product for quick reaction.) When spring growth begins, the soil's pH should be near the desired level.

If drainage is a problem, the soil can be mounded, terraces can be constructed, or in very poor soils, raised box gardens can be built and filled with a good sandy loam soil.

Fruits such as peaches, plums, nectarines, apricots, blueberries, and strawberries and nuts such as pecans require the best drainage. Use your plot plan to determine where pecans and these fruits should be planted. Generally, fruits should be planted in their native soil, aided by few improvements.

Mulching can be very beneficial. Over time, the decomposing organic matter will be worked into the soil, adding needed nutrients and keeping the soil light and fluffy. Mulch is also invaluable in controlling weeds, helping to regulate moisture levels and maintaining a more stable soil temperature. Do not pile very heavy layers of mulch around the crown or trunk of some fruits. Excessive mulch piled at the base of the plant can increase problems with crown rot due to excessive moisture. This is easily solved by raking the mulch a few inches away from the base of the tree.

Growing in Containers

There is a growing interest in container gradening. Our society is so mobile and space is often so limited that containers are an excellent option. Blueberries, strawberries, citrus, and many of the dwarf fruit trees serve as attractive accent plants, with delicious fruit, for the patio.

Select a container that is large enough to support the mature fruit tree. Use no smaller than 15-gallon containers for most dwarfing-type trees and up to 30-gallon containers for larger trees. Large drain holes are essential for good plant health.

Place a few bricks in the bottom of the container to add stability. Commercially made synthetic soil mixes containing peat, perlite, vermiculite, bark, or sand are widely available. You may mix your own soil mix, but don't use garden soil in the mix. Garden soil doesn't work well in containers and should be avoided.

Container gardening is a little different than growing fruit trees in the ground. The plants must be watered often and all year round. A slow-release fertilizer should be used each spring and a liquid fertilizer, containing minor elements, should be applied at least twice a month throughout the growing season. With a little extra care, container gardening may become your favorite way to grow some fruits.

Topography: The Lay of the Land

The topography can have a great influence on the planning of your orchard. Finding those microclimates can help you decide the best location for certain fruits.

Low spots tend to hold the cold longer. Fences and buildings help block the north wind, possibly keeping the air temperature a degree or two warmer. Sometimes this is all a plant or tree needs to survive a late frost that could destroy the crop.

Most fruit crops do best on high, open areas that have good air drainage. This allows the cold to settle in low pockets away from the trees. Crops sensitive to hard or mild freezes can be planted in courtyards and on the south side of buildings where more protection can be added when needed.

Figuring Out the Spacing

Spacing is very important when laying out an orchard. The variety of rootstocks (the root system the tree is grafted on) and training systems being used have greatly complicated the layout process. The tables below outline the standard spacings for the individual fruits. The spacing range column gives the distance rows should be planted apart (first measurement) and the distance that should be between the trees within the rows (second measurement). Closer spacings are often used in the home orchard due to space limitations. Remember close spacing will require more aggressive pruning if you expect the tree to perform properly.

Fruit/Nut	Rootstock Size	Spacing Range	Approximate Number of Trees or Plants Per Acre	Approximate Yield Per Tree or Plant	Years to Bear
Apples	Standard	18′ × 24′ to 30′ × 30′	45 to 100	1 to 4 Bushels	4 to 5 Years
	Semi-dwarf	6′ × 10′ to 12′ × 18′	200 to 726	20 to 60 Pounds	3 to 5 Years
	Dwarf	3′ × 6′ to 8′ × 12′	450 to 2400	20 to 40 Pounds	2 to 3 Years
Pears	Standard	15′ × 18′ to 25′ × 25′	70 to 160	2 to 4 Bushels	5 to 9 Years
	Semi-dwarf	10′ × 15′ to 12′ × 18′	450 to 726	1 to 2 Bushels	3 to 5 Years

Fruit/Nut	Rootstock Size	Spacing Range	Approximate Number of Trees or Plants Per Acre	Approximate Yield Per Tree or Plant	Years to Bear
	Dwarf	6′ × 6′ to 8′ × 12′	450 to 1200	1 to 1½ Bushels	3 to 5 Years
Peaches	Standard	12′ × 18′ to 24′ × 24′	80 to 200	2 to 4 Bushels	2 to 4 Years
Nectarines	Standard	12′ × 18′ to 24′ × 24′	80 to 200	1 to 3 Bushels	2 to 4 Years
Apricots	Standard	12′ × 18′ to 24′ × 24′	80 to 200	1 to 2 Bushels	3 to 5 Years
Plums	Standard	10′ × 15′ to 18′ × 24′	100 to 290	1 to 2 Bushels	3 to 5 Years
Grapes	Standard	6′ × 10′ to 8′ × 12′	450 to 726	100 Pounds	2 to 3 Years
Muscadine Grapes	N/A	15′ × 10′ to 20′ × 12′	180 to 726	20 to 50 Pounds	3 to 5 Years
Blueberries	N/A	5′ × 10′ to 8′ × 15′	450 to 726	8 to 15 Pounds	2 to 4 Years
Blackberries	N/A	3′ × 6′ to 4′ × 12′	900 to 2400	1 to 2½ Gallons	2 Years
Raspberries	N/A	2′ × 6′ to 4′ × 12′	900 to 3600	1 Quart to 2 Gallons	2 Years
Strawberries	N/A	1′ × 1′ to 1½′ × 1½′	N/A 40,000	1 Pint to 1 Quart	6 Months to 1 Year
Figs	N/A	8′ × 15′ to 12′ × 20′	180 to 360	1 to 5 Gallons	2 to 3 Years
Sour Cherries	Standard	12′ × 18′ to 30′ × 30′	45 to 200	500 to 100 Pounds	4 to 5 Years
Citrus	Standard	6′ × 10′ to 12′ × 18′	200 to 726	50 to 100 Pounds	3 to 5 Years
Persimmons	Standard	10′ × 15′ to 24′ × 24′	80 to 726	1 to 4 Bushels	2 to 4 Years
Pecans	Standard	35′ × 35′ to 50′ × 50′	17 to 36	200 to 400 Pounds	5 to 9 Years

Number of Trees Needed Per Acre When Planted at These Spacing Intervals

SPACE (IN FEET) BETWEEN TREES WITHIN ROWS	SPACE (IN FEET) BETWEEN ROWS												
	6	8	10	12	14	16	18	20	24	28	30	35	50
3	2420	1815	1452	1210									
4	1815	1361	1089	907									
6	1218	907	727	605									
8	907	680	544	453	358	339	302	272					
10	726	544	435	363	311	272	242	218					
12	605	453	362	302	259	226	201	181					
14			311	259	222	194	172	155	129	111	103		
16			272	226	194	169	151	136	113	97	90		
18				201	172	151	134	121	100	86	80		
20				181	155	136	121	108	90	77	72	62	
24						113	100	90	75	64	60	52	
28								77	64	55	51	44	
30								72	60	51	48	42	29
35										44	42	36	25
50												25	17

Pest Control

In order to grow certain fruits successfully in the South, you must use pesticides. Gardeners who wish to go strictly organic should select only those fruits that require little or no spraying, or whose pests are readily controlled by organic means and products. Pears, figs, feijoas, jujubes, blueberries, citrus, brambles, strawberries, and persimmons will grow successfully with a minimum of sprays. Peaches, nectarines, apricots, plums, grapes, pecans, and apples all require numerous applications of fungicides and an occasional use of insecticide. Consider this when planting these fruits and make sure spray drift is not going to affect your neighbors' vegetable gardens or children's play areas. Pesticides are a valuable tool if used safely and responsibly. Keep pesticide needs in mind while you are in the planning process.

Fruits Easily Grown Organically

Fruit	Comments
Figs	Use heavy mulch to keep the roots healthy. The only problems you'll encounter are birds and varmints.

Fruit	Comments
Blackberries	A natural for the southeastern United States. Petal blight and stink bugs can be a problem some years.
Blueberries	Where soil pH is right and water quality good, blueberries will thrive.
Asian Persimmons	No major problems with disease or insects. Birds and possums can be devastating.
Pears	Select fire blight-resistant varieties and this crop is easy to grow.
Feijoa (pineapple guava)	An excellent landscape shrub in the lower South. It may get damaged by freeze in the upper South.
Jujubes (Chinese date)	Very easy to grow with little or no care.

Creating an Orchard Design

Many fruits work well as ornamentals in a landscape. Blueberries, some peaches and plums, strawberries, and persimmons are among those that work well as ornamentals. Raspberries need a little protection from the west sun, so select a site such as

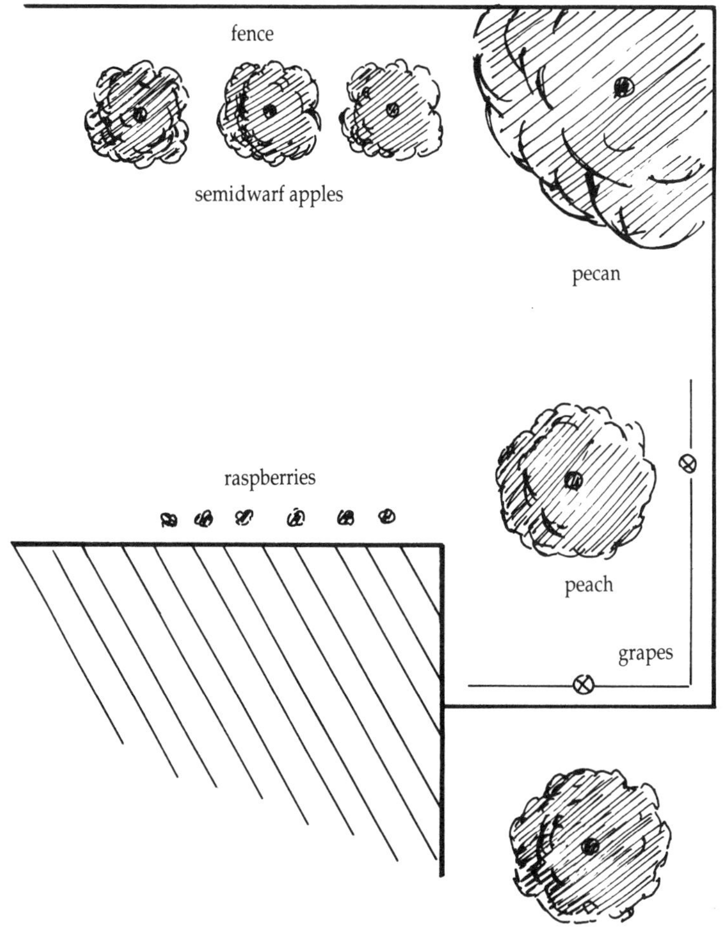

Sample orchard layout.

the eastern wall of a building, a fence, or a tree line. Strawberries make an excellent ground cover for sunny beds. Many of the tree fruits make excellent specimen plants, which add interest and variety to the landscape.

When laying out an orchard, reserve your best soil for planting peaches, plums, nectarines, apricots, and pecans. Group similar fruits together to improve pollination. Rows make irrigation, spraying, and weed control easier. Spacing is important; plants that are planted too close together will be more difficult to spray, prune, and work around. Excess shading can reduce yields or even stop production altogether.

Selecting Varieties

Variety selection is probably second in importance to soil selection. The varieties you select should be given considerable thought because they will be with you for a long time.

There are several things to consider when selecting a fruit variety. Quality should be high on your list. Next you should consider adaptability, yield, and disease resistance. There are a number of very high-quality fruits that just don't yield enough to make growing them worthwhile.

Pollination requirements are also important. Peaches, nectarines, apricots, strawberries, blackberries, raspberries, and citrus are all self-fruitful. Most other fruit will produce better if planted with one or two other varieties that bloom at the same time. Keep this in mind when laying out your orchard.

Rootstocks are also important and are used for several reasons. In the case of pears, apples, and citrus, they are used to help dwarf the trees. Other benefits like disease or insect resistance and increased adaptability to certain climates or soils can be achieved by using rootstocks.

When purchasing a fruit tree, try to choose a nice vigorous medium-sized plant. Very large trees are difficult to establish and often don't survive the shock of transplanting. Small plants can indicate a problem; there is a reason when a plant doesn't reach its full potential. It could indicate a root problem, a poor graft union, or a possible disease problem.

Irrigation

Regardless of your location, you will be required to irrigate your orchard from time to time. Whether you install a permanent drip irrigation system is not important as long as you're prepared to water when needed. Most fruits require the equivalent of at least 1 inch of rainfall each week and 2 inches during the hottest time of the year. This is especially important during the fruit development stages.

A drip irrigation system is easy to build and very inexpensive. The trees you grow will do much better if they are watered regularly.

Planting

There are two main ways to purchase fruit trees. Container-grown (plants grown and well rooted in a pot) and bare-rooted (plants dug and shipped without soil on the roots) fruit trees are readily available from local nurseries and mail-order sources. Most people prefer bare-rooted trees because they are less expensive, easy to plant, and grow vigorously. Bare-rooted trees should only be planted during their dormant season. Container-grown trees can be planted any time. But be aware that the root systems of container-grown trees can be girdled by the container. The root girdling can cause serious problems in the mature fruit tree.

Where possible, till or disk the soil several times prior to planting. Work on raising the bed, if necessary, months before planting to allow the soil a chance to settle.

Bare-rooted trees should be soaked in water for 2 to 6 hours before planting. It is critical that the roots be kept moist until the tree is planted; only a few minutes of exposure to the dry winter wind can kill the small feeder roots. All bare-rooted fruit trees should be pruned at planting time. (See individual fruits for specific pruning information.)

A hole should be dug in the location where the tree is to be planted. In heavy soils, score the sides of the hole with a shovel to prevent a slick, clay potlike hole from resulting and causing circling roots. It should be just large enough to accommodate the roots without crowding. Any very long or broken roots should be trimmed at this time. The hole should not be too deep. Place the tree in the prepared hole to see how it fits. The tree should be placed so that it is even with or just above the previous soil line. Fill the hole with the native soil. Rake the soil up around the tree, covering the roots up to the original soil line on the trunk. A water well can be built a foot or so away from the tree to hold water while the tree is becoming established. While you are filling the hole, water occasionally to wash the soil in and around the roots. Plant tabs (compressed fertilizer tablets) can be placed in the soil at planting time to provide the newly planted tree with a little nutrition while it is establishing itself. You may also use a root stimulator. Once the plant has been planted, a good layer of mulch will finish the job.

Many gardeners loosely wrap the lower 12 inches of the trunk with aluminum foil to help protect it from sunscald, rabbits, and rodents, to prevent suckering, and to shield the trunk from herbicide sprays. Check the foil periodically to make sure it's not wrapped too tightly around the trunk.

Weed Control

It is very important that you maintain a weed-free zone around young fruit trees. Weeds compete with a tree's ability to absorb nutrients and water, which can reduce the tree's rate of growth. Using mulch is an excellent way to control weeds around your fruits. Lightly tilling or hoeing weeds will work as well as careful use of herbicides.

The careful use of herbicides and mulches is better than tilling or mowing. The use of such equipment can damage the thin bark on the trunk and the shallow feeder roots. Glyphosate and surflan are commonly used on weeds around nonbearing trees. **Whenever using chemicals, read all label directions before applying.**

Environmental Influence on Fruit Culture

Water plays a significant role in climate regulation—a fact that is widely apparent in the southern states. The warm gulf water tends to moderate the temperatures along the coast. As you travel away from the coast, you'll see a dramatic change in rainfall, temperature (winter and summer), and humidity.

This diverse environment is indicated by the variety of fruits that are grown across the Southeast. Fruit crops range from tropicals such as oranges, grapefruit, avocados, and guava (which are grown in the deep South) to many temperate fruits such as cherries and northern apple varieties (which are grown in Arkansas, Tennessee, and North Carolina). Before selecting the fruit to grow in the southeastern United States, it is important for a fruit grower to understand his or her environment and its influence on fruit growth and development.

SPRING FREEZE

Spring comes quickly in the South. We move from cold to warm temperatures and back again to cold temperatures with little notice. This up-and-down spring weather plays havoc with fruits. Spring freezes can catch fruits in full bloom, destroying an entire crop in a matter of hours.

ROW COVERS

There is a newcomer to the gardening field, called the floating row cover, that can be a valuable tool in preventing late-season freezes. The row cover, which is made of a tightly woven gauze, helps to modify the temperature by trapping heat. This helps to accelerate the bloom, increase the yield, and hasten harvest. The trapped heat can give as much as 2 to 3 degrees of frost protection. By wetting the row cover just as it freezes, you can get a few more degrees of protection.

Row covers can be used on any fruit when it is practical to cover the crop. It is especially valuable on small crops like strawberries, brambles, and dwarf fruits.

OVERHEAD SPRINKLERS

Overhead sprinklers can also be a useful tool in protecting a vulnerable crop from an unexpected freeze. Sprinklers should be turned on before the temperature falls below the freezing point (around 34°F). Keeping the water running until the ice has melted will keep a mix of ice and water, holding the developing flowers or fruit at 32°F. This is usually just above the temperature that will cause damage.

Sprinklers will only work when a short, unexpected freeze occurs. Prolonged periods of freezing temperatures will result in excessive ice buildup, causing limbs and trellises to break.

CHEMICAL SPRAYS

Researchers have found a class of bacteria that nucleates ice crystals. This means the bacteria actually encourages the formation of ice crystals on the plant. Once the freeze damage occurs, the bacteria can then attack the damaged tissue.

Frostguard and a number of other chemicals are being tested and used to inhibit the development of these ice-nucleating bacteria. When combined with other frost control measures, these chemicals appear to reduce frost damage.

VARIETIES

Where late spring freezes are a common occurrence, late-blooming varieties should be selected. You should also avoid varieties that bloom very early. Selecting the proper varieties for your particular environment can be one of the most important decisions you make in planning a home orchard.

SUMMER HEAT

Spring quickly turns to summer and with it comes hot days and warm nights. The southern summer can stress your fruit trees. When temperatures rise into the mid-90s, many plant functions slow to a standstill.

It is important to keep trees well watered during the heat of summer, especially during the fruiting season, to keep the trees in good health. A healthy tree consistently produces more high-quality fruit, and has fewer disease and insect problems.

In the South, fruit ripens earlier than in the northern United States. Because of this, many fruits are ripening during the extreme heat of late summer and early fall. This can affect quality, color, and storage life. For example, red apples require cool night temperatures in order to develop good red color. In the South, these fruits ripen from July through September, when night temperatures are less than cool. This is the reason many southern apples are barely red.

WINTER CHILLING

Winter weather is still the most potentially limiting factor in fruit growth. The United States Department of Agriculture and Rutgers University publish plant hardiness zone maps, which are based on the average lowest temperatures any given area is likely to have. These maps help us determine which fruits will tolerate the lowest temperatures of the season (see page 75).

The low temperature of the year is important, but the chilling is the key. Temperate fruit have what is called a chilling requirement. This is the number of hours of chilling (temperatures between 32° and 45°F) needed to develop flower and leaf buds.

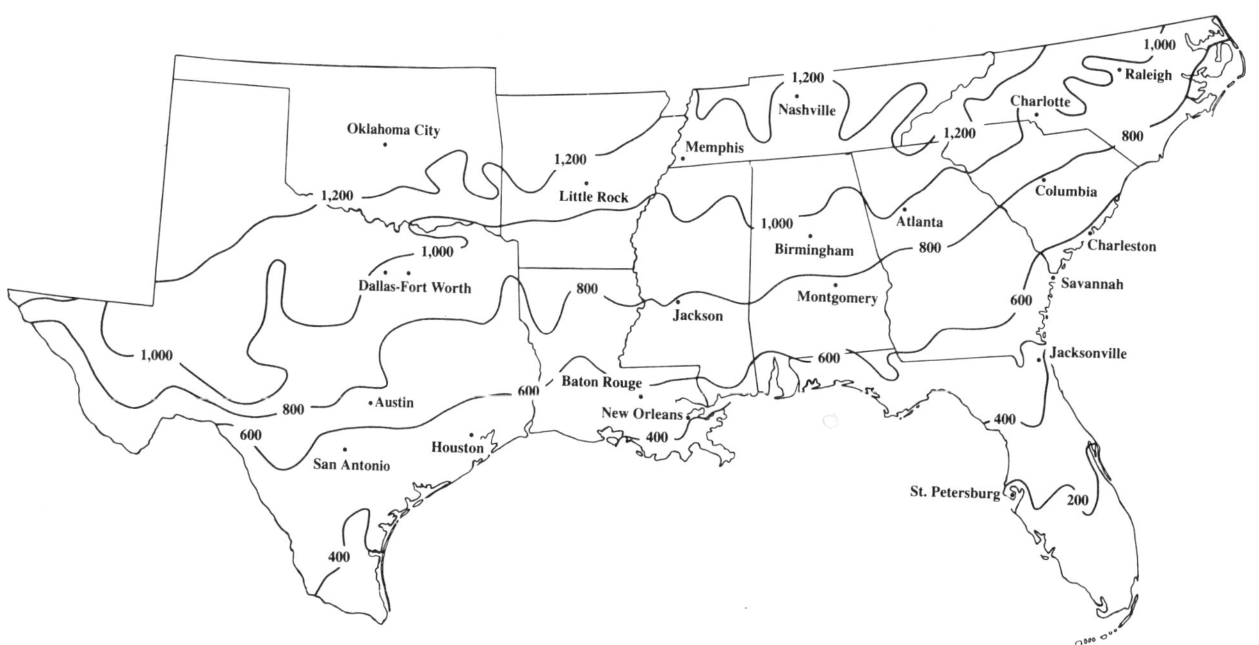

Approximate chilling hours for the southeastern United States.

When the tree becomes dormant the buds are present, but not prepared to grow. The chilling is required to give the buds time to complete their development so that they are ready to grow when the weather warms in the spring.

Trees have an internal gauge that turns on development when the temperature is in the range of 32° to 45°F. When the temperature is out of this range, the gauge shuts down development. It may even reverse development, if the temperature gets too warm.

Different areas of the South receive different amounts of chilling hours (see map). Try to select fruit varieties that have a chilling requirement within 100 hours plus or minus those your area receives. This means if your region receives 700 hours of chilling each year, select trees that need between 600 and 800 hours. Varieties requiring 300 to 400 hours will bloom too early and freeze, and varieties requiring 900 to 1000 hours may only bloom every 5 to 6 years when the winter is very cold. Always keep the chilling requirements in mind when selecting fruits to cultivate.

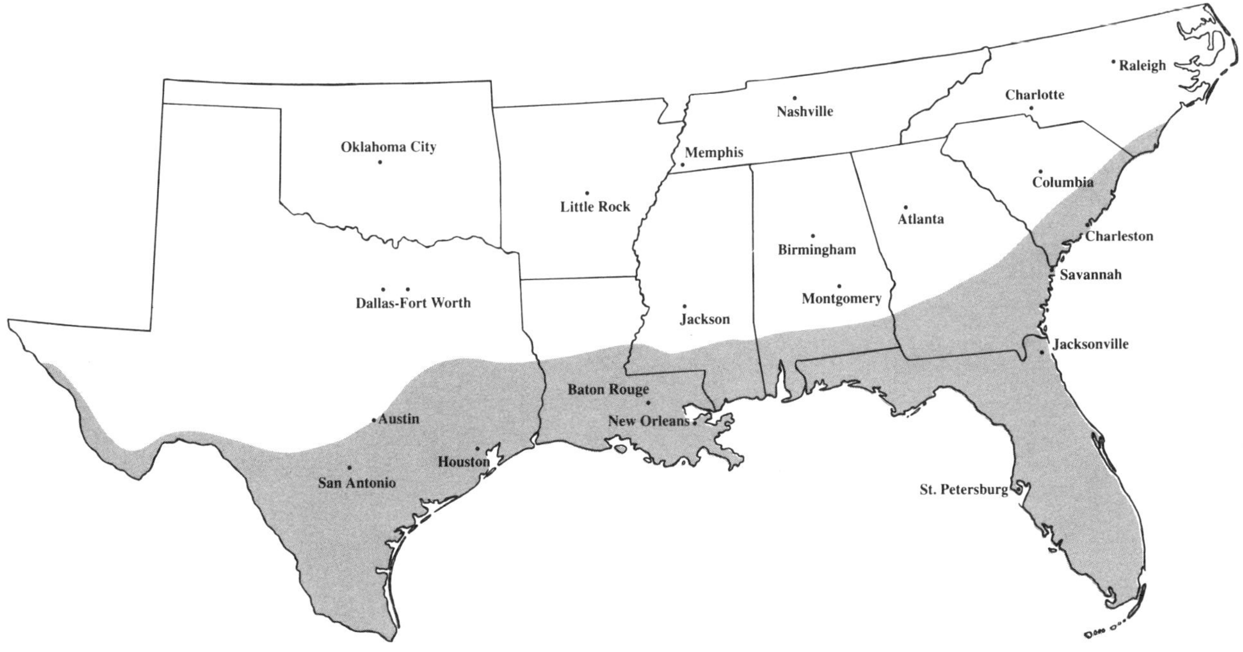

APPROXIMATE UPPER AND LOWER PLANTING ZONES FOR THE SOUTH.

Water and Rainfall

Water, or rainfall, is one of the few environmental factors we can control. Because water is essential for good tree health and growth, and because most fruits will benefit from a minimum of 1 inch of rain per week and 2 inches during the hottest months, it's a good idea to monitor your watering. One way to monitor watering, which takes into account temperature, humidity, and wind, is to place a shallow pan in the orchard. Fill it with water and mark the starting level. Cover it with a wire screen to prevent birds and pets from altering the results. When the water drops 1.5 inches, it's time to irrigate. Rainfall will also be recorded and will help replace the water that evaporates.

Modern fruit growers are using moisture meters called tensiometers to monitor soil moisture. This device can even be rigged to turn on the water when the soil moisture reaches a certain level.

Humidity and rainfall also affect fruit disease. The total climate of an environment determines which diseases and insects will be a problem and how often control measures will be needed. One of the major problems affecting the southern fruit grower is disease. The abundance of rain and high humidity contribute to the disease pressure.

Keep the environment in mind when selecting fruit varieties and types. We, as gardeners, try to control as many factors as possible to ensure our success. The environment is the most difficult to control. Maybe this is what makes the challenge of fruit culture the most interesting and, sometimes, the most frustrating.

Pruning

Pruning is one of those chores that scares almost everyone. But you don't have to be afraid of pruning. Learn the general principles of pruning for each of the fruits you grow, then just get out and do it. Remember that next season the tree will most likely correct any mistake you make this season.

It is important to understand the basic principles of pruning:

1. Prune to remove dead and diseased wood.
2. Prune to correct structural problems and to create strong scaffold branches.
3. Prune to open up the tree and allow light to reach the leaves, buds, and fruit.
4. Prune to remove undesirable, improperly placed branches.
5. Prune to maintain tree size and shape.

A properly pruned tree should bear fruit evenly. An unpruned or improperly pruned tree will produce on the outer branches and branch tips only.

Each of the following chapters reviews the pruning method used for that particular fruit. A number of terms that you may be unfamiliar with will be used in these chapters. Reviewing the following definitions will increase your understanding of pruning techniques:

ALTERNATE BEARING—a characteristic that some trees have that causes them to bear a heavy crop one year, followed by a light crop the next. Alternate bearing is usually caused by poor management or plant stress.

ANGLE CUT—when cutting limbs and branches, cut the ends at a slight angle and just above a bud.

APICAL DOMINANCE—the terminal or apical bud displays a dominance over the buds just below it. Removal of this bud breaks the dominance and allows the other buds to develop.

BRANCH COLLAR—there is a collar at the point where a branch attaches to the trunk, a ring of rapidly growing tissue that helps the wound heal fast when a branch is removed. The collar should be left when removing branches.

BUD—a cluster of protective scales that encase the embryonic leaves, shoots, and flower parts.

CORDON—means rope or cord and refers to a tree or vine being trained with a main trunk and lateral branches. The cordons are trained horizontally or vertically from these laterals.

CROTCH—the angle where branches fork or where limbs join the trunk. The ideal crotch angle is 45° to 60°. Narrow crotch angles are weak because bark becomes trapped in the crotch and prevents a strong union from forming.

CROWFEET—the development of 3 or more narrow-angled shoots, arising from the same point. Pruning is used to discourage this condition.

DORMANT—the period during the year when the plant is not actively growing.

ESPALIER—training a tree, shrub, or vine to grow on a single plane. Commonly done on walls, fences, and trellises and often shaped in a decorative design.

FORCING—pruning to cause a branch bud or shoot to grow in a particular way or direction.

FRUIT THINNING—the deliberate removal of fruit to increase size and quality of remaining fruit and to reduce the chance of alternate bearing.

GRAPE SPUR—not a natural spur like apples and pears. Short one-year-old twigs that bear fruiting canes created during the pruning process.

Hanger—a drooping branch or a branch growing toward the ground on a tree that normally doesn't have a weeping habit.
Heading back—cutting back a vigorous branch by one-third or more to reduce height and encourage lateral branching. Results in crowfeet regrowth.
Internode—area located between 2 nodes or buds.
Lateral bud—these buds are located below the terminal bud.
Leader—a dominant branch or trunk. Strong central leader has 1 leader; open center has 3 or 4 leaders.
Leggy—thin, weak shoot growth where buds are too far apart. Legginess is frequently caused by excessive shading and overfertilization.
Multiple leader—more than one main trunk competing for dominance. Multiple leaders should be discouraged by removing weaker leaders or by propping them out, using spreaders, to form branches.
Node—location on a twig or branch where a bud arises.
New wood—the growth that has occurred since the last dormant season. New wood is smoother, has lighter bark, and lacks side growth.
Pinching—nipping the tip out of a tender new shoot, usually done to slow growth and increase bushiness.
Scaffold—a main limb usually arising from the trunk. Scaffolds are usually permanent or semipermanent, being retained for several years or even the life of the tree.
Spreaders—any device that spreads developing branches to wider angles. Spreaders may be made of anything from a 1 × 1 with nails in it to specially constructed plastic V-shaped devices.
Suckers—vigorous shoots arising from the main trunk usually below the graft union.
Stubs—a short limb left after pruning. Stubs should be removed to the branch collar because they tend to rot and attract borers.
Terminal bud—the bud located at the end of a shoot or branch. It usually develops into the strongest shoot.
Thinning—selective removal of entire branches back to where they join another branch to open up the tree, allowing more light into the center.
Tip pruning—pruning out the growing point to stimulate branching or slow growth. Tipping done during the growing season slows growth. When done during the dormant season, it stimulates growth. Tipping just as growth begins encourages branching.
Topping—uniformly trimming a tree so it is at the same height all the way around. Topping is commonly done on peaches, plums, nectarines, and apricots to maintain a tree's given height.
Water sprouts—very vigorous upright shoots arising from dormant buds on older branches. Water sprouts can usually be removed when they are first noticed.

SANITATION

Many disease problems can easily be transmitted from tree to tree during pruning. **Always** soak or wash your tools with a 20% solution of chlorine bleach (1 part bleach to 4 parts water) after pruning each tree. I like to take two sets of pruning tools out to the orchard—that way one set can be soaking while the other set is being used. Bleach is extremely corrosive so always lubricate your tools when you are finished pruning. Rubbing alcohol, although more expensive, is less corrosive and may also be used to sanitize pruning tools.

All limbs and trimmings should be removed and disposed or shredded and composted. Many diseases grow on old dead wood.

2 apples

The apple probably originated somewhere in southern Asia or southern Russia and has been cultivated for over two thousand years. Early colonists brought the apple to the Americas and successive waves of European colonists took the fruit westward. Johnny Appleseed (John Chapman) was the most notable of these apple lovers.

Many of us have a bit of Johnny Appleseed in us—even though the odds are probably one in ten thousand that our seedling fruit will be as good as existing varieties, it's a chance that many gardeners take. In spite of breeding programs sponsored by universities and private organizations, many popular varieties originated as chance seedlings. In the case of apples, these include Delicious, Golden Delicious, Dorsett Golden, and Granny Smith.

Varieties are divided into those for the lower South that require relatively limited chilling temperatures below 45°F and those for the upper South. Very often there will be an overlap—varieties recommended for the lower South will grow in colder regions, but some years they will break dormancy early after an unseasonably warm spring only to have the flower buds freeze during a late spring freeze. Conversely, higher chilling varieties may produce very well some years after a cold winter in the lower South, but most years they will be very slow to break dormancy in the spring and they will not grow with vigor.

Many apple varieties have originated through bud mutations. These varieties are often very similar to the original variety, but may vary in skin color or in the tendency to form fruiting spurs early in their development. The latter varieties are termed "spur type" trees and are named appropriately: Spur Winter Banana, Greenspur, Granny Smith, and so on. In most cases the fruit characteristics of "spur type" trees are identical to those of the original cultivar.

There are so many local varieties planted from seed throughout the South that it is impossible to mention them all. Most are virtually unavailable in the nursery trade. If they prove worthy, they may be propagated eventually, but in the meantime they languish in obscurity with names like Chandler, Hartwell Cook, Bo Griffen, and Mary's Seedling.

Other varieties are of such poor quality or produce so poorly that they are gradually being dismissed. These include Elah, Slor, Slomit, Einshiemer, Beverly Hills, and Gordon.

Soils and Fertility

Apples tolerate a wide range of soils if certain conditions are met. When selecting a site to plant an orchard, choose the best possible soil. Unfortunately, home orchardists don't usually have many choices when picking the location for orchards.

Apples should ideally be grown in a rich, fertile, loamy soil with good internal drainage. The optimum pH for apples is between 6.0 and 6.5. This will allow for extensive root development, strong vigorous growth, and optimum production.

Apples, however, can grow in a variety of locations; most good garden soils will be adequate. Apples will tolerate soil pHs from 5.5 to 8.5. On alkaline soil (pH 7.0 to 8.5), apples should not be planted where cotton root rot has been a problem.

They can be grown in sands or clays with equal success as long as the drainage is good. During the winter months, while the trees are dormant, apple trees can tolerate a little water around the roots. But once growth begins in the spring, wet soils can lead to root rot, poor tree vigor, and even death. The rootstock used with any given variety can affect the tree's tolerance to certain soil. For example, M 7 and MM 106 rootstock adapt well to a wide variety of soils, MM 111 and M 9 don't do well in light sandy soils, and M 26 won't tolerate wet soils.

Those who have low, poorly drained locations should consider changing to raised beds. A 64-square-foot box 8 to 12 inches tall, made from used railroad ties or landscape timbers is adequate for most semidwarf to standard-sized apples. A 16-square-foot bed should be adequate for most dwarf varieties.

Even in many of the high rainfall areas along the coast you will need to irrigate during short periods of drought, so always locate trees near water. Apples perform well on drip or sprinkler irrigation and sprinklers can be used for freeze protection during the early spring season.

Soil fertility will play a major role in fruit production. A soil analysis can be obtained from your cooperative extension service for a nominal fee. This analysis will provide you with invaluable information needed to develop a fertility program for your trees. Most southern soils contain adequate amounts of phosphorus and potassium, but need to have nitrogen added on a regular basis. If your soil analysis shows a deficiency of phosphorus or potash, then a balance fertilizer can be used in the early spring.

Apples should be fertilized rather aggressively during the early years. Monthly applications of a high nitrogen fertilizer from March through June will aid in growth and promote earlier fruiting. Use only one fertilizer for each application and place it around the tree at the branch dripline.

Amount of Fertilizer Applied Monthly from March through June

FERTILIZER	YEAR			
	1	2	3	4
Ammonium Nitrate	⅛ Cup	¼ Cup	½ Cup	1 to 2 Cups*
Ammonium Sulfate	⅛ Cup	¼ Cup	½ Cup	1 to 2 Cups*
13-13-13	½ Cup	1 Cup	2 Cups	2 to 4 Cups*
Cottonseed Meal	2 Pounds	4 Pounds	8 Pounds	10 to 20 Pounds*
Blood Meal	½ Cup	1 Pound	2 Pounds	4 to 6 Pounds*
Fish Meal	1 Pound	2 Pounds	4 Pounds	8 to 10 Pounds*
Sewage Sludge (Sterilized)	5 Pounds	10 Pounds	15 Pounds	20 Pounds*
Urea Formaldehyde (Slow Release)	¼ Cup	½ Cup	1 Cup	1 to 2 Cups

*Amount applied per inch of trunk diameter in March and May only.

Fruit Thinning

Well-cared-for apple trees will set more fruit than they are capable of supporting. Excess fruit production can cause stunting, limb breakage, and alternate bearing (bearing fruit every other year). In order to produce high-quality, large, well-shaped fruit every year, thinning should be done when the danger of late freezes has passed and the apples are about the size of marbles.

Fruit can be thinned by hand or chemically. Hand thinning involves removing all but one fruit per cluster, preferably leaving the center or "king" blossom, so that the clusters are spaced 4 to 6 inches apart along the limbs. Care should be taken not to damage the spurs and short branches that support the fruit and flower buds.

The insecticide carbaryl (Sevin) is a photo inhibitor (inhibits photosynthesis) and does an effective job of thinning apples. Care should be used to ensure the proper results. Carbaryl should be applied no later than 30 days after flowering at the recommended rates on the label. Carbaryl should not be used on apples within 30 to 45 days of flowering if hand thinning is to be done.

Tree Training Systems

For years apple tree training has been rather straightforward and apple growers throughout the United States have used only a few simple systems. Recently the development of such systems as the Tatura trellis and many others has stimulated the imagination of creative inventors the world over.

There are several principles that must be followed to optimize flower development, light penetration, and fruit coloring. In much of the deep South, light levels can be limiting, and too many layers of leaves can actually reduce production. Heavily shaded leaves still respire and use photosynthates produced by other leaves. For this reason, many systems will need modification to promote maximum yields in your area. Shade from landscape trees and buildings may also have an effect on the system you use.

Scaffold branches should be trained to grow at 45° to 65° angles from horizontal because this encourages early fruiting. Keep the distance between scaffolds wide enough to afford good light penetration, aeration, and even spray coverage. The area between scaffolds should always be kept open. Crossing and vertical branches should be removed.

Winter pruning stimulates regrowth and is often used to develop a strong framework for freestanding trees. Summer pruning, on the other hand, tends to reduce vigor, and if done too heavily or early in a tree's life may even cause increased stunting. Summer pruning can be a valuable tool in managing dwarf and semidwarf trees but should not be done during the establishment years.

TRAINING FREESTANDING TREES

Freestanding trees are trained to a modified central leader system. This system is used for standard trees on seedling rootstock and vigorous well-anchored clonal rootstocks like MM 106, MM 111, or Mark (Mark requires staking when young).

The modified central leader system is commonly used on a wide variety of fruits and nuts. The principles of training are basically the same regardless of the tree.

Traditionally, we have conducted major pruning chores on apples and pears during the dormant season. This type of pruning encourages the development of a few very vigorous upright shoots. The strong upright growth is difficult to train and slower to come into production. Research conducted in Oregon suggests that delayed heading will devigorate the tree slightly while encouraging the development of a strong upright growth and numerous horizontal branches. This is the kind of strong growth pattern to strive for.

The young bareroot tree is planted in the proper location during the dormant season. As soon as the terminal bud begins to swell (greentip stage), the young whip should be headed back to 32 to 36 inches. All side branches (feathers) should be removed.

A number of upright shoots will develop from near the top of the trunk. When these shoots are 4 to 6 inches long, select the strongest shoot to become the central leader, the others should be cut back to 1-inch long stubs. By cutting back those upright shoots instead of removing them, more shoots with wider branch angles will develop below them to form the scaffold branches. Try to select 3 to 5 evenly spaced branches and remove the rest.

As the growth begins next spring, you should conduct your second year's delayed heading. The central leader is cut back to 24 to 30 inches above the highest scaffold branch. The scaffold branches should be cut back to about 18 inches. Continue to conduct this delayed pruning at the greentip stage until the tree has developed 3 to 5 tiers of branches on a strong main trunk (central leader).

The modified central leader system has a strong main trunk with scaffold branches radiating from it and evenly spaced up the length of the trunk. The scaffolds will need training using spreaders or weights tied to branches, pulling them down and out to an angle of between 45° and 65°. Once the main framework of the tree is established, the only pruning required will be removing excessive internal branches, vertical shoots, and suckers. Remember your objectives are to keep some space between scaffolds to allow light and air to get to the interior of the tree. When light doesn't reach a part of a tree, the fruit development stops in that area. If fruit production becomes limited to the outer fringes of the tree, additional pruning is required to allow more light to penetrate and restimulate interior growth and fruiting.

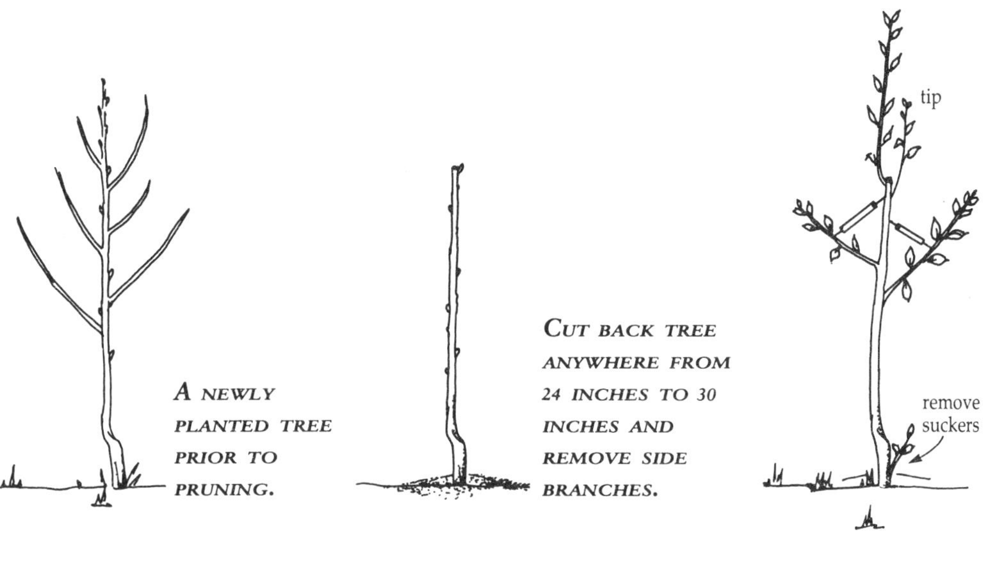

A newly planted tree prior to pruning.

Cut back tree anywhere from 24 inches to 30 inches and remove side branches.

During the growing season, select 4 to 6 well-spaced scaffold limbs and begin spreading them.

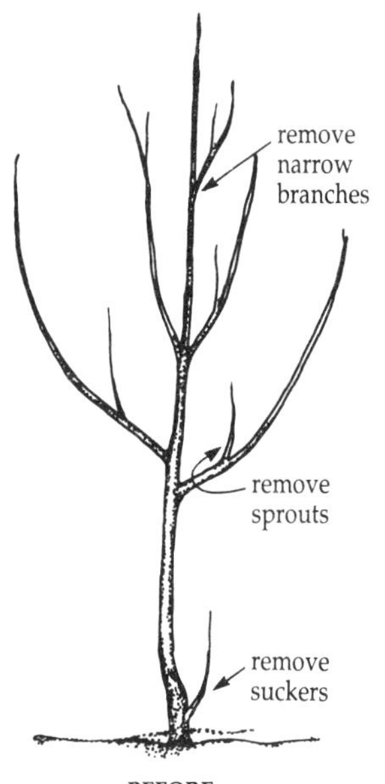

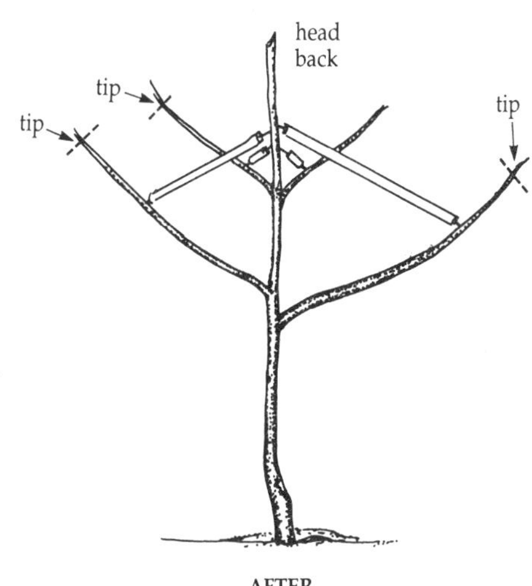

Vertical shoots and suckers should be removed, selected scaffolds should be tipped, and the main trunk should be headed back one-third. Spreaders should be inserted to increase branch angles.

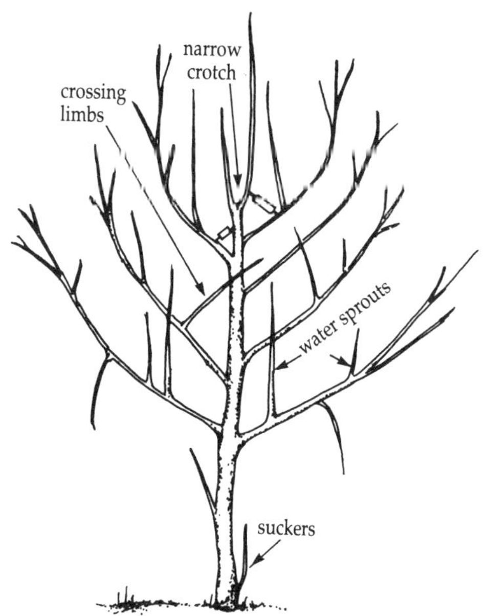

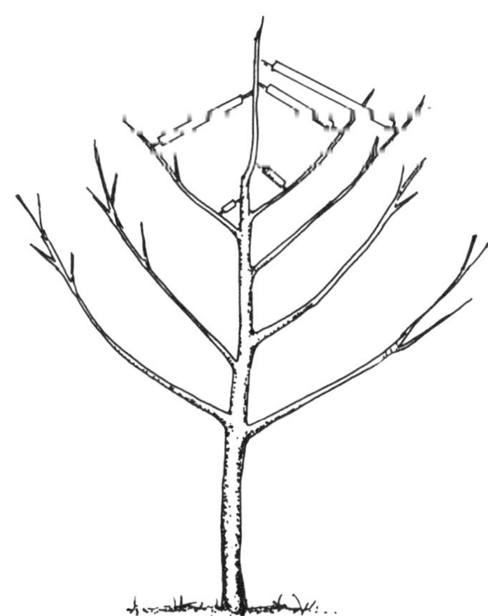

LEFT • REMOVE SUCKERS AND WATER SPROUTS (VIGOROUS UPRIGHT SHOOTS); OPEN UP BRANCHES. REMOVE NARROW BRANCH ANGLES, CONTINUE PROPPING OUT SCAFFOLDS, HEAD BACK THE TERMINAL ONE-THIRD, AND TIP SCAFFOLDS. DON'T ALLOW FRUIT TO DEVELOP ALONG THE MAIN TRUNK UNTIL THE TREE IS FOUR TO FIVE YEARS OLD. RIGHT • CONTINUE THE PRUNING AND TRAINING PROCESS UNTIL THE TREE IS TOO LARGE TO HEAD BACK THE TERMINAL.

TIPS FOR PRUNING A MATURE TREE

- Avoid excess pruning—when heavy pruning is needed, do it over a 2- to 3-year period.
- Light is critical to flower bud development—keep the trees full, but open and spreading.
- Heading back branches should only be done when necessary, but a few should be done each year.
- Try to maintain the tree at a manageable height.
- Always remove suckers and water sprouts.
- Try to maintain a cone-shaped tree, or a tree that is wide at the base and narrow at the top.
- Scoring and undercutting branches can be used to reduce vigor and to promote fruiting.

VERTICAL TRELLIS

Apple growers around the world are using numerous variations of vertical trellises. The trees are trained a variety of ways, but the trellis structure is basically the same. Vertical posts are spaced out along the row; posts vary in height from 5 to 12 feet with wires that are spaced 18 to 24 inches apart, depending on the exact system being used. The narrow wall of branches allows for good light and spray penetration and the posts and wires help support the heavy fruit loads these systems produce.

VERTICAL TRELLIS KNIFFEN TRAINING SYSTEM

The Kniffen System uses a 6-foot trellis with 3 wires that are spaced 24 inches apart.

The main trunk is trained to grow straight up to the top of the trellis and 6 branches are trained to grow down the wire. These 6 scaffolds support the spurs and short branches that carry the fruit. Trees are planted 4 to 8 feet apart and M9, Mark, M26, and M7 rootstocks are commonly used with this system.

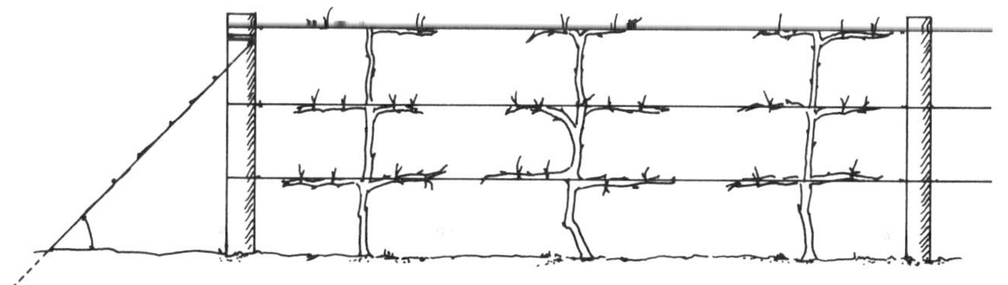

Mature trees trained with the Kniffen training system.

VERTICAL TRELLIS
PALMATE OR FAN SYSTEM

The Palmate or Fan system is very similar to the Kniffen training system. Instead of selecting 6 horizontal branches, select 4 to 8 branches and angle them in a fan or palm shape. The branches are attached to the wires with ties to help support the fruit and to assist in orienting the branches correctly. This system lends itself to ultrahigh density plantings of 1,000 trees or more per acre.

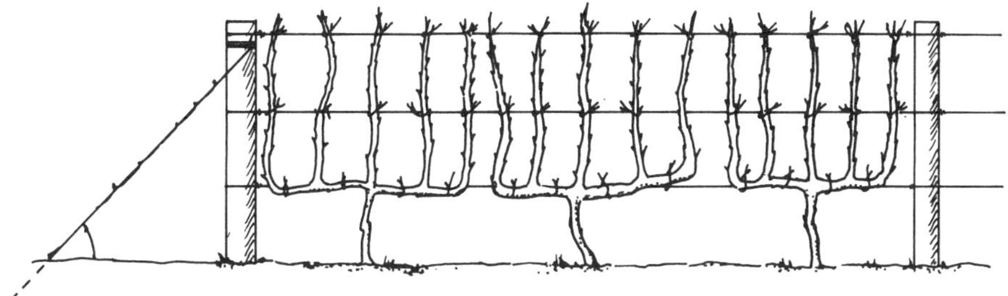

The Palmette, or fan, pruning system. This system is recommended for close tree spacing.

SLENDER SPINDLE

The Slender Spindle training system utilizes a 3-wire trellis or stalks to support the dwarf trees grown on M9, Mark, or M26 rootstocks.

At planting time, the tree should be pruned back to a height of 32 to 40 inches. If horizontal side branches (feathers) exist, prune them up to 12 to 15 inches above the highest branch that will be kept. Do not tip or head back the side branches.

During the growing season, spread the branches horizontally using weights, strings, or clothespins. Remove any vigorous upright shoots.

The trees will require dormant-season pruning each year. Strong vertical shoots should be removed. Do not tip the leader or side branches. Remove the leader by cutting into 2-year-old wood to a weak upright growing branch. This will become the new leader, giving the trunk a zigzag appearance. Tie the new trunk to the wire or stake.

This same procedure should be continued until the tree reaches its ultimate height of 7 to 8 feet, at which time the leader should be cut back to become a weak lateral branch.

The trees should be cone shaped. As the tree matures, maintain the conical shape by shortening limbs by cutting back to a side branch or by stub cutting (cutting back a branch 1 to 2 inches to produce a short weak shoot). Remember to keep the tree opened up by removing vertical limbs and thinning limbs as needed.

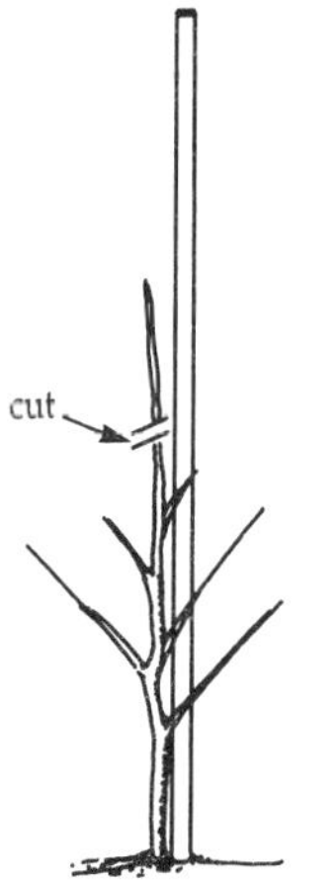

Cut back tree 12 inches above the last branch at planting, or to 30 inches to 36 inches if tree is not branched. Do not head back side branches.

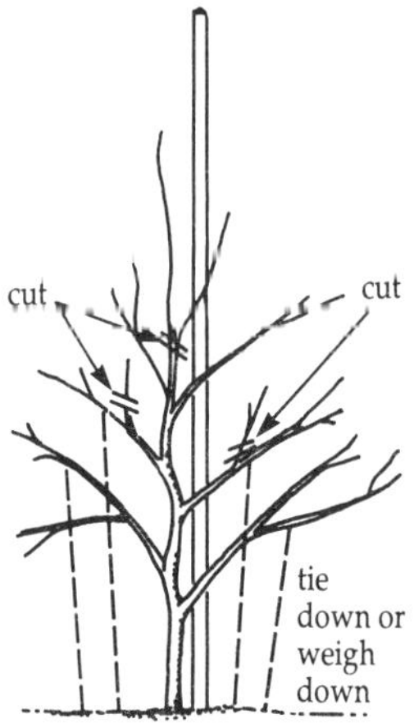

During the first dormant season, tie down the horizontal branches. Remove the strong leader to second-year wood at weak vertical branch. Do not head back branch.

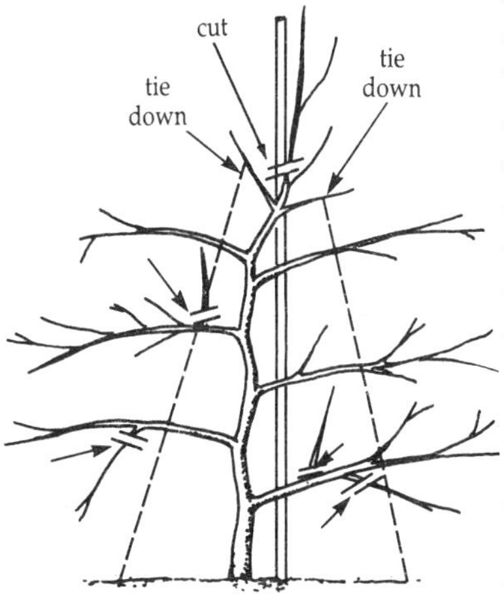

During the second and third dormant seasons, tie down the horizontal branches. Remove the leader to second-year wood at a weak vertical branch. Do not head back branches.

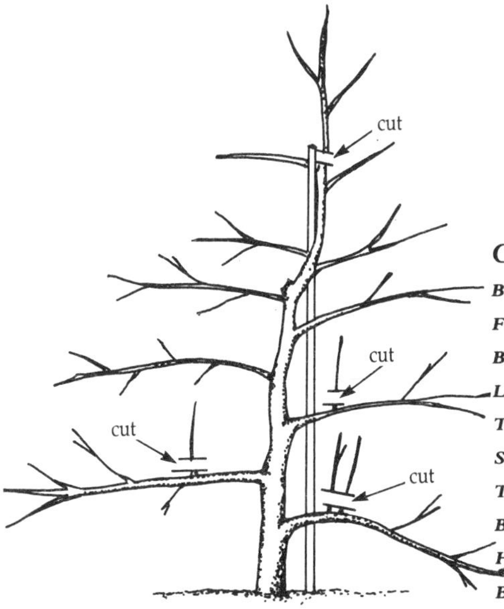

Cut back branches when fruit weight bends them too low, leaving the renewal stub. Cut terminal back to weak horizontal branches.

VERTICAL AXIS

Young trees should be planted along a wire trellis or staked for support. When planting, remove all side branches (feathers), but *do not* head the central leader. During the growing season, remove all vertical growing branches before they make 6 inches of growth, leaving a 1- to 2-inch stub. These stubs will be left to form weak horizontal branches. The central leader should be tied to the trellis or support poles

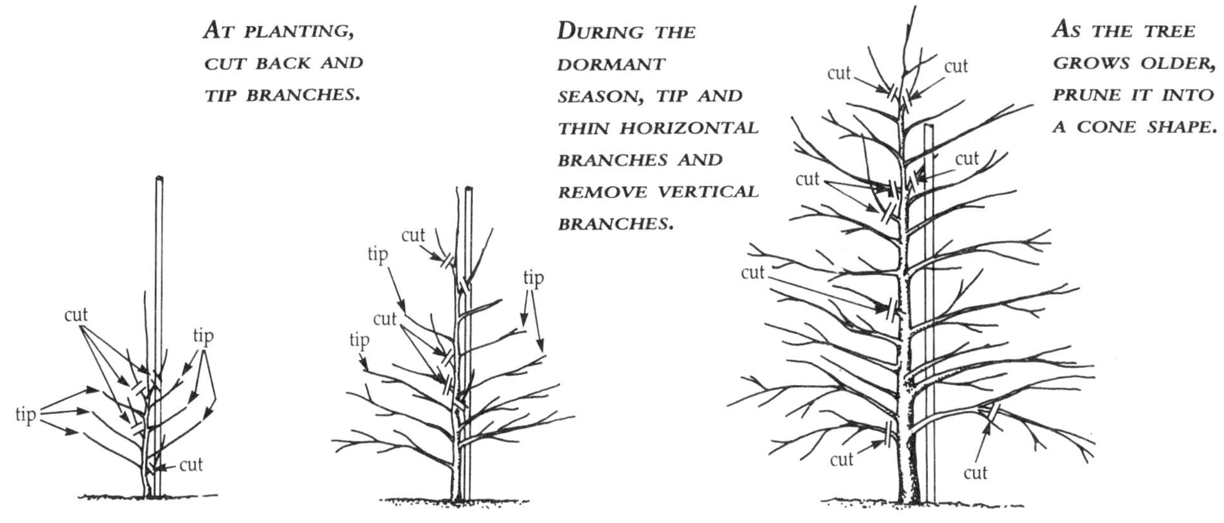

At planting, cut back and tip branches.

During the dormant season, tip and thin horizontal branches and remove vertical branches.

As the tree grows older, prune it into a cone shape.

as needed. Dormant-season pruning should consist of thinning horizontal branches, leaving 4 inches between branches, and removing vertical branches.

The practice of stub pruning and thinning should be continued until the tree reaches the height of the trellis or support. Remember: At no time during the training process should the central leader be cut back, tipped, or pruned.

As the tree begins to bear, the vigor of the leader will decrease. Once the tree grows above the support, the leader will droop from the weight of the fruit. As the tree ages, maintain a cone shape and remove low hanging branches, leaving short renewal stubs.

Y-TRELLIS

The Y-trellis is a smaller, less complicated version of the Tatura trellis. It utilizes high tree density, early-producing dwarf rootstocks that need minimal early pruning, and high light interception and distribution.

The trellis consists of a frame built of landscape timbers and 2×4s. The landscape timbers are sunk 2 feet in the ground 40 to 50 feet apart. Two 6.5-foot supports are attached to the posts at a 60° angle from horizontal. A horizontal crosspiece is used to give strength to the V-shaped structure. Three pairs of wires are connected to the structure at 20 to 40 inches and 60 inches above the base of the V.

The apple trees should be planted 4 to 8 feet apart (depending on rootstocks) and pruned back to 24 to 30 inches. As growth begins, select 8 to 10 shoots and spread them using clothespins or weights when the branches are 2 to 3 inches long. The object is to select 4 to 5 evenly spaced branches for each side of the trellis, creating wide crotch angles.

Over the next 3 to 4 years, the branches should be trained in a fan shape, evenly spaced and attached to the wire support with tie tape or trellis clips. The scaffolds should not be tipped or headed back until they reach the top of the trellis support.

Once the tree reaches 8 to 10 years of age, the renewal process begins. Each year an upright vigorous shoot is selected to replace one of the scaffolds. This process leads to the complete replacement of scaffolds every 8 to 10 years.

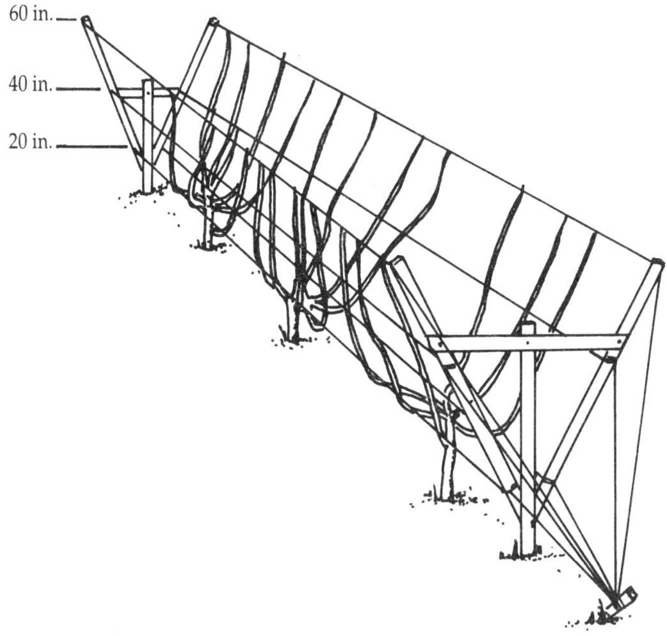

Y-TRELLIS SYSTEM.

Summer pruning is required each year to maximize fruit color. This consists of removing upright shoots, thinning weak branches, and keeping the center of the Y-trellis open.

The Y-trellis is a new system that shows real promise for producing high-quality apples on small acreage.

LINCOLN CANOPY

The Lincoln Canopy was developed in New Zealand at Lincoln College. It was one of the first attempts to train apple trees for mechanical harvest. The single layer of branches allows the apples to hang below the trellis where the fruit can be shaken off the tree without hitting branches or wires before falling onto a canvas collection tarp. One of the most interesting aspects of this single-plane system is the unusually even fruit maturity. The disadvantage of using the Lincoln Canopy is poor coloring in red apple varieties, which is caused by heavy shading and excess vertical shoot growth. This training system should use dwarfing rootstocks like M9, M7, or Mark.

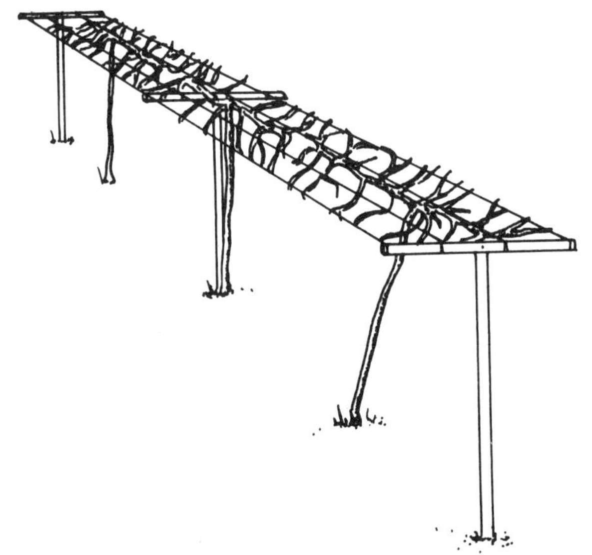

Lincoln Canopy system.

KEARNEYSVILLE DOUBLE T

The Kearneysville Double T is a modification of the Lincoln Canopy. The lower canopy is planted in a green or yellow variety and the upper canopy is planted in a red variety. M9 rootstock is used on the lower canopy and M7 and Mark are used on the upper canopy. This system doubles the planting area and increases blossom pollination, resulting in yields about 30% higher than those produced by the Lincoln Canopy.

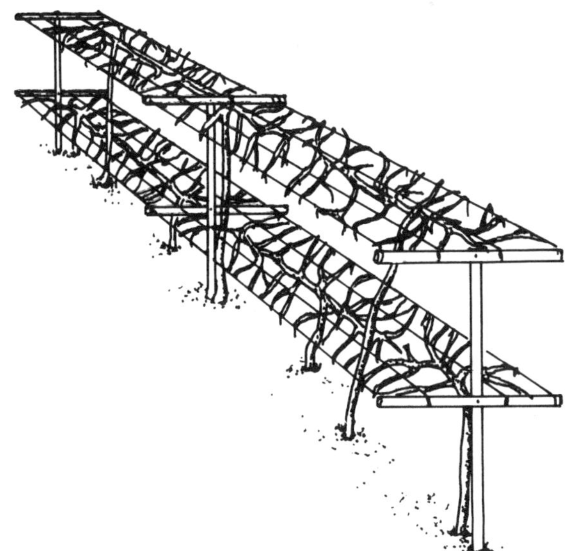

Kearneysville Double-T system.

VERTICAL TRELLIS

FRENCH MARCHARDT SYSTEM

The French Marchardt system, sometimes known as the Belgian Cordon, supports the tree's main trunk at a 45° angle. Short side branches are trained at a 90° angle to the trunk to form a narrow latticework of branches. Dwarf rootstocks such as M9, M7, and Mark are used. The training of the main trunk to a 45° angle provides for the optimum balance of fruiting and vegetative growth. This system lends itself to ultrahigh density plantings of 1,200 to as many as 2,400 trees per acre.

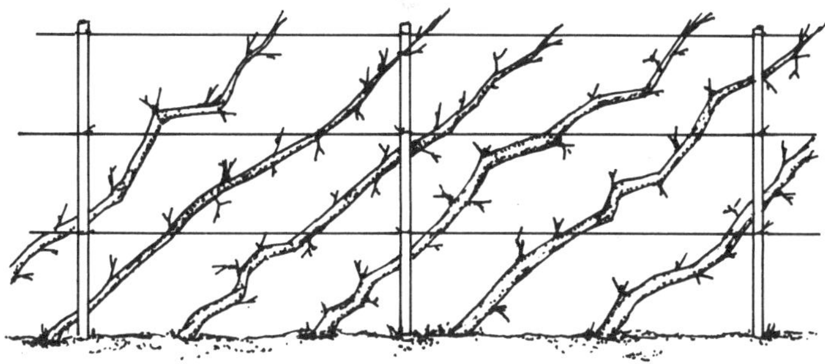

Belgian Cordon or French Marchardt system.

SMITH TREE WALL

Stanley Smith from South Africa developed a system using a semidwarf rootstock such as M7, MM 106, or MM 111 that eliminates the need for expensive trellises. The Smith Tree Wall produces a 9- to 15-foot wall of interlocking branches capable of supporting heavy fruit loads at an early age. Each tree has 3 to 15 leaders arranged in fan shape and interlocking with the adjacent tree.

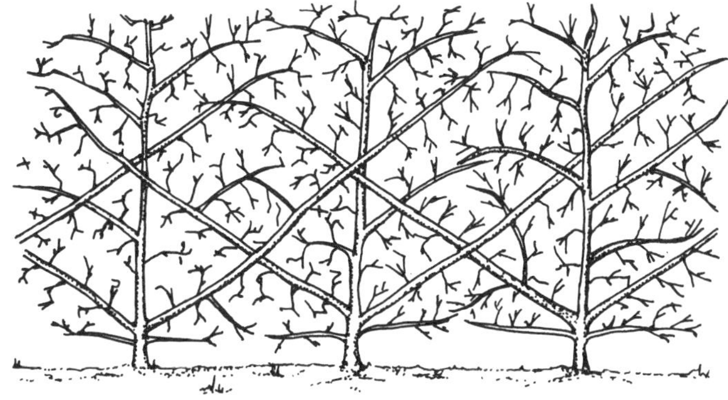

Side view of Stanley Smith tree wall.

EBRO-ESPALIER

The Ebro-Espalier patented system, developed by Roger Evans in New Zealand, has 4 layers of branches on either side of the specially designed supports. MM 111

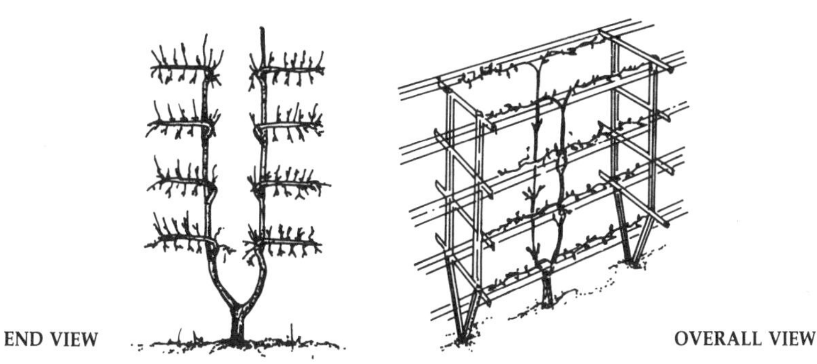

The Ebro-Espalier system is a complex system of frames and wires.

rootstock is being used with this system in trial orchards in Washington. This system, however, may not allow enough light to reach the lower layers of the fruit for good color to develop. This system may be especially problematic for southern gardeners because the light intensity is lower along the Gulf Coast than in Australia or New Zealand.

Factors to consider when designing a high-density apple orchard:

1. The maximum tree height should not exceed the distance between the rows.
2. Avoid excess pruning until the support is covered. Stunting can occur.
3. Build trellises to support heavy loads. Many growers are surprised to find their trellises knocked down by excessive production and strong winds.
4. Trellis systems have the potential for unbelievable yields. But, in order to be successful, the intensive labor requirements must be met.

Apple Varieties for the Lower South

Variety	Chilling Requirement	Ripe/Color	Comments
Adina	500 to 600	early summer pale red, striped	Vigorous tree, but fruit is only of average quality and production is low.
Anna	100 to 300	late spring yellow-red blush	Developed from Yellow Delicious. Probably the best choice for southern gardeners to date. Quality is excellent within a narrow window of 2 to 3 weeks. When picked too early it is sour and lacks flavor, picked too late and its texture is mealy. When grown in the upper South, Anna may bloom in January and lose its crop in a freeze every year. Self-pollinated fruit may develop an elongated shape.
Brogden	500 to 600	mid-summer red	Fruit has a hint of anise flavor.
Calville Blanc d'Hiver	600 to 700	early fall yellow with red splotches and irregular ribs	Introduced in the sixteenth century, high-quality fruit with aromatic, perfumelike, and complex flavors. Has a reputation for limited production.
Cox's Orange Pippin	600 to 700	late summer red stripes over pale orange	One of the world's great dessert apples. Blooms late and may require more chilling than it usually receives in the lower South. Poor producer.
Dorsett Golden	100 to 200	late spring yellow	Like Anna, it is at its prime for only a few weeks. Slightly sweeter than Anna, it is also about the only variety that will bloom at the same time. Either variety will produce some fruit without cross-pollination, but production will be increased if both varieties are planted. This is another

Variety	Chilling Requirement	Ripe/Color	Comments
			very low-chilling variety that will often suffer frost damage in the upper South.
Early Dawn	500 to 600	late summer yellow, blushed red	Medium-sized, aromatic fruit. Vigorously growing tree.
Ein Shemer	400 to 500	mid-summer yellow, slight blush	Golden Delicious parentage, like Anna and Dorsett Golden, but inferior quality—more tart than sweet.
Fuji	400 to 600	early fall Yellow-green with pale red stripes, Red Fuji is more highly colored. It may be of lesser quality.	In spite of its poor appearance, this is one of the finest quality apples in the world. As a result, it is being widely planted and consumers quickly empty the shelves once they've tried it. The tree requires detailed pruning. Fruit harvested before full ripeness is mediocre.
Golden Delicious	700 to 800	late summer yellow, often russeted	Parent of many low-chilling apple varieties. Often planted in the lower South with good success, except along the Gulf Coast.
Granny Smith	600 to 800	early fall waxy green	Marginal along the Gulf Coast, but generally adapted in the lower South. Widely planted and a heavy producer. Good quality tart, sweet fruit. Late maturity makes disease control difficult.
Irazu	500 to 600	mid-summer green	Average quality, limited planting to date.
Michal	400 to 500	mid-summer red	Average quality. Israeli variety.
Mollie's Delicious	700 to 800	mid-summer red	Excellent quality but slow to break dormancy in the lower South. Also susceptible to bacterial fireblight.
Mutsu or Crispin	600 to 700	late summer greenish yellow	Crunchy texture with anise-like, spicy flavor. Very delicious and juicy: Excellent fresh-eating quality. Unfortunately, not very productive for most growers. Susceptible to Brook's spot. Pollen sterile—will not pollinate other varieties.
Reverend Morgan	700 to 800	late summer green with pink blush	Granny Smith seedling with good-quality fruit.
Tropical Beauty	500 to 600	fall dull red over green	Sweet and crisp, but not strongly flavored. Late maturity for a low-chill apple.

Variety	Chilling Requirement	Ripe/Color	Comments
Winter Banana	300 to 400	fall pale yellow, pink blush	Poor-quality fruit but outstanding as a pollinator. Also used as an interstem with M9 apple rootstock because it is compatible with pears—results in a dwarf pear on a productive rootstock.

Apple Varieties for the Mid- to Upper South

Variety	Chilling Requirement	Ripe/Color	Comments
Akane	800	early summer bright red	Crisp, juicy variety developed in Japan. May be slow to bear and foliage has a tendency to develop chlorosis.
Arkansas Black	800 to 900	fall dark, almost black-red	Beautiful Winesap-type fruit. Crisp, firm, and tart. Tree is large and vigorous with a tendency to produce poorly though the spur type produces more abundantly.
Ashmead's Kernel	800 to 1,000	late fall greenish yellow russet	Not a pretty apple, but one of the most superb in flavor. Yellowish flesh is crisp, aromatic, and juicy. Very highly rated in taste tests. Large, vigorous tree.
Black Twig	1,000	fall yellowish green with red flush	Tart, yellow-fleshed apple with firm texture. Good for fresh eating, cider, or cooking, and has good keeping qualities.
Blairmont	800 to 1,000	mid-summer red striped	Similar to Winesap, but larger and the tree is more heat tolerant.
Braeburn	800 to 1,000	fall orange-red over yellow	New variety from New Zealand growing in popularity. Early bearing, but the tree is low in vigor. Excellent fruit is tart, sweet, and crisp.
Criterion	800 to 1,000	late summer yellowish with pink blush	Mild and sweet with Golden Delicious character.
Delicious, Red (Starkrimson)	800 to 1,000	late summer red (typically striped)	Good quality, typical Red Delicious type. Comparatively low chilling. One of the best for the upper South. Often has better quality fruit compared to similar varieties grown in the Northwest.
Elstar (Lustre Elstar)	700 to 900	fall yellow with red stripes	Excellent quality apple from Holland. Creamy white flesh, sweet-tart flavor.
Early Harvest	800 to 1,000	late summer yellow with slight orange blush	Cooking apple that is acceptable for fresh consumption when ripe.
Fuji			See low-chilling variety description.

Variety	Chilling Requirement	Ripe/Color	Comments
Gala	800 to 1,000	early to mid-summer to fall gold with red stripes	Superb apple, somewhat small and poorly colored. Excellent fruity flavor. Extensive commercial plantings. Several cultivars have been selected. Production is excellent though fire blight is a problem.
Golden Delicious		late summer yellow, some russet	See low-chilling variety description. Prime Gold has done well in the upper South.
Golden Russet	1,000+	fall greenish bronze russet	Excellent apple. Crisp, sugary, and tart. Like all russet varieties, it has little "eye appeal."
Granny Smith			See low-chilling variety description.
Gravenstein	700 to 800	early summer yellow with red stripes	Good cooking apple. Popular in California. Needs frequent picking.
Grime's Golden	1,000+	late summer golden yellow	Good-quality apple reported to be the parent of Yellow (Golden) Delicious.
Jerseymac	1,000+	early summer primarily red over yellow	Probably the earliest quality apple for this region. Crisp, sweet McIntosh-type apple good for cooking or fresh use. The best McIntosh variety for warm areas.
Jonagold	800 to 1,000	late summer red stripes over yellow	High-quality triploid variety; requires a pollinator (usually a third variety will be needed to pollinate the pollinator—a common problem with triploids). Widely planted in Europe, the fruit is crisp and richly flavored. Summer heat may take this variety out in most areas of even the upper South.
Jonalicious	1,000+	fall red with slight yellow undertones	Like Jonagold, this variety is a cross between Golden Delicious and Jonathan. It is another good-quality cooking and fresh-eating apple.
Jonathan	800 to 1,000	late summer yellow washed with red	Great cooking and cider apple. Fair quality for fresh use. Tart flavor.
Liberty	800 to 1,000	late summer red striped	Small apple, but has good flavor and tolerates heat.
Limbertwig	800 to 1,000	late fall greenish yellow with red blush	Hard-fleshed apple prized for cider, but also good for cooking and fresh use.
Lodi	800	summer light green with a yellow blush when fully ripe	Summer cooking apple, sweet-tart flavor—good for fresh use when fully ripe. Very productive but susceptible to fire blight.

Variety	Chilling Requirement	Ripe/Color	Comments
McIntosh	1,000+	mid- to late summer red to dark red with yellow undertones	Old variety with many sports, and it has been used to produce a number of hybrids. Good for cooking and, if not stored too long, crisp, tart and sweet for fresh use. Often withers away in areas with high summer temperatures.
Mollie's Delicious	700 to 800	late summer to early fall red	See low-chilling variety description.
Mutsu	600 to 700	late summer greenish yellow	See low-chilling variety description.
Newtown Pippin	800 to 1,000	fall greenish yellow with russeting	Primarily a cooking apple, but it is also good for cider. Its aromatic yellow flesh is considered excellent for fresh use.
Ozark Gold	800 to 1,000	midsummer yellow gold	High-quality fruit similar to Golden Delicious, but better adapted to summer heat. Beautiful color; resists russeting.
Priscilla	1,000+	late summer red blush over yellow	Crisp, sub-acid apple with good disease resistance (especially to scabbing).
Stayman Winesap	700 to 800	mid-fall yellow with red	Primarily a cooking apple; spicy, tart, and winelike. Often mealy after prolonged storage. Also suffers in high heat areas.
Vista Bella	800 to 1,000	early summer dark red	Early, good-quality fresh-eating apple.
Winter Banana			See low-chilling variety description.
Yates	800 to 1,000	late fall dark red, dotted skin	Very small fruit. Firm, tart, and juicy. Vigorous tree with heavy production—good pollinator.

Note: Exact chilling hour requirements for all of the apple varieties listed have not been determined. In some cases an estimate has been included for reference.

Apple Rootstocks

Researchers are still looking for the perfect apple rootstock. Chances are that the perfect rootstock for every grower will never be found. Some want a very small tree, and others must have disease or insect resistance tailored for their soil. Although there are many apple rootstocks to pick from, some compromise will always be necessary.

Variety	Size	Remarks
Antanovka (most seedlings)	100%	Results in a well-anchored, full-sized tree. Hardy and does not sucker.

Variety	Size	Remarks
Budagovski 9	25%	Well anchored, but fruit load requires support. Resistant to Phytophthora (collar rot), recommended as a dwarfing interstem.
Budagovski 490	75%	Possible alternative to EMLA 106. Well anchored and does not need to be staked. Some resistance to collar rot.
Budagovski 491	25%	Well anchored, but would still require support and would be susceptible to collar rot, so potential may be as an interstem. Foliage has a prominent red coloration.
EMLA 7	50%	Virus-free stock adapted to heavy soils. Trees are moderately well anchored. May be short-lived in the South. Suckers considerably.
EMLA 9	30% to 40%	Adapted to heavy soils and typically the varieties propagated on this stock bear early and bear high-quality fruit. Roots, however, are brittle and the trees must be staked. Some resistance to collar rot; also used as an interstem. Fire blight may take it out, even as an interstem in some areas.
EMLA 26	40%	Produces good-quality fruit on trees that are better anchored than on EMLA 9; however it is more susceptible to collar rot and trees still need support on most sites.
EMLA 106	60%	Well anchored, no staking required, but susceptible to collar rot. Resistant to Wooly Apple Aphid. Often recommended with a dwarfing interstem.
EMLA 111	75%	Better adapted to heavy soils and resistant to collar rot. Also used with an interstem and for spur-type varieties. One of the most promising rootstocks for the southern grower. Resistant to Wooly Apple Aphid.
MARK	40%	Strongly anchored, may be grown without support. Some resistance to collar rot and fire blight. Resistant to suckering.
OTTAWA 3	30%	Freestanding and drought-resistant but difficult to propagate. Also used as an interstem.
POLAND 2 (P2)	25%	Reportedly freestanding and resistant to collar rot; best on rich soils. May need support in some areas. Also used as an interstem. Trees go dormant early in the fall and break bud late in the spring.
POLAND 16 (P16)	30%	Nonsuckering and resistant to collar rot. Best on rich soils and does not require staking.
POLAND 18 (P18)	75%	Tolerates wet soils, resistant to collar rot and only moderately susceptible to fire blight. Good candidate for use with an interstem.
POLAND 22 (P22)	20%	Better anchored than M9 and induces early fruiting, but would still need support. Usually suggested as an interstem. May be too susceptible to fire blight.

Apple Rootstock Interstem Combinations

Variety	Size	Remarks
Budagovski 490/ EMLA 27, EMLA 9, Mark, Ottawa 3, P2, P22	50%	This series of potential combinations should be similar to the same combinations on EMLA 106. Potentially more resistance to collar rot.
EMLA 106/ as above	40%	A somewhat tried and proven combination. Collar rot susceptibility and the increased cost of producing trees on interstems are major concerns.
EMLA 111/ as above	50%	Another combination that has been used and should be more acceptable where collar rot is a potential problem.
POLAND 18/ as above	50%	Tolerant of wet soil, collar rot, and fire blight, this may well be the best rootstock for many southern fruit growers.

Rootstock Spacing

ROOTSTOCK	*BETWEEN TREES IN ROW*		*BETWEEN ROWS*		*NUMBER OF TREES PER ACRE*
	NONSPUR	*SPUR*	*NONSPUR*	*SPUR*	
seedling	18	12	22	18	nonspur 110 spur 202
Bud 9	8	not recommended	14	not recommended	nonspur 389
Bud 490	16	8	20	14	nonspur 136 spur 389
Bud 491	6-8	not recommended	12 to 14	not recommended	nonspur 605 to 389
EMLA 7	12	8	18	14	nonspur 202 spur 389
EMLA 9	8	not recommended	14	not recommended	nonspur 389
EMLA 26	10	not recommended	16	not recommended	nonspur 272
EMLA 106	16	10	20	16	nonspur 136 spur 272
EMLA 111	16	8	20	14	nonspur 136 spur 389
MARK	10	not recommended	16	not recommended	nonspur 272
OTTAWA 3	8	not recommended	14	not recommended	nonspur 389

ROOTSTOCK	BETWEEN TREES IN ROW		BETWEEN ROWS		NUMBER OF TREES PER ACRE
	NONSPUR	SPUR	NONSPUR	SPUR	
P2	8	not recommended	14	not recommended	nonspur 389
P16	8	not recommended	14	not recommended	nonspur 389
P18	16	8	20	14	nonspur 136 spur 389
P22	6	not recommended	12	not recommended	nonspur 605
EMLA 111/dwarfing interstem	10	not recommended	16	not recommended	nonspur 272

3 pears

Most gardeners think pears are an easy-to-grow fruit that are not worth investing much effort. No doubt the hard-sand pear varieties most often grown in the South have encouraged this attitude. Kieffer is the main culprit. Although it is adequate for processing (in products such as jelly and pear butter), it requires several months of storage before it approaches fresh eating quality. Garber is similar to Kieffer and even though LaConte is better, it is too susceptible to bacterial fire blight for most growers.

Pears were introduced into the United States around 1630. The European pear is noted for its quality but is also known for its susceptibility to fire blight. Asian varieties introduced later, like the sand pear (*Pyrus pyrifolia*), enjoy increased resistance but also have more grit cells. Very little effort has been invested in breeding pear varieties for the South. The University of Tennessee introduced Ayers and the University of Florida introduced Floridahome, but Ayers is slow to produce and is not adapted to the lower South, and Floridahome is extremely susceptible to fire blight. There is some hope that varieties found surviving around old farm sites may be worth growing. Almost every fruit-growing enthusiast is cultivating a few of these varieties, which have names like Oakhill, Utopia, Victoria, Golden Boy.

Asian pears, erroneously called "pear apples," are increasingly in demand. The fruit is mostly round like an apple but that's where the similarity ends. The flavor is very mild—some might say bland—and the fruit is very juicy. In fact, you need a bib to eat one. These pears are very popular with the Asian community and command a high price because they are in relatively short supply. Unfortunately, Asian pears have their problems. Most varieties have been very susceptible to bacterial fire blight and some, like 20th Century, require too much chilling to grow in the lower South. If many of these pears were planted, the market could quickly become glutted. Asian pears are definitely worth trying, but proceed with caution before planting a large acreage with them in the South.

Fire blight isn't the only pest that damages pears. The pear psylla insect transmits pear decline mycoplasma—not a problem in the South, but a threat to West Coast production. Pears in the South suffer from fungal leaf spot diseases that often defoliate trees by mid-summer, causing them to set a new crop of leaves and often causing them to bloom in the fall. Eventually this begins to reduce tree vigor and hurt spring production. Several applications of fungicide during rainy periods in the spring and summer can limit this damage.

Healthy pear trees can be extremely productive. They can be expected to produce between 15 and 25 tons of fruit per acre. The standard planting distance has been 18 feet (distance between trees within rows) × 22 feet (distance between rows), but other spacings such as 8 feet × 12 feet and 14 feet × 22 feet have been used with dwarfing rootstocks. Unfortunately there aren't many dwarf rootstocks for pears. Quince is used in some areas of the country, but it is susceptible to fire blight and productivity is often low. The Old Home X Farmingdale series (OHF) shows promise, but typically the rootstocks that dwarf trees the most are the hardest to propagate. Some haven't been very productive either. Trees are rather vigorous—it appears they will attain at least 80% of the size expected when these varieties are grafted on *Pyrus calleryana* roots. The OHF 40 rootstock does seem to promote early production and is reported to have good disease resistance.

Soils and Fertility

Pears are very tolerant of both soil condition and moisture problems. They grow and produce best in well-drained sandy loam soils. Excessively fertile soils should be avoided, because they tend to stimulate too much growth, which can lead to fire blight. Pears will grow in clay soil, light sandy soils, dry soils with a little additional irrigation, and wet soils if mounded slightly.

Fertilizing is easy when it comes to pears. Basically, the best fertilization program is no program. On all but the poorest soils, fertilizer should be withheld to keep growth to a minimum. On very poor soils, one pound of 13–13–13, or a similar complete fertilizer, can be applied to young trees in February or March. Mature trees, even in poor soils, should not be fertilized.

Pruning and Training

Young pear trees should be trained using the modified central leader system outlined in Chapter 2. Pears have an upright columnar growth habit. It is critical that you prop the branches at an angle between 45° and 60° as you train the young trees. This will encourage early production, strong branch angles, and better open-growth habits.

Summer pruning can be used to direct growth and increase the development of fruiting spurs and branches. Vigorous shoots can be tipped to slow growth and stimulate the development of side branches. Removal of water sprouts and suckers should be done as soon as they are noticed. You'll have less regrowth of these sprouts if you break them off as soon as they appear, so check your trees often.

Mature trees should be pruned as little as possible. Annual thinning of internal shoots, water sprouts, and an occasional older branch is recommended instead of a heavy top pruning.

Pears can be trained using almost any of the systems described in the chapter on apples. Remember there are not as many rootstocks available for size reduction for pears as there are for apples. As a result, training systems that require a highly dwarfed tree will be very difficult to manage. Pears can be used for an espalier, creating beautiful living fences or fancy designs on walls and fences. When espalier systems are being used, heavy production should be encouraged to reduce vigor and the need for heavy pruning that could increase fire blight problems. It is generally wise to remove young, tender growth from the trunk and basal area of major scaffolds or leaders to protect a fireblight strike from destroying a large portion of the tree.

Flowering, Pollination, and Fruit Thinning

Fruit buds or spur development on pears is similar to that on apples. A spur is a short, leafy shoot that terminates in a cluster of 5 to 7 flowers. Any given spur will generally fruit every other year for 7 or 8 years. This means that about half of the spurs are producing each year. Young pear trees will also bear fruit on both the lateral and terminal buds.

A prolonged period of dry weather can often cause a false dormancy to occur.

When fall rains and milder weather start, the trees will begin to bloom, thinking it is spring again. This summer-fall blooming can greatly reduce the size of the crop and will often force the tree into alternate bearing (bearing every other year). This can be avoided by watering during periods of prolonged drought.

Pears are, for the most part, self-sterile. This means that two or more varieties that bloom at the same time are required for good fruit development. If space is limited, a limb can be budded or grafted to a second variety to provide the needed pollen. Another way to encourage pollination would be to ask a neighbor or friend with another pear tree for a few flowering shoots that can be placed in water in a mason jar or coffee can and hung in the tree each spring.

Pear trees, like most fruit trees, tend to overproduce. While the trees are young, this tendency should be encouraged. Heavy fruit loads will help reduce vigor, weigh down limbs, and increase formation of short spurs. However, overloaded limbs should not be allowed to bend below horizontal or to break under a heavy fruit load. Also, the main trunk should not bear fruit until it's large enough to support it.

As the tree matures, the fruit should be thinned until each cluster has 1 to 2 fruit and the clusters are spaced 4 to 5 inches apart. This will help increase fruit size and quality without breaking limbs or forcing the tree into alternate bearing. Thinning should be done as soon as frost season has passed and the pears have reached the size of a quarter.

Top Working

Many gardeners already have large, established pear trees in their landscapes. These trees may be the wrong variety for the area or hard-fleshed pears with poor fruit quality. Rather than removing the tree and starting over, graft an improved variety onto the tree and you will have it in production again in 2 or 3 years. If you're really creative, you can create your own fruit basket and graft several pear varieties on 3 or 4 large limbs.

The most common techniques used to top work old pears is the cleft graft, done during the dormant season, and the bark graft, which uses dormant graft wood on an actively growing root and is usually done in April or May. See Chapter 13 for details.

Girdling for Early Production

Pears, unlike most fruit crops, can take as long as 10 to 12 years to begin producing. This delay can be shortened by pruning and training properly. Limb and trunk girdling can also be used to speed up the fruiting of large juvenile trees.

Girdling involves the removal of a thin sliver (3/16 inch) of bark on both sides of the trunk, leaving a small amount of undisturbed bark to allow transport of nutrients to the roots.

This process disrupts the flow of carbohydrates, produced in the leaves, to the roots. When these carbohydrate levels build up in the upper portion of the trees, the trees are forced into the blooming process. Girdling done during the spring and early summer will usually result in flowering the next season. Care should be taken not to girdle the tree all the way around. This process should only be done on large, nonbearing, vigorously growing trees.

Variety	Chilling Requirement	Ripe/Color	Remarks
Baldwin	200	October light green with russet	Old variety with some resistance to fire blight. Fair to good quality.
Comice	600 to 800	September greenish yellow with red blush and some russet	Too susceptible to fire blight for most areas of the South, but high quality and worth trying on a limited basis.
Garber	200	August green with some russeting	Good fire blight resistance and overall vigor, but the fruit quality is only fair—roundish in shape and hard with grit cells; best for processing.
Golden Boy	150	August yellow	Old homestead variety found in northern Florida near Newport, Florida and propagated by the Just Fruits nursery in Crawfordville, Florida. Fruit is typically pear-shaped, soft, sweet, juicy, and has a small neck. The tree is resistant to fire blight.
Hood	150 or less	August yellow-green	Very low chilling variety used to pollinate other low-chilling types, but only of fair quality. Fruit tends to be brown and soft in the center.
June Sugar	400 to 600	June yellow-green, some russeting	Small pear with good fresh-eating quality.
Kieffer	300 to 400	September/October yellow rough skin with some blush	Large, coarse pear used mainly for canning because of its hardness and grit cells. May be stored for several months and eaten fresh (in desperation). Slight musty flavor, which adds character to pear butter and other foods. Tolerates fire blight.
Le Conte	300 to 400	August attractive yellow pear	Above average, fresh-eating quality, but rather susceptible to fire blight. Typical pear shape.
Monterey	150 or less	August yellow fruit with red blush	Has been very susceptible to fire blight in the Houston, Texas area, but reportedly grows well in San Antonio. Roundish in shape.
Oakhill	300 to 400	August yellowish green with pink blush	Some fire blight, but seems to tolerate it. Typically pear-shaped, an old farm variety found near Bellville, Texas. Good-quality fruit, free of russeting.
Orient	300 to 400	August yellow, and somewhat russeted	Hard, round pear, of fair to good quality, with good blight resistance. Best for processing.

Variety	Chilling Requirement	Ripe/Color	Remarks
Pineapple	150 or less	August large yellow fruit unless it overbears	Somewhat self-fruitful, but will set larger crops with a pollinator like Hood. Neither is particularly good, however. Reported to have pineapple-like flavor. Store for fresh use or use for processing.
Pound Pear	300 to 400	early to late August russet-colored	Extremely large old-home variety from the southeastern United States. Dubbed Pound Pear because each piece of fruit literally weighs about 1 pound.
Tenn (Tennessee)	200 to 400	August red blush with some russeting	Promising variety from a Tennessee breeding program that was never released—probably because it didn't have the desired appearance. Shows good blight resistance and has good to excellent quality fruit. Medium-sized and somewhat rounded bell shape.
Turnbull Giant	200 to 400	August/September yellow with russeting	Large and round in shape, it tastes a lot better than it looks. Crisp, yet suitable for fresh use. Also good for cooking.
Warren	600 to 800	August pale green free of russeting	Very high quality fruit, similar to Magness. Trees are slow to begin bearing and leaf spot may be severe. Resistant to fire blight.

Pear Varieties for the Mid- to Upper South

Variety	Chilling Requirement	Ripe/Color	Remarks
Ayers	600 to 800	August yellow with red blush	High-quality fruit, but notorious for being slow to come into production. Good blight resistance.
Bartlett	800	August/September yellow with red blush	Excellent for fresh use or processing. Blights severely in most areas of the South.
Harrow Delight	600 to 800	August yellow with red blush	This variety was developed in Canada, but has shown promise in the South. The tree is resistant to fire blight and the fruit is excellent for fresh use.
Honeysweet (Stark)	600 to 800	September yellow	An excellent quality fruit for fresh use—reportedly on par with Seckel. Also good for processing.
Magness	800	September greenish yellow with russet	Not very pretty, but good-quality fruit with a tough skin. Needs a pollinator and doesn't produce viable pollen for other varieties.

Variety	Chilling Requirement	Ripe/Color	Remarks
Maxine	800	September yellow	High-quality fruit, sweet but not strongly flavored. Fireblight resistant.
Moonglow	700 to 800	September yellow with pink blush, some russeting	Excellent quality. Another variety with mild flavor and trees that have good blight resistance.
Seckel	600 to 800	August/September yellow to brownish red	Extremely high quality and sweet, with many complex flavors. Fine-grained texture and very small in size. Affected some by fire blight.

Asian Pears

Variety	Chilling Requirement	Ripe/Color	Remarks
20th Century	600 to 700	August golden yellow	Highly desired variety. Thin skin, mild flavor, and very juicy—this is characteristic of all Asian pears. Very susceptible to fire blight and slow to break dormancy in the vicinity of Houston, Texas.
Hosui	400 to 500	August brownish orange with russet	Crisp with more flavor compared to other Asian varieties. Has shown considerable blight in recent years, but still produces crops. Whether this variety can live with the disease like some others (Kieffer, for example) remains to be seen.
Kikusui	500	August greenish yellow	This variety doesn't store well but the fruit is crisp, sweet, and juicy.
Kosui	500 to 600	late July-August yellow with russet	Small fruit with very sweet taste.
Pai Li	500 to 600	August yellow	Attractive, round fruit. Blooms early and may be only moderately productive.
Shinko	600 to 800	September-October brownish green	Slow to break dormancy in the lower South. Medium-sized fruit has a distinctive flavor and stores comparatively well.
Shinseiki	600 to 800	August yellowish green	Medium-sized fruit with very mild flavor. Hangs on the tree in good condition and stores well. Very large and vigorous tree with healthy foliage. In fact having lush dark green foliage, when standard pears have spotted foliage or lose most of their leaves in late summer to fall, is a distinguishing characteristic of Asian pears.

Variety	Chilling Requirement	Ripe/Color	Remarks
Ya Li	300 to 400	September light green to yellow	Chinese variety with a typical pear shape. It has shown some susceptibility to fire blight. Fruit has a slight tartness and is good for fresh use.

Note: Exact chilling hours have not been determined for all pear varieties, so in some cases an estimate is given.

Pear Rootstocks

Variety	Size	Remarks
M9/Winter Banana	20% to 30%	Winter Banana apple is reportedly compatible with most pear varieties. Thus, it bridges the incompatibility between this well-known apple dwarfing rootstock and pears.
OHF 333	50%	This rootstock is difficult to propagate and appears to be a slow producer. However with maturity production, it may be adequate. Resistant to fire blight and suckering.
OHF 40	80%	One of the most promising of the Old Home X Farmingdale rootstocks. It is hardy with good disease resistance and is not as difficult to propagate as OHF 333 is. Varieties with a reputation for slow bearing begin production in 2 to 3 years.
Pyrus betulifolia	100%	A favored rootstock for Asian pears on the West Coast. However, fire blight may be a problem in the South. Pears grow vigorously on this rootstock.
Pyrus calleryana	100%	This is the standard rootstock for pears in the South. Excess vigor typically produces large trees that are slow to begin bearing.
Quince	60% or less	Incompatibility problems and intolerance of southern soils—especially tight clays make the various Quince rootstocks unacceptable for most areas of the South.
Standard pear seedlings	100%	Pears grow quite well on their own roots—actually, sometimes people root favorite varieties. The existence of seedling varieties that may be 100 years old proves that pears can grow very successfully on their own roots. The main drawback would be inconsistency and the potential susceptibility to fire blight.

peaches & nectarines 4

Peaches and nectarines come in various shapes, colors, and sizes. They originated in China, but have been available throughout the world for many centuries; it was the Spanish who brought the peach to Florida and the Southwest. Later, England and France introduced peaches to the colonies. The Spanish peaches had yellow flesh, but most of those from northern European countries had white flesh. A Chinese cultivar 'Chinese Cling' produced the seedling selections 'Belle of Georgia' and 'Elberta,' which have contributed genes to many of the cultivars grown today.

Peaches have often developed from stands introduced as "wild" in the United States and in other areas of the world. There are still untapped gene pools in China—fruit quality may be poor but it's interesting to speculate what qualities these wild peaches might have. Disease resistance is an appealing possibility, but new flavors and textures might also be waiting to be discovered and incorporated into today's limited peach and nectarine genetics. It's only been in the last 10 to 15 years that good quality low-chilling varieties have become available for southern growers.

Genetic dwarf varieties are relatively new and so far the quality has been only fair to good. Scale insects seem to love the coziness of the close leaf internodes. A tree that would produce large, high-quality peaches and that would be only a bit larger than a tomato bush has yet to be developed, but would solve many problems.

Peaches and nectarines don't increase in sugar content after harvest. They eventually soften and improve in flavor compared to the green-ripe stage that they're picked in, but they will never achieve the flavor of fruit that is picked when some softness is detected. The public's disappointment with fruit grown in one area of the country and shipped long distances has strengthened the market for locally grown produce. To satisfy this demand southern growers need varieties that have good flavor and texture. Flordaking is a good example of such attempts. It produces a very large, very early attractive peach that is barely fit to eat when tree-ripened and even worse when picked firm-ripe. Sunfre nectarine is a beautiful dark red fruit long before it is soft enough to eat. In fact, the birds will probably damage every nectarine before it could ever become soft-ripe on the tree.

The development of varieties for the South has really just begun. One of the main advantages southern gardeners have is an early ripening date. As a result, many early varieties have been developed for the South. Typically, early varieties don't develop much flavor. Perhaps the complex flavors we appreciate in quality peaches take more time. There are other reasons to look for these early varieties: disease pressure, insects, late summer heat, and grower "burnout" make it hard to grow quality fruit that ripens after the last of June in the lower South and after the end of July in the upper South. Apparently some of these early varieties develop more flavor when they mature in a dry climate—probably the sugars are more concentrated—but serious evaluation of fruit quality is a must before any grower invests in a large planting.

The potential for new peach and nectarine varieties adapted to the South is exciting. So far genetic dwarfs haven't been very good because of poor quality and pest problems, but they certainly have great potential. The bagel-shaped Peen To peach is interesting—one could almost eat it like a doughnut. As a fuzzless peach (nectarine) it is an ideal fruit to pack for snacks.

Soils and Fertility

Peaches and nectarines are among the most challenging fruits to grow successfully in the South. The high humidity and abundant rainfall provide the ideal conditions for a host of leaf spots, fruit rots, vascular wilts, and root problems.

These fruits are also among the most treasured of fruits grown in the home orchard. Don't let the challenge discourage you, just be prepared to spend a little more time selecting a planting location, preparing the soil, planting, controlling insects and disease, and pruning.

Peaches and nectarines should be planted in the best soil available with ideal drainage. Short periods of wet weather can mean disaster for peach trees planted on tight clay soils and sands with poor internal drainage. An ideal soil would be 12 to 36 inches of sandy loam with an acid pH and a ferrous red subsoil. This allows for a deep, well-anchored root system. When selecting a site for planting new trees, try to avoid soils where peaches and nectarines have been grown before.

Where soil drainage is marginal, plant on raised beds. The height of the bed will vary according to the drainage. The poorer the drainage, the higher the bed. If you plan to bring in soil, I would suggest washed bank sand, river sand, or a loose sandy loam top soil. Commercial soil mixes aren't recommended because many have a very high percentage of partially composted pine bark mixed with a sandy soil. As the bark decomposes it will become soggy, or possibly sour, and will settle too much.

Peaches and nectarines won't tolerate prolonged periods of drought either. Water is very important for consistent production. Locate your trees near a dependable water source. A mature tree loaded with fruit requires between 30 and 40 gallons of water each day. Fortunately Nature supplies the bulk of this, but watering is still necessary, especially in late summer when the trees are developing fruit buds for next year's crop. Soaker hoses or drip irrigation are the most efficient ways to water, but almost any way of thoroughly soaking the soil around your trees will work.

Peaches and nectarines are heavy feeders (they require high levels of fertility), especially during the trees' early stages of development. Once trees reach maturity (4 to 6 years), fertility must be cut back to reduce their growth to only 12 to 24 inches each year. Agriculture extension services at most land-grant universities will do a leaf analysis, which is the most definitive way to determine your fertilizer needs. Although specific fertility programs are difficult to develop without doing a soil test, some general recommendations are helpful for most fruit growers.

Each year in March a complete fertilizer like 15–5–10 should be applied around the tree under the farthest-reaching branches, about 12 to 24 inches from the tree. Apply ½ cup the first year, 1 cup the second year, and 2 cups per inch of trunk diameter the third year. Select only one fertilizer for each application.

Amount of Fertilizer Applied Monthly April through June

POSSIBLE FERTILIZERS	YEARS		
	FIRST YEAR	SECOND YEAR	THIRD YEAR
Ammonium Nitrate	½ cup	1 cup	2 cups*
Ammonium Sulfate	½ cup	1 cup	2 cups*
Cotton Seed Meal	4 pounds	6 pounds	12 pounds*

POSSIBLE FERTILIZERS	YEARS		
	FIRST YEAR	SECOND YEAR	THIRD YEAR
Blood Seed Meal	2 cups	3 cups	6 pounds*
Fish Meal	2 pounds	3 pounds	6 pounds*
Sewage Sludge (Sterilized)	10 pounds	15 pounds	20 pounds*
Urea Formaldehyde (Slow Release)	½ cup	1 cup	2 cups*

*Amount applied per inch of trunk diameter

Mature trees (4 years or older) are fertilized according to their growth rate. A tree growing less than 12 inches per season should be pruned heavily and fertilized monthly following the program outlined for a 3-year-old tree. Between 12 and 24 inches of growth per season is considered ideal. This will promote the proper balance of flower bud and vegetative bud development. These trees should be fertilized in March with a balanced fertilizer, like 15–5–10, at the rate of 1 pound per inch of trunk diameter and again in early May with a nitrogen fertilizer, like ammonium sulfate, at the rate of 2 cups per inch of trunk diameter.

More than 48 inches of growth per season is considered excessive. This type of rapid growth will produce mostly vegetative buds, which can reduce yields and create a pruning nightmare. When you have trees producing excess growth, discontinue fertilizing until tree vigor decreases.

Pruning and Training

The pruning and training process begins the day the tree is planted and continues until the tree dies. Because peach and nectarine trees bear on 1-year-old wood, they must be pruned each year to continue to grow vigorously. The open center training system is by far the most popular for peaches and nectarines, but other systems like the Tatura trellis and the V or Y training systems are being tested.

Open Center Training System

The trees are planted 16 to 24 feet apart with rows 24 feet apart during the dormant season. A 3- to 5-foot unbranched grafted whip is ideal. Large trees are more difficult to train, suffer more transplant shock, cost more, and usually don't bear any earlier.

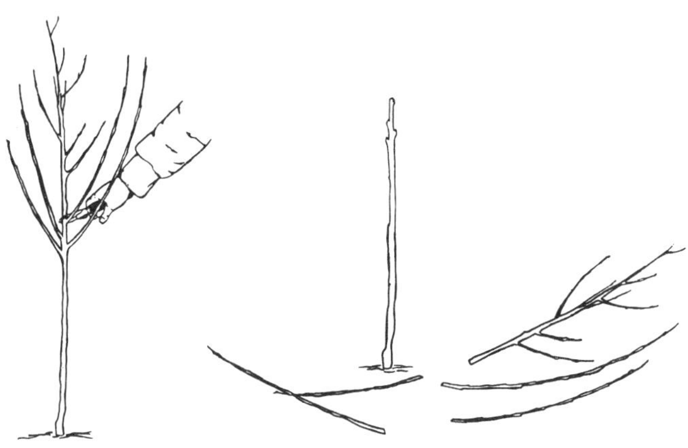

At planting stage, top the tree approximately 2 feet above the ground. Remove all side branches regardless of tree size.

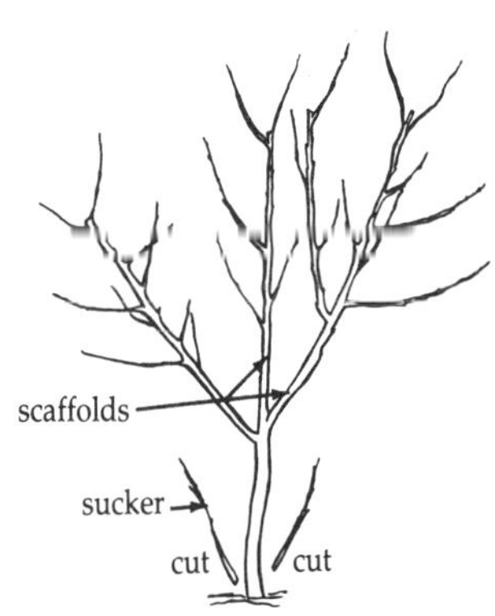

TRAINING DURING THE FIRST OR SECOND YEAR DEPENDS ON THE TREE'S RATE OF GROWTH. CLIP THE TIPS ON MAIN BRANCHES 24 TO 32 INCHES FROM THE MAIN TRUNK TO FORCE THE SIDE SHOOTS TO DEVELOP. REMOVE SUCKERS REGULARLY. LEAVE THREE OR FOUR WELL-SPACED, WIDE-ANGLED BRANCHES TO FORM A BOWL-SHAPED FRAMEWORK OR SCAFFOLD SYSTEM.

After the tree is planted and well watered, it should be cut back to 24 to 28 inches. This will encourage the development of numerous branches, which will be used to form the first set of permanent scaffold branches.

Select 3 to 4 of the strongest, most evenly spaced branches to become the scaffold branches; all others should be tipped to slow their growth. Years ago this was commonly done in the summer, but bacterial canker is such a serious problem along the Gulf Coast that summer pruning should be avoided. By leaving these branches through the first season, and tipping them to control their growth, a strong root system will be encouraged to develop.

By the end of the first growth season, your trees should have 4 to 6 feet of growth. This establishes the main framework for a tree trained with the open center training system. Once the tree is completely dormant, (December through February) it will need its first major pruning. Select the 3 to 4 permanent scaffolds. They should be evenly spaced and angled outward at a 45° to 65° angle from vertical. Remove all other branches from the main trunk and tip the remaining scaffold branches at 36 to 38 inches.

The second season, allow the trees to grow with little or no pruning. The only thing to look for is suckers or water sprouts arising from the main trunk. These sprouts can be removed easily if caught early, so check the trees often. You may get a light crop of fruit the second season, but they should be thinned heavily. It's more important to develop a strong, vigorous tree than to allow it to set an early fruit crop. Once the tree is dormant, it will need its second major pruning.

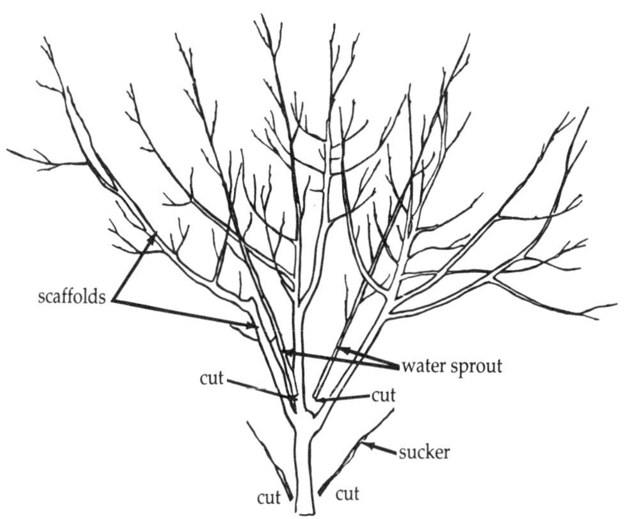

TRAINING DURING THE SECOND OR THIRD YEAR ALSO DEPENDS ON THE TREE'S RATE OF GROWTH. REMOVE WATER SPROUTS. SUBSCAFFOLDS DEVELOP AFTER CLIPPING THE TIPS FROM THE SCAFFOLDS. REMOVE SUCKERS REGULARLY. REMOVE LARGER INTERIOR BRANCHES THAT USUALLY FILL THE BOWL-SHAPED CENTER OF TREE BUT LEAVE SUFFICIENT SHORT, LEAFY GROWTH IN THE CENTER TO PROVIDE SHADE PROTECTION FOR THE SCAFFOLDS.

Remove all branches on the main trunk except the permanent scaffolds. Top the tree at a workable height. This height will vary according to your needs. For years a height of 7 to 8 feet has been recommended, but recent research data indicates that allowing the tree to reach heights of 9 to 12 feet will greatly increase yield without significantly increasing labor. Once the tree's height has been reduced, the tree should be thinned. The center should be opened up to allow maximum light penetration, and strong upright shoots and low hanging limbs should be removed. After the second growing season, treat the tree as a mature tree.

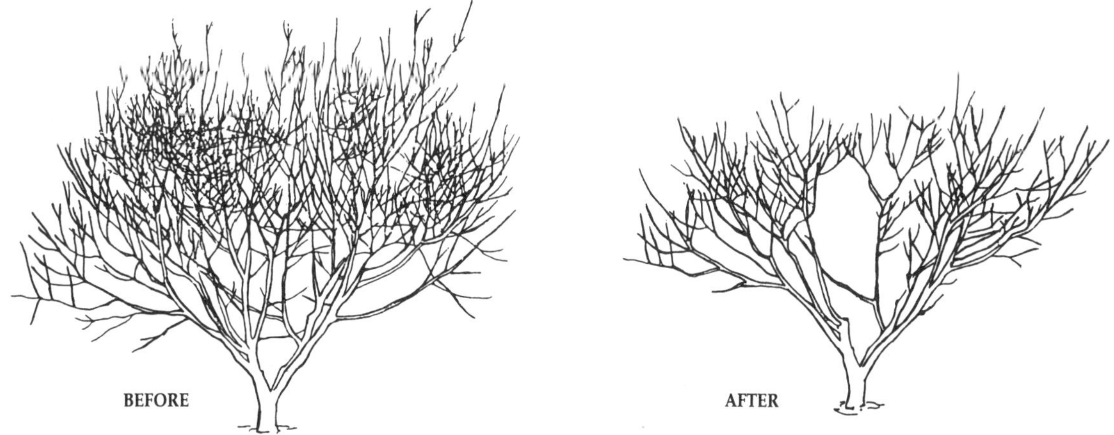

When trees begin to bear, clip subscaffolds and other branches to maintain a practical tree height (usually 7 to 10 feet above the ground). Fruit are set on one-year-old shoots so these must be regrown from year to year. Thin out crowded shoots that will receive little sunlight. Remove low-hanging branches that may sag to the ground when loaded with fruit.

PRUNING A MATURE PEACH OR NECTARINE

1. Each year remove 40% to 60% of the growth to keep the trees vigorous and productive.
2. Top the tree at a workable height (7 to 12 feet).
3. Remove all suckers and water sprouts (vigorous upright shoots).
4. Thin the tree, removing all crossing branches and low hanging limbs.
5. Open up the center to allow light into the tree to help ripen the fruit more evenly and to encourage new growth from the permanent scaffolds.
6. Prune early bearing varieties heavily to increase fruit size.
7. Dead twigs in the center and lower part of the tree is evidence of too little pruning in the center of the tree.

Y or V Training System

Trees are planted 6 to 10 feet apart in the row with rows 14 to 22 feet apart. Newly planted trees are pruned back to 20 to 24 inches. Two scaffolds are selected and trained into the row at 30° to 40° angles from vertical. These 2 scaffolds form the Y or V that hold the short fruiting shoots. Each year the center is opened up and the shoots are cut back to maintain vigor and a balance between fruiting and shoot growth. This system has many advantages, including high yields during early years, the potential for mechanical pruning, more efficient pesticide application, and more even fruit ripening.

Tatura Trellis

The Tatura trellis is a V-shaped trellis system that was developed in Australia. It involves an elaborate system of poles and wires to support the limbs and the heavy fruit load. The Tatura trellis was developed for mechanical hedging and harvesting. The wide canopy angles tend to stimulate fruitwood development and high yields. Trees are planted very close together (2 to 6 feet apart). The primary disadvantage is the high cost of establishment and replanting.

Pollination, Fruit Thinning, and Harvesting

Peaches and nectarines are self-fruitful and most don't require a pollinator for good production. Bees are required to assist in pollination so avoid using insecticide during the flowering season.

Peaches and nectarines, like most fruit, tend to overproduce. A medium-sized tree will set 1,500 to 3,000 fruit but only 200 to 300 fruit should be allowed to ripen. The tree can only manufacture and store so much food (carbohydrates). Thinning will encourage large flavorful fruit without overloading the tree.

Thin the fruit until they are 4 to 6 inches apart when the danger of frost season has passed and the fruit is about the size of a nickel. Early varieties should be pruned heavily and have their flowers thinned.

Girdling Increases Fruit Size

Girdling limbs can be used to increase fruit size. This practice has been studied under controlled conditions and proven to be a viable way to grow larger peaches, enhance color, and advance ripening. Girdling is the removal of a thin strip of bark from around the limb of the tree. This blocks the movement of food produced in the leaves to the roots and diverts it to the fruit. Girdling should be done 1 to 2 weeks before pit hardening occurs (mid-April in the lower South, early May in the upper South).

This practice has a number of drawbacks. It increases split pit (a splitting of the seed often extending to the skin of the fruit). Girdling can also decrease growth and may increase disease problems.

Peach Varieties for the Lower South

Variety	Chilling Requirement	Ripe/Color	Remarks
Babcock	300 to 500	June white flesh	Old variety with good quality, but easily bruised.
Chelena	100 to 200	July dull red overblush, yellow flesh	Slight bitterness near the pit, but good quality for a low-chilling peach. Also a somewhat late producer. Semidouble flowers are a dark reddish pink, perhaps the most striking of any variety with edible fruit.
Earligrande	200 to 300	April/May yellow with red blush, yellow-fleshed cling	An improvement over Early Amber. Well adapted to the lower South.

Variety	Chilling Requirement	Ripe/Color	Remarks
Flordacrest	400 to 500	May yellow with yellow-fleshed, semicling	Good size and better quality than Floridaking though slightly later to mature.
Flordaglobe	100 to 200	May yellow with yellow-flesh, cling	Very early, large, and has good flavor. One of Florida's newer releases.
Flordaprince	100 to 200	May yellow with red striping, yellow-fleshed cling to semicling	Considered one of the best of the very low-chilling varieties. It also has good size.
Idlewild	600 to 700	late May-June almost solid dark red, yellow-fleshed, semicling	Heavy producer of good-sized fruit. Spicy peach flavor with red speckled flesh.
June Gold	600	late May-June yellow with red blush, yellow flesh	Considered a moneymaking variety for much of the South. Quality is poor to good. Split pits and stringy flesh are typical. May produce a prominent, pointed tip in some seasons. Unforgiving of inadequate chilling.
Juneprince	600 to 700	mid-June red blush over yellow, yellow flesh, semifreestone	One of the highest flavored varieties for this season and for the upper region of the lower South. Round shape with a small nipple end. Deserves wider planting in the upper Gulf Coast.
La Feliciana	550 to 600	late June yellow-fleshed freestone	Has been widely tested in the South. Quality is good to excellent.
La Percher	400 to 500	early June to late June (may ripen over a long season) yellow with red blush, yellow flesh, semicling	June Gold season, but a much better peach. May have the best flavor of the Louisiana varieties so far.
Mid-Pride	200 to 300	mid- to late June yellow-orange with distinctive red striping, yellow-fleshed freestone	One of the few California varieties to show promise for the South. Good tree vigor and good to excellent quality fruit.
Red Baron	500 to 600	mid-June to early July yellow with	This may be the ultimate home variety. It has spectacular pinkish red, semidouble flowers and

Variety	Chilling Requirement	Ripe/Color	Remarks
continued		red blush, yellow flesh, semifreestone	high-quality fruit that ripens over an [illegible]
Starlite	600	mid-May pale yellow with red blush, white-fleshed, cling	One of the better quality early-bearing peaches. Soft and deteriorates rapidly after harvest.
Texroyal	600	mid- to late June bright yellow with red blush, yellow-fleshed, freestone	New release from Texas A&M University. High quality with a good rounded form. May require too much chilling for much of the lower South. Much better quality than the clingstone variety Texstar, which requires 450 chilling hours. Ripens just behind Juneprince.
Tex Star	200 to 300	mid-June yellow, semicling	Often produces a pointed tip, fair to good quality, more vigorous than June Gold.
Tropic Sweet	150 to 200	mid-June yellow with red blush, yellow flesh, cling	A new variety worth trying in the lower south.
Tropic Snow	150 to 200	May pale yellow with red blush, white flesh, freestone	High-quality white peach, not quite as soft as others.

Peaches for the Mid- to Upper South

Variety	Chilling Requirement	Ripe/Color	Remarks
Bicentennial	800 to 900	mid- to late May yellow with a red blush, yellow-fleshed clingstone	One of the earliest peaches for this region. Fair to good quality.
Cresthaven	800 to 900	late July yellow with red blush, yellow-fleshed freestone	Excellent round shape and tough skin. Ripens about as late as is practical for southern growers. Fruit cracking may be a problem.
Denman	800	July yellow with slight blush, yellow-fleshed freestone	Tends to bloom later so may escape late freezes. Nice round shape, fair to good quality.
Dixieland	700 to 800	late July yellow with medium blush, yellow freestone	A long-time standard variety.

Variety	Chilling Requirement	Ripe/Color	Remarks
Harvester	700 to 800	mid- to late June yellow with strong red blush, yellow-fleshed freestone	Fair to good quality.
Jefferson	800	mid- to late July bright yellow with red blush, yellow-fleshed freestone	Good to excellent quality, but only fair production.
June Gold	600 to 700	late May to early June yellow with dull red blush, yellow-fleshed cling	Often planted in the mid-South, but still produces only average quality fruit with a tendency toward split pits. Try La Percher as a substitute.
Juneprince	650	mid- to late June yellow with red blush, yellow-fleshed freestone	About a week earlier than Texroyal with similarly excellent quality. Slightly greater tendency to develop points on the end of the fruit.
Loring	650 to 750	mid-June to mid-July attractive red blush over yellow, yellow-fleshed freestone	Very large, high-quality peach. It has not been a reliable producer in the Texas Hill Country. Well-known by the consumer and much in demand.
Majestic	800	late June to early July yellow with red blush, yellow-fleshed freestone	Good to excellent quality. Becoming an important mid-season variety.
Red Globe	800 to 900	late June to early July mostly red over yellow, yellow-fleshed freestone	Good quality and also a good shipper. Becoming well-known with consumers.
Redskin	700 to 800	mid- to late July mostly red over yellow, yellow-fleshed freestone	Long blossom period and very high-quality fruit. A major variety for this area.
Sentinel	650 to 750	early to mid-June dark red blush over yellow, yellow-fleshed semiclingstone	Fair to good quality for an early season peach.
Texroyal	600	mid- to late June yellow with attractive red blush, yellow-fleshed freestone	High-quality fruit with nice round shape. Along with Juneprince, this variety should be planted for mid-season production in the mid-South region.

Nectarines for the Lower South

Variety	Chilling Requirement	Ripe/Color	Remarks
Karla Rose	600 to 700	June mostly red, yellow-fleshed cling	Good quality, but can be very small unless thinned adequately. May have disease problems.
Mayglo	500 to 600	late May red, yellow-fleshed cling	Fair to good quality. Nice round shape, burgundy red color.
Nectar Babe	500 to 600	June July red, yellow-fleshed cling	Modest producer of fair-quality fruit. Perhaps a forerunner of genetic dwarf varieties to come. The major advantage is the ease of caring for trees that have a maximum height of 6 feet.
Snow Queen	650 to 750	early to mid-June dull red over pale yellow, white-fleshed cling	Extremely high-quality fruit—people will suck the pits on this one. Not real pretty, but large with unforgettable flavor. Also soft so is probably limited to local market sales.
Sungold	200 to 300	late May to early June red over yellow, yellow cling	Sungold is quickly being passed by as an old variety, but it has very tasty fruit, good production, and it's early to bear. It still has a place in home plantings, pick-your-own setups, and local market plantings.
Sunred	150 to 200	June red, yellow-fleshed cling	A newer generation nectarine for the lower South.
Sungem	150 to 200	early to mid-May red, yellow-fleshed cling	Another new one. Good-quality fruit and showy flowers.

Nectarines for the Mid- to Upper South

Variety	Chilling Requirement	Ripe/Color	Remarks
Armking	400 to 500	late May some red over yellow, yellow-fleshed cling	May also be used in lower South as far as the Gulf Coast.
Crimson Gold	600 to 700	mid-June red over golden yellow	Productive variety with attractive fruit, nonbrowning.
Double Delight	700 to 800	July dark red, yellow-fleshed freestone	Attractive semidouble pink flowers, plus good quality fruit makes this an excellent tree for homeowners.
Durbin	850	mid-July to early August red over yellow,	Large size and good flavor with excellent disease resistance.

Variety	Chilling Requirement	Ripe/Color	Remarks
		yellow-fleshed semifreestone	
Fantasia	650 to 750	late July predominantly red over yellow, yellow-fleshed freestone	Excellent quality egg-shaped fruit. Relatively small tree.
Red Gold	850	early to mid-July mostly red, yellow-fleshed freestone	Vigorous, productive tree. Fruit resists cracking and remains firm during storage and shipping.
Snow Queen	650 to 750	late June dull red over light yellow	Better adapted to the upper South, this is one of the most delicious white-fleshed nectarines in existence. It's not real attractive and it doesn't ship well but you won't care.

5 plums, apricots, & cherries

Wild plums are the most common of native fruits. They are found worldwide—in the Americas, Asia, and in Europe. Most are edible, though some are very small and a few are mostly seed. For fresh consumption, the Japanese plum is most popular. The European plum is perhaps best known as the prune, a variety with a high sugar content free of fermentation at the pit, which is why it is often dried. American plums have been used in breeding fresh consumption varieties because they contribute disease resistance, but they are rarely known for high quality on their own. The Wild Goose plum (*Prunus musoniana*), Hortulan plum (*P. hortulana*), and Hog plum (*P. Umbellata*) are examples. Sloe is a name often used to denote a large-fruited American plum.

In the United States, most plums and prunes are grown in California. In fact 90,000 acres of California land is planted in plums and prunes, including 25,000 acres of Japanese plums for fresh use. Cultivated plum varieties were brought to California in 1870. In 1885, the famous plant breeder Luther Burbank imported twelve Japanese plum (*P. salicina*) seeds, and from these seedlings, many of the fresh plums commonly available in today's market were developed. Santa Rosa, Burbank, and Beauty are a few of the many Burbank varieties.

Soils and Fertility

Plums, apricots, sour cherries, and the assorted hybrids all have the same requirements for soil, fertility, and general tree management. Ideally, the soil should be a deep, sandy loam that is slightly acidic and has good internal drainage. A soil that works for peaches and nectarines should be well adapted to the other members of the stone fruit family. However, plums seem to tolerate a wider range of soils than the rest of the family. Care should be taken to avoid soil that remains soggy or water-soaked for even a short period of time.

Irrigation is important if you expect consistent growth and production. Prolonged periods of dry weather may not cause tree death, but can reduce future production and can weaken the tree and increase the possibility of disease or insect problems.

Young trees should be fertilized the same as peaches and nectarines. Once the trees reach maturity, you'll find that fertilizers can be reduced greatly. On many soils you may not need to fertilize mature trees at all.

Plums, apricots, and sour cherries produce fruit on new growth like peaches and nectarines do, but the major production comes from short branches and spurlike twigs. This means that the need for abundant growth is not as important for plums, apricots, and cherries as it is for peaches and nectarines.

On soils low in fertility, mature trees can get by with a single application. In March, a balanced fertilizer such as 13–13–13 or 10–10–10 should be applied at the rate of 1½ to 2 pounds per inch of trunk diameter. This is all that is needed to ensure good tree health and production.

Pruning and Training

The training and pruning procedures for young plums, apricots, sour cherries, and the assorted hybrids (plumcots, pluots, apriuims, cherry plums, etc.) are identical to the open center pruning system outlined in Chapter 4, except that the scaffold angles tend to be a bit more upright and development of 4 scaffolds is quite common.

As the tree matures (when it becomes 4 years old or older) the pruning procedure changes slightly. This group of trees produces the bulk of their fruit on lateral spurs rather than on one-year-old shoots.

Pruning Mature Plums, Apricots, and Sour Cherries

1. Remove water sprouts, broken and diseased limbs, and crossing branches. Cut back flush to other branches; don't leave stubs.
2. Trees should be maintained at a workable height (often between 11 and 14 feet).
3. Topping the trees at the same height year after year can cause crowfeet that may require periodic thinning.
4. Thin fruit wood (lateral spurs) throughout the tree to reduce crop load and encourage renewal growth for later fruiting.
5. Trees making 6 to 8 feet of growth should be pruned lightly and a tree making 1 to 2 feet of growth should be heavily pruned.
6. Heavy pruning can cause the production of excessive vegetative growth, which will reduce yields. Light pruning can cause overproduction and reduce the growth of new fruiting wood.

Pollination, Fruit Thinning, and Harvesting

Sour cherries and apricots are self-fruitful and will usually set adequate crops without help from an additional pollinator. Plums, on the other hand, will set heavier crops if a pollinator is present. There are a few self-fruitful varieties of plums, such as Santa Rosa, Methley, Ozark Premier, and Beauty. But in general, your trees will set more fruit if you plant another plum variety nearby to help with pollination.

Where space is limited, you can graft another variety on one limb of the tree.

Filling a jar or can with water and flowering plum branches of another variety and placing it in the tree at blooming time is another way of getting good pollination.

Plum Varieties for the Lower South

Variety	Chilling Requirement	Ripe/Color	Remarks
Au Roadside	500 to 600	June cherry red fruit, flesh color	Good quality, but the fruit often develops a pronounced nipple at the end.
Au Rosa	400	June purplish red, amber flesh	Santa Rosa-type plum with reported disease resistance.
Beauty	300	late May to early June reddish purple, yellow flesh streaked with red	Like most Japanese varieties developed in California it is susceptible to leaf spot and leaf scorch. Fruit quality is good.
Bruce	200	May yellow with reddish purple blush	Commonly available in southern nurseries and has good disease resistance, but the fruit is barely edible. Most wild plums are better.
Burbank	400	June purplish red with yellow flesh	Good-quality plum, but it is extremely disease susceptible and an inconsistent producer.
Byron Gold	400 to 500	June golden yellow, yellow flesh	Fair quality, but most yellow plums are rather tasteless. The tree is disease resistant and a good grower. Fruit is very attractive.
Cocheco	500	late May to June pinkish bronze, light red flesh	This is a beautiful reddish purple-leaf plum. It produces medium-size fruit, which is only of fair quality.
Discover	400 to 500	June dark purple, flesh is also dark	Produces very tasty fruit, but it has been an inconsistent producer.
Elephant Heart	500	June reddish purple with a green tint, flesh is burgundy red	Good-quality fruit. The tree is relatively strong growing, but still has the potential disease problems of other California varieties.
Laroda	500	mid- to late June dark red with light red flesh	Slightly later maturing than other California varieties. Fruit has good quality. The tree still has potential disease problems.
Mariposa	200 to 300	June greenish bronze with heavy white bloom, burgundy red flesh	Excellent-quality fruit. Unfortunately it's not very pretty. It's a California variety, but the tree stays fairly healthy when planted in the South.
Methley	200	May small reddish purple fruit, burgundy flesh color	Excellent quality, but the fruit rapidly develops a jellylike texture when too ripe. Home or local market variety only. The tree has good disease tolerance.

Variety	Chilling Requirement	Ripe/Color	Remarks
Red Ace	500 to 600	late June small red fruit, red flesh	Excellent quality, but leaf diseases may almost defoliate by late summer, causing the tree to weaken with each succeeding season.
Robusto	400	June red, red flesh	California variety. Good pollinator and good-quality fruit, but disease problems mentioned for other California varieties will limit its use.
Santa Rosa	400	June relatively large purplish red fruit, flesh mostly yellow with red near skin	This is an excellent-quality plum widely grown on the West Coast. It usually succumbs to bacterial canker within 7 to 10 years, but it is good enough that the homeowner may want to try it. It is also fairly self-fertile and a good pollinator for other varieties.
Starking Delicious	400	mid- to late June red with some bronze, bright red flesh color	Good quality and somewhat disease resistant.
Wade	300 to 400	late May dark red with red flesh	Southern variety, could be described as a large Methley. The flavor, however, is not quite as intense. Good disease resistance.

Plums for the Mid- to Upper South

Variety	Chilling Requirement	Ripe/Color	Remarks
Morris	600 to 700	June red with red flesh	Fair to good quality. Production has been erratic, probably due to pollination requirements.
Ozark Premier	700 to 800	June large red fruit with some yellow, yellow flesh	If thinned properly, this can be one of the largest plums grown. It is also one of the best tasting. Somewhat self-fertile but benefits if pollinated with other Japanese plums.
Shirley	700 to 800	June purplish red with yellow flesh	This is an excellent-quality plum with many complex flavors; it even has a hint of pineapple. It certainly warrants planting where adapted.
Romeo	700 to 800	June/July dark pink over yellow with yellow flesh	Thought to be a chance seedling of Burbank. The fruit is of very high quality.

Note: The varieties recommended for the mid- to upper South require more chilling hours. Virtually all of the lower South varieties can be used in these upper regions.

Apricots

The apricot is one of the world's most elusive temperate-climate fruits. In the world's northern regions the flowers are often frozen in the spring; in its southern regions varieties don't receive enough chilling hours to break dormancy or they break too soon and freeze again. Even when fruit sets, diseases such as the fungus brown rot can ruin a promising crop. Most varieties are susceptible to cracking, especially in areas where heavy spring rains follow relatively dry periods. The fruit's skin simply can't expand rapidly enough to accommodate the intake of water.

Nothing can compare to the quality of a tree-ripened apricot. Even though the apricots grown on the West Coast often look good in crates at the produce market, they have usually been picked too green. Chances are they are flavorless. On the other hand, a tree-ripened apricot bursts with juice and flavor. It's an unforgettable assault on the senses—worth trying thousands of seedlings and testing hundreds of varieties to find an adapted and productive variety.

Apricots for the South

Variety	Chilling Requirement	Ripe/Color	Remarks
Afghanistan	variable	May/June white with pink to red blush, white flesh	The development of white apricots is still in its infancy. The fruit typically has very high soluble solids and is very sweet. Color preference for golden-colored apricots will probably hamper its popularity. So-called Turkish varieties are similar.
Blenheim	500	June light orange with red dots, yellow freestone flesh	Often grown successfully in the South. It is delicious when tree-ripened. The Royal variety is very similar.
Flora Gold	500	May yellow, yellow-fleshed freestone	One of the early varieties developed for the South and West. Matures early, but only fair quality and production.
Gold Kist	300 to 400	May golden yellow, orange-fleshed freestone	Large, vigorous tree capable of producing sizable crops of good-quality fruit. Unfortunately it is very susceptible to cracking and the fruit will be small if not thinned.
Harriet	500	May yellow	Promising new variety. Relatively untested.
Katy	300 to 400	late May to early June yellow, yellow-fleshed semifreestone	Another new variety developed in California. Limited testing in the South.
Royal Rosa	500	May yellow with pink blush, yellow-fleshed semifreestone	Early bearing with delicious, high-quality fruit.

Variety	Chilling Requirement	Ripe/Color	Remarks
Surecrop	800	early June yellow orange, yellow flesh	Medium-sized fruit that has produced somewhat reliable crops in the upper South.
Daecker	600 to 800	May yellow, yellow flesh	Texas Hill Country variety. Has shown some tendency to produce reliable crops.

Note: Exact chill hours for many apricots have not been determined, so in some cases an estimate is given.

Cherries

Cherries are not a realistic crop for most southern growers. In the upper South the sour cherries offer the most hope. The standard variety is Montmorency. Sweet cherry varieties may succeed, especially in higher altitudes, but have limited commercial potential. Even where chilling hours are adequate (most varieties need 700 to 1000 hours), late spring freezes often ruin entire crops.

Tropical cherries have tempted growers in the lower South for a number of years—the Capulin cherry (*Prunus salicifolia*) in particular. Though the fruit is quite edible, the seed is relatively large. Selections have been made of this species in South America but it remains to be seen if it can survive the pathogens—especially soil-borne ones—found in the southern states. The temperature is also a factor since these cherries are most often found at high elevations where hard freezes aren't a problem and high summer temperatures aren't common.

The Nanking bush cherry can also be grown in most areas of the South, even along the Gulf Coast. Out of a group of seedlings some won't be happy in the lower South, but others will grow with limited chill hours. Unfortunately this is another species that produces fruit with large seeds and little flesh.

6 berries

The berry category includes a large and somewhat diverse group of plants. It could be subdivided into brambles, blueberries, strawberries, and miscellaneous. Most of the miscellaneous—currants and others—don't grow well in the majority of southern gardens, which simplifies gardeners' decisions.

Brambles are quick to produce. Blackberry root cuttings planted in the winter will be fruiting about 16 months later. Primocane bearing raspberries may produce some fruit the first fall after dormant-season planting.

Blueberries will require 2 to 3 years before they bear significant crops, but this is still relatively early. Blueberries are the most demanding of the berry crops. They need very acidic, sandy soil. It is doubtful that one could add enough sulfur, aluminum sulfate, or other soil acidifier to an alkaline clay soil to make blueberries happy. The home gardener with an alkaline clay soil would need to build a raised bed 12 to 18 inches deep and fill it with an acidic soil mix to ensure good growth free of iron chlorosis. One other alternative would be to plant rabbiteye blueberries grafted to farkleberry rootstock (*Vaccinium arboreum*). The farkleberry is much more tolerant of soil types, but West Texas gardeners can still forget about growing blueberries because even the farkleberry won't grow in this region. A number of propagation techniques can be used with farkleberries, but the use of the inlay bark graft on established farkleberries has been especially successful.

Strawberries are also quick to produce. In fact, for most of the South they are an annual crop that is planted in the fall (October), harvested in the spring (March to June), and plowed under and replanted in the fall. The summer, with its leaf spot fungi, spider mites, and other pests, usually takes too much of a toll on the plants for good plantlets to be produced for next year's crop. And of course with summer's heat, berry production also stops. Growers willing to carry over plants will need to contend with weeds through the summer and keep plants well watered to avoid stresses, which will reduce the following season's production. Homeowners may be able to carry over plants for several years, but they will occasionally want to renew their planting with fresh stock.

Blackberries

Blackberries and their relatives are one of the easiest fruits to grow in the South. Many people avoid growing these cooperative fruits because they have the reputation for getting out of control. With proper pruning, plants can be kept within workable boundaries.

Many of the productive varieties will produce as much as 1 gallon of fruit per foot of row. Plants are planted 3 feet apart. As few as 3 or 4 plants can provide the average family with more than enough berries for their needs.

SOILS AND FERTILITY

Blackberries are especially tolerant of soil conditions. Although blackberries prefer well-drained, sandy loam and slightly acidic soils, they will tolerate sands or clays with a pH ranging from 5 to 8. Strongly alkaline soils may require the addition of chelated iron to correct yellowing problems. Where drainage is poor, raised beds will work well.

Pruning can be difficult with large home or commercial plantings. When the size of the planting prohibits hand pruning, a system of mechanical pruning can be used. Every other row should be shredded to the ground as soon as the berries are harvested. These rows will produce a small crop the following season. The unpruned rows will produce a large crop and be shredded next year. This rotation will help maintain plant size, remove the old canes, and save the labor required to prune by hand. It is important to collect and discard the old canes after the plants are pruned.

Blackberries should be fertilized with a complete fertilizer, such as 15–5–10 at the rate of 1 pound per 10 feet of row just prior to bloom and again after the fruit is harvested.

PRUNING AND TRAINING

Blackberries can be divided into two groups: upright varieties requiring no support, and trailing varieties requiring a trellis of some sort to control their growth and support the fruit load. (See page **66** for information about trellis structures that can be used for raspberries and blackberries.)

Blackberries produce their crop on the last year's growth. Once the cane has produced a crop, it must be removed and discarded to help reduce disease problems. Blackberries should be pruned each year as soon as the fruit is harvested. The old woody canes should be removed at ground level and only the vigorous new growth allowed to remain. Once this new growth reaches 48 to 60 inches in height if it's an upright variety or the top of the trellis if it's a trailing variety, the canes should be tipped to encourage branching. Blackberries must be contained by mowing or digging suckers. The row should be maintained at 2 to 3 feet wide to make picking easier. If blackberries are allowed to grow unchecked, they will become a thick, unmanageable bramble jungle.

Last year's canes will bloom and bear fruit as the new canes begin to grow and develop. Thin the developing shoots so that 5 to 7 per plant remain.

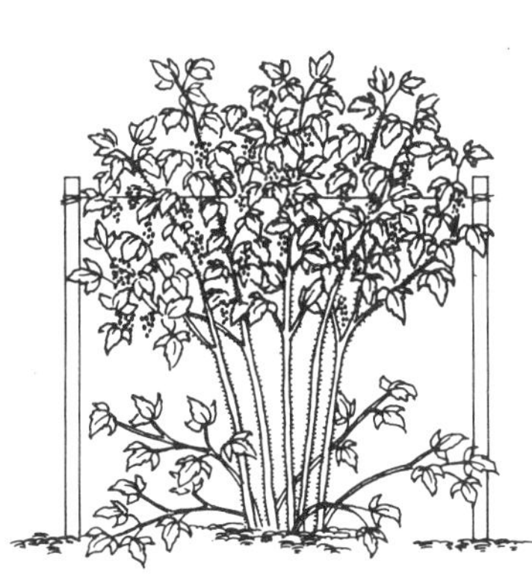

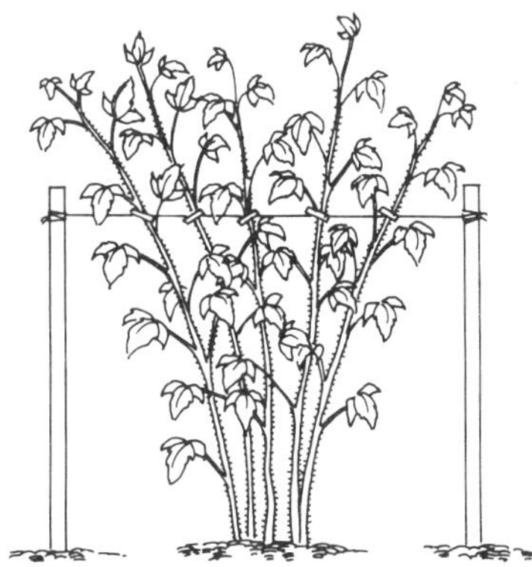

After harvest, remove all old canes at ground level. On trailing varieties, tie the canes to the trellis or support.

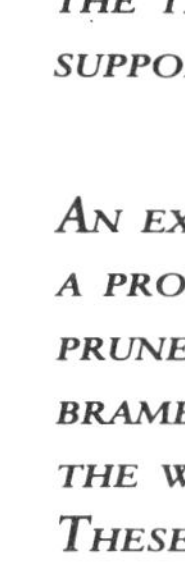

An example of a properly pruned bramble during the winter. These one-year-old canes will support the spring crop of berries.

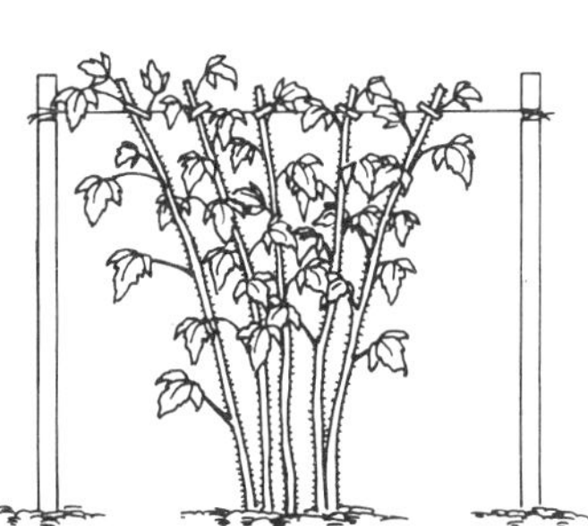

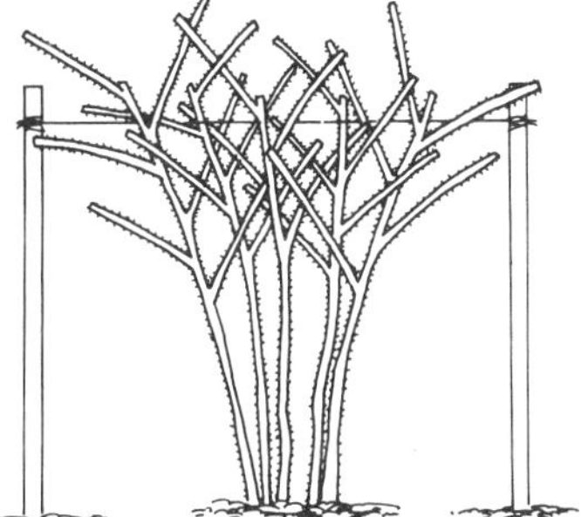

Cut back the new canes at 3 to 4 feet to encourage branching.

Exotic brambles seem to have a good bit of potential for southern gardens. The Tayberry is a cross between the loganberry and black raspberry. The Keriberry is thought to be of black raspberry origin, probably from Thailand. Many of these hybrids, like the Youngberry, prove to be of marginal value. The Youngberry produces good quality, subacid fruit, but its crop is disappointingly small and its trailing canes require high maintenance. Nevertheless, the potential for complex hybrids should entice fruit breeders to give this group of fruiting plants more attention.

HARVESTING

Blackberries should be harvested when fully ripe. The berries should be dark black-purple, slightly soft, and release easily from the fruit stem. If you plan to make preserves or jellies, a few red berries will help add the pectin needed to make the fruit jell.

Weed control is important because blackberries are very shallow rooted. Herbicides are difficult to use because of the suckering nature of the plant. A thick layer of mulch can be used to control weeds without damaging the new shoots.

Blackberries for the South

Variety	Upper (U) or Lower (L) South	Remarks
Black Satin	U	Large sweet berry produced on a semierect, thornless cane. Seeds fairly large.
Boysenberry	U, L	Considered a premium berry, it is large, soft, and dark maroon in color. However, productivity is lacking and the berries do not hold up well. Vines are trailing and require support for best production. The thornless variety is even less productive.
Brazos	U, L	Large crops of good-quality berries are produced on this variety introduced by Texas A&M. The berries are large, but unfortunately so are the seeds. Like most blackberries the majority of the crop comes off in May. Disease problems may prevent fruit forming even though plants still look healthy.
Cherokee	U	Fruit is produced high on the erect-growing plant, making it convenient for mechanical harvest. Medium-large, very sweet berries adapted to wide range of uses.
Cheyenne	U	Excellent quality, large berries. Should appeal to the pick-your-own customer.
Choctaw	U	This high-quality berry is an early ripener and has produced high yields.
Comanche	U	Large, somewhat soft, but high-quality berry. Better for fresh use than for processing. Should appeal to the pick-your-own customer.
Hull	U	The best summer-ripening, semierect, and thornless variety. It doesn't have much competition in this category.
Loganberry	U, L	Thought to be a blackberry-raspberry cross. Productivity is low, but the red berries have a unique

Variety	Upper (U) or Lower (L) South	Remarks
		flavor that is much in demand. Vines are thornless and trailing.
Navaho	U, L	One of the most exciting new berries to come along in years from Dr. Jim Moore at the University of Arkansas. It is a strong upright-growing variety producing high-quality berries on thornless canes. Though not thoroughly tested, it does not appear to be adapted from the Gulf Coast south.
Olallie	L	Large, sweet berries are produced on thorny, trailing canes. This variety is popular in Southern California and is best when planted in the lower South.
Rosborough	U, L	An improved variety of Brazos also developed by Texas A&M University, it has a similar upright growth habit and is a heavy producer of sweeter berries with smaller seeds. Brison is a similar variety that was released at the same time. Probably the best variety for its combination of size, flavor, and yield.
Shawnee	U	This is becoming one of the main commercial varieties in the upper South. Yield and quality are both excellent. Another University of Arkansas release. Especially erect, freestanding canes.
Womack	U, L	Another Texas A&M University release, similar to Rosborough, but has smaller berries.

Blueberries

In the past, growing blueberries was out of the question for southern growers. Except for the upper South and a few high-altitude regions that could grow the highbush blueberry, most Southerners never even considered this crop. Finally the potential for native rabbiteye blueberry cultivation was realized and this became the hot new crop for the South.

SOIL, WATER, AND FERTILITY

Rabbiteye blueberries have one of the most demanding cultural requirements of any fruit. When blueberries have the growing conditions they like, they almost grow like weeds; when blueberries do not have the best growing conditions they struggle along for years, bringing the gardener nothing but problems and disappointment.

Rabbiteye blueberries require very acidic (pH from 4.5 to 5.8), well-drained, sandy soil with an abundance of organic matter. Many fruits tolerate a wide variety of soil conditions, but not the blueberry. Sulfur can be used to help lower the pH where needed (see table in Chapter 1). It should be used cautiously, being mixed into the soil thoroughly in the fall, months before the plants are to be planted.

Blueberries have a shallow fibrous root system, similar to azaleas. They benefit greatly from the use of mulch and the addition of organic matter. Mix about 2 to 3 cubic feet of peat moss or composted pine bark with the existing soil prior to planting. The organic matter should be mixed with existing soil to a depth of 8 to 12 inches. Southern Highbush varieties require copious amounts of organic matter in their planting beds as well as a surface mulch for best results. However, some southern Highbush varieties that warrant trial in the upper South are being developed.

Bareroot- or container-grown plants (container-grown are easier to establish) are placed in a shallow hole in the winter or early spring, and the soil mix is packed around it. Cut the root ball of container plants in 3 to 4 places to tear the roots up a little bit. Most nurseries let plants grow for too long in containers, causing them to become so rootbound they cannot recover. A thick layer of mulch is placed around the plants to help retain moisture and to control weeds. Because of the suckering nature of the plant, some herbicides are difficult to use around blueberries, so mulches are much preferred.

Water quality for the other fruits has not been discussed, mainly because most water available in the South is good enough for most irrigation needs. With blueberries, this is not true. High pH or high levels of bicarbonates, carbonates, and salts such as sodium can cause blueberries all kinds of problems. An irrigation water test is usually available from the state soil testing labs at the states' agricultural universities. Check with your extension agent about water testing information.

Water Quality Standards for Rabbiteye Blueberries

WATER CONSTITUENTS	*IDEAL*	*MARGINAL*	*NOT RECOMMENDED*
Salinity in PPM	less than 160	160 to 960	greater than 960
SAR (sodium absorption rate)	less than 1.0	1.0 to 3.0	greater than 3.0
Bicarbonates PPM	less than 92	92 to 153	greater than 153
Chlorides PPM	less than 142	142 to 355	greater than 355
Boron PPM	less than .75	.75 to 1.2	greater than 1.2
pH	less than 7.0	7.0 to 8.4	greater than 8.4

***PPM** — 1 MILLIGRAM PER LITER OR 1 PART PER MILLION.*

Blueberry Recommended Fertilizing Program

	13–13–13	*AMMONIUM SULFATE*			*15–5–10*			
Year	*March*	*April*	*May*	*Sept*	*March*	*April*	*May*	*Sept*
1	1.0	1.0	1.0	1.0	1.0	1.0	1.0	1.0
2	2.0	1.0	1.0	1.0	2.0	2.0	1.0	1.0
3	3.0	1.0	1.0	1.0	2.5	2.5	1.0	1.0
4	4.0	2.0	2.0	2.0	3.0	3.0	2.0	2.0
5	5.0	2.0	2.0	2.0	3.5	3.5	3.0	2.0

AMOUNTS GIVEN IN OUNCES PER PLANT. APPLY EITHER 13–13–13 AND THEN AMMONIUM SULFATE, OR 15–5–10 EXCLUSIVELY.

Be careful with commercial fertilizers; they can burn young plants. Cottonseed meal applied at the rate of 1 to 2 cups per plant in March and again in May is an organic fertilizer for blueberries. Also, "azalea-camellia food" works well.

PRUNING AND TRAINING

Blueberries require very little pruning or training. Removal of dead or diseased wood is about all that is needed during the early years.

As the bush matures (in 7 or 8 years), it may become quite tall and the lower branches may become unproductive. You will also find that the newer, vigorous canes are more productive than the older canes.

Each year, remove one or two large, old canes at ground level, allowing room for new canes to develop. This type of thinning will keep the plants in bounds and encourage the production of new, more productive growth. Selective topping or heading back can also be used to control height.

HARVESTING

Rabbiteye blueberries begin turning blue weeks before they are ripe. They also ripen over a 2- to 5-week period, making mechanical harvesting difficult.

The good old taste test is the best way to determine when the berries are ripe. Sample a few and you will immediately be able to distinguish the ripe fruit from the others.

The way I distinguish between the two is that a truly ripe berry has a plump look to it. The flower scar on the bottom of the fruit is flattened and the fruit has a slight softness when squeezed.

Blueberries for the South

Variety	Harvest	Remarks
Aliceblue	May	Tall, spreading bush. Good for early pick-your-own growers in the lower South. Production often frozen out in the upper South. Pollinator for Beckyblue.
Avonblue	early June	Small spreading plant that needs pruning to reduce overproduction. Rabbiteye type adapted to mechanical harvest.
Baldwin	mid-June to early July	Vigorous, upright plant not adapted to mechanical harvest. Recommended for trial to extend the pick-your-own season. The berries are medium-sized, dark blue, and have a dry stem scar.
Beckyblue	May	Plants are tall and vigorous. This is one of the earliest and also one of the best hybrids. Needs Aliceblue as a pollinator. Fruit is medium blue and medium in size with a small, dry stem scar.
Bonita	May to early June	Vigorous, upright-growing rabbiteye variety. The fruit is medium-sized and light blue. Potential for fresh use or processing.
Brightwell	June	Plants are upright and spreading. The fruit of this rabbiteye variety is medium-sized and medium blue with a small, dry stem scar. The berries are firm and separate easily, making this a variety adapted to mechanical harvesting.
Briteblue	June to July	This is one of the mainstay varieties for southern growers. The fruit is light blue because of a heavy wax bloom. It is also large and firm and has a small, dry stem scar. Color develops before maturity so it's important not to harvest too early. Plants are moderately vigorous and spreading.
Centurion	July to August	Fruit is medium to large and rather dark. This makes it excellent for processing but it may have less appeal to the pick-your-own customer. Unfortunately it also is not well adapted to mechanical harvesting.

Variety	Harvest	Remarks
Chaucer	late May to June	Good for the early pick-your-own season but may be lost to frost. Rabbiteye variety with medium to large fruit on a vigorous, spreading bush.
Choice	June	Medium-sized plant with dark fruit. Good fresh or for processing.
Climax	May to late June	Plants are upright and spreading with medium-sized fruit. Seed is somewhat prominent resulting in a gritty texture. Ripening is concentrated so this variety is excellent for mechanical harvesting.
Delite	Late June to July	Upright plant, but with a weak leaf canopy. The berries are light blue, but quality is acceptable even when some red is showing through. Good variety to end the pick-your-own season or it can be mechanically harvested when a majority of the berries are ripe. Poor production in the lower South.
Floridablue	May	Hybrid variety producing medium to large fruit. Primarily for fresh use.
Garden Blue	May to early June	Small, good-quality berry. Ripens over a long period. Strong grower and good backyard variety.
Powderblue	June	Vigorous, upright plant with medium-sized, light blue fruit. Suitable for mechanical harvest.
Premier	May to June	Rabbiteye variety with light blue fruit. Very high quality, but crops may be lost to a late frost. Plants are vigorous and upright.
Sharpblue	April to May	Very early hybrid variety with large, high-quality fruit. Wet stem scars limit this variety to "pick-your-own" customers.
Southland	June	This variety is several years slower to come into production, but produces good, regular crops. The fruit is medium to large in size and light blue. Skins toughen late in the season.
Sunshine Blue	May to June	Excellent quality fruit on a relatively dwarfed plant (3 to 4 feet). Possible container plant.
Tifblue	June to July	Very vigorous upright plant with many suckers. Fruit is medium to large in size and light blue. Ready to harvest when all reddish color is gone. Consistent, high-yielding variety.
Woodard	June to July	Plants are medium-sized and spreading. The fruit is light blue and of excellent quality, but the stem scar is large. Best for pick-your-own setups.

Raspberries

If blackberries are the easiest bramble crop to grow, raspberries are by far the most difficult one to grow. Raspberries need lots of organic matter, fertility, and water. They even need afternoon shade in the heat of summer to survive. All varieties are best when grown on a trellis.

SOILS AND FERTILITY

The raspberry is considered by many to be the best of the best when it comes to fruit. Their culture in the South has not always been easy. The extreme heat makes it a challenge to grow, but with a little extra care and the proper variety selection, raspberries can be added to almost any southern orchard.

Proper soil preparation can be the difference between success and failure. When planting most fruits, we use our existing soil with little or no improvements with the possible exception of raising the planting beds to improve drainage. Because raspberries need good drainage, adequate moisture, and high organic matter, it is recommended that generous amounts of organic matter be added to the soil before planting.

Ideally, raspberries require a sandy to sandy loam, slightly acidic soil (pH 6 to 7) with good internal drainage. A pH ranging from 5 to 7.5 is considered acceptable. Raspberries enjoy a location where they get a little protection from the hot afternoon sun.

Once you've selected the site, remove the weeds or grass and till the soil to a depth of 8 to 12 inches. A 3-foot-wide bed is usually adequate with plants being planted every 3 to 4 feet in the row. Three to four inches of compost, black bark (partially decomposed bark), or other available organic matter should be deeply tilled into the existing soil. A raised planting bed should be constructed if drainage is poor. You are now ready to plant your raspberries.

Root cuttings, suckers, or established plants can be used, but the large established plants will require less care the first year. Once you've planted your raspberries, a thick layer of mulch should be added (3 inches is a minimum and 5 to 6 inches is not too much). (Remember, mulching is an annual event and an excellent way to eliminate yard wastes like grass clippings and fall leaves.) Raspberries require an abundance of moisture and drip lines or soaker hoses can be laid down the row before applying the mulch. This will make watering easier and increase your chances for success. Just a few weeks without water in the summer can result in plant death.

Raspberries should be fertilized twice a year using a balanced fertilizer. In alkaline soils (pH above 7.5), phosphorus should be avoided because it tends to tie up iron and nitrogen by forming insoluble compounds that plants can't absorb.

A light application (2 to 3 pounds per 100 feet of row) of an 8–8–8, or 10–10–10 fertilizer should be applied just prior to bud break in the spring and again in late May or early June. Organic fertilizers like cottonseed meal or well-rotted manure can be applied at the rate of 10 to 12 pounds per 100 foot of row in early to mid-winter. Very fresh manure should not be used until it has had a chance to rot for a few months.

PRUNING AND TRAINING

Raspberries can be divided into three main groups: spring-bearing, fall-bearing, and everbearing (in the South, everbearing varieties produce in the spring and fall). We primarily grow the fall- and everbearing varieties.

We should take just a minute to explain how raspberries grow before discussing pruning and training. Spring-bearing varieties produce what is called a primocane the first year. This primocane goes through the winter and becomes a floricane (flowering cane) the second season. This floricane fruits that spring and dies. While the floricanes are producing fruit, new primocanes are being produced for next season.

Fall-bearing varieties produce primocanes that terminate in a cluster of flowers each fall. These canes usually die in the winter. The everbearing varieties produce a fall crop from the newly developing primocanes and these canes remain through the winter to become floricanes and fruit again that spring.

Raspberries will grow best on a trellis or support. The canes tend to get very long and floppy. There are many trellis designs used for raspberries, but they all have the same qualities in common. They control the vigorous canes and support the fruit. The most simple system is a 3- to 4-wire, 5-foot fence. Poles are set in the ground and wires are strung out at regular intervals. The T- and V-type trellises are very common and work well for everbearing varieties. The current season's primocanes can be tied to one side of the T or V trellis. Next year the old floricanes are removed and the new primocanes are tied to the other side of the trellis. This helps to keep pruning simple.

Everbearing varieties are easy to prune when cultivated for a fall-only crop. Each winter, all the canes are cut off at ground level and the old canes are destroyed. In the spring, the new primocanes grow and are tied to the wires. Once the canes reach the top wire, they should be tipped to encourage branching, which should also increase yields. Try to avoid tipping after mid-July to allow plenty of time for the fall crop's flower development. This procedure is just repeated each year. Suckers will develop some distance from the main plants. Try to limit the width of the planting to 2 feet and thin the canes to 2 to 3 strong canes per foot of row. Strong canes will outproduce thin, weak canes.

The everbearing varieties may also be cultivated for spring and fall crops. As the primocanes grow, they should be tied to the support wires. Once the canes reach the top of the trellis, they should be tipped to encourage branching. Don't tip canes after mid-July. These primocanes will terminate in a cluster of flowers for the fall harvest. Once harvesting is complete, cut back the canes a few inches to remove the old fruit clusters.

The old canes (floricanes) will overwinter and bear a spring crop. Once the spring harvest is complete, these old floricanes will be cut to the ground and destroyed. The newly developing primocanes should be thinned to 2 to 3 strong canes per foot of row so the process can start over again.

HARVESTING

Raspberries will develop their best quality fruit if allowed to ripen completely before harvesting. The berries should develop a rich dark red color and be soft to the touch, and should release easily from the fruit stems. The most difficult part of harvesting is getting to the house before eating the crop, but if you're like us, you'll have to try a few berries.

Raspberries for the South

Variety	Harvest	Remarks
Bababerry	May and June and again from September to December	Good-tasting red berry with a waxy bloom. Has produced excellent crops in Southern California, but has yet to prove a commercial success in the South. Recommended for trial planting.
Dorman Red	June	This is by far the strongest grower for the South. It is also a good producer, but the quality is poor to good—not really in a league with varieties like Heritage. It's a red variety as are all of the raspberries that will grow in the South.
Heritage	light in July, heavy in September to December	This variety isn't supposed to grow in the lower South. It has produced in the upper Gulf Coast—especially in the fall. Given afternoon shade, mulch, lots of fertility, and organic matter, it

Variety	Size	Remarks
continued		would at least seem to have home garden potential. It produces excellent-quality fruit.
Oregon 1030	light in July, heavy in September to December	Excellent quality fruit and potential for production from the upper Gulf Coast north.
Redwing	September to December	Heritage offspring worth trying for fall crops in the South.
Ruby	August to December	Recommended for trial planting.
San Diego	light in June and July, heavy in September to December	Southern California variety worth trying in the South.
Southland	June	Upright variety with good-quality fruit.

Strawberries

Our modern garden strawberry is a complex hybrid whose story begins in the seventeenth century. The colonists discovered a delicious native berry in America and sent it back to England and Europe, where they produced natural hybrids with strawberries of those regions. Some of these hybrids returned to the United States and later included the genetics of a large, pale Chilean strawberry after its discovery in the mid-eighteenth century. Though large, the Chilean strawberry lacked flavor, wasn't bright red, and tended to be male sterile. Plus, its hairy foliage made it more susceptible to disease. Finally, the California beach strawberry contributed glossy foliage and long-season bearing characteristics.

Today's modern hybrid combines the best characteristics of its progenitors with the possible exception of flavor. Varieties like Chandler produce large, red berries that have good storage and shipping qualities. But frankly, even when protected by bird netting and allowed to become burgundy red, they aren't much to eat fresh from the field. Strawberries don't continue to ripen if picked too soon, so you can imagine that it takes a lot of sugar to make them edible if they are picked when they only have a bit of red coloration.

Growers anxious to make a profit from their "pick-your-own" gardens will be tempted to plant strawberries because they can be produced using an annual planting system. The plants are set in October, berries are harvested from April to June and then plowed under. To date it's been difficult to find plants ready to grow in the fall, however. The home gardener may find that even if he can locate plants at the proper planting time, come spring the birds get the top half of the berry, the pill bugs get the bottom half, and all that's left is the white core. Bird netting works, of course, and there are chemicals available to use for slugs and pill bugs, but wood ashes sprinkled around the bed also seem to help—at least with the pill bug problem. Apparently the ashes get in the pill bugs' "gears."

Although they are fast growing, strawberries are demanding. Most acreage must be sterilized prior to planting because strawberries are so sensitive to soil-borne pests. This usually adds between $500.00 and $1000.00 per acre to the cost of production. The soil should be worked up into planting beds and is often covered with plastic or paper mulch. The plants must be irrigated immediately and regularly to get them off to a good start. Once established they will need supplemental fertilization to keep them growing vigorously.

SOILS AND FERTILITY

Strawberries are the smallest of the fruit plants we commonly grow in the South. The small rosette has a compact fibrous root system that enables it to grow well in containers or raised beds. The glossy green foliage, white flowers, and shiny red fruit make strawberries an excellent ornamental ground cover for sunny, well-drained areas.

Strawberries require a very well-drained, sandy acidic soil with at least 40% air space to ensure good root health. For container culture, a good commercial peat-lite (soilless) mix is best. Strawberries do best in most of the South if planted in a raised bed or box garden. Bank sand with the addition of 20% composted organic matter by volume will make an excellent planting medium. If your existing soil is sandy and well drained, the planting bed can be prepared by deeply tilling in organic matter and building raised beds that are 24 to 36 inches wide and at least 8 inches high.

Using plastic or organic mulches will help to retain moisture, control weeds, and maintain a more consistent soil temperature. Floating row covers or frost blankets protect tender plants from winter freezes, and are an invaluable way to protect newly planted plants from the elements. Using row covers will also result in larger, more productive plants if left on during the winter and a lightweight type is used.

Because of the nature of the plant and its small fibrous root system, strawberries should be fertilized often in small amounts. You must apply the fertilizer very close to the plants for good uptake to occur but you must be careful not to burn them. To prevent fertilizer burn, water thoroughly.

There are several approaches that work well. Of course, the use of a slow-release fertilizer placed just under the plant at planting is recommended regardless of the program you follow.

A weekly application of a liquid fertilizer is easy and an excellent option. There are a number of hose-end sprayers designed to apply soluble fertilizers. Just put the granules in the jar, hook it to the hose, and spray. The foliage takes up the nutrients and the plants do quite well.

A light application of a balanced fertilizer, like 13–13–13 or 8–8–8, every 3 to 4 weeks throughout the growing season, at the rate of 1 to 2 pounds per 100 square feet, will also work.

Try to avoid the use of animal manure around strawberry plants. The manure contains high levels of salts that can damage the tender strawberry plants.

PLANTING SYSTEMS

Strawberries are generally grown using one of two techniques. In the upper South, the matted row system is usually used. With this system, the plants are planted as a short-lived perennial and the bed is maintained for two to three years. New plants can be planted in the spring or the fall. The first year's crop should be removed to allow all the energy to develop strong plants.

In the fall, the plants will produce runners that develop into new plants. Each fall you will need to thin the bed, leaving only the large vigorous plants. Small, weak, and old, diseased plants should be removed and destroyed. Try to thin the plants so they are 12 inches apart.

In the lower South, strawberries are grown commercially as annuals. But home gardeners resist the annual method. The average home gardener has a difficult time removing plants each summer and replanting again in the fall.

The South's mild winters allow adequate time for strawberries planted in the fall to grow large enough before the spring bloom. During the hot summer, the soil rests and new healthy plants can be replanted without the chore of keeping the plants alive all summer. If diseases become a serious problem, the bed can be rotated to new sites around the garden.

PLANTING

It's important that you take a little time to plant your strawberries correctly. The strawberry plant is a small rosette with a small, fibrous root system, a crown, and a whorl of leaves. The plants produce runners each fall. Nodes located along these runners form into new plants that, once they root, are dug and shipped to fruit growers to plant.

When you receive the plants, they should be unpacked and planted immediately. Soak the plants in water with a little fungicide added. Dig a hole and place a tablespoon or so of a balanced slow-release fertilizer in the bottom. Place a little soil in the hole to cover the fertilizer slightly. Place the plant in the hole and spread out the roots. The crown of the plant (the point where the roots and the stem meet) should be placed right at grown level. If the plant is placed too deep the crown will rot and the plant will die. If the plant is placed too high, the roots will be exposed and the plant will die.

Once the plants are in, they should be watered thoroughly and covered with floating row cover to protect the young plants until they become established. Plants should be watered every day for about a week to ensure good survival.

Keep the row cover handy because winter will follow shortly and the cover can be used to protect your plants from frost damage.

The shallow-rooted plants required frequent, regular watering. Drip, sprinkle, or furrow irrigation all work well. The plants should not be kept soggy, but they also should never be allowed to dry. The use of mulches is extremely important. Much less water will be needed to maintain healthy plants where heavy layers of organic mulch are used.

HARVESTING

Strawberries are one of the first fruits harvested in the garden. The fruit should be allowed to ripen fully on the plant. The berries should be fully red but still firm. These delicious fruit are highly prized by the gardener and almost everyone else. Netting and mulches should be used to help keep the berries safe from above and below.

Strawberries for the South

Variety	Upper (U) or Lower (L) South	Remarks
Cardinal	U, L	Good for the matted row system. Berries held up on stalks.
Chandler	L	Probably the best berry for the Gulf Coast and lower South. It is a productive and attractive variety with firm flesh. Red color extends to the berry's center. Quality fair to good.

Variety	Upper (U) or Lower (L) South	Remarks
Douglas	U, L	Not as productive as Chandler, similar quality.
Florida 90	L	This was once the most important commercial variety in the South. Quality is better than the California varieties but virus-infected plants may be responsible for reduced productivity.
Selva	U, L	Vigorous day neutral variety. Day neutral varieties stop producing during southern summers and rarely produce in the fall. Generally they are less productive than varieties that bear in June.
Seascape	L	Day neutral variety. May produce longer into the season. Large, high-quality berries.
Sequoia	U, L	Large, high-quality berries but productivity is often low. Soft and consequently not good for shipping.
Sunrise	U, L	Vigorous, red stele-resistant variety. Berry color is lighter than desirable, but the variety holds up well in storage. Good overall disease resistance.
Tangi	L	A Louisiana variety. Resistant to some disease problems.
Tioga	L	Older California variety. Firm flesh, but good flavor.

grapes 7

Bunch grapes are difficult for southern growers to cultivate, even though there are more grape species native to the South than there are to Europe. Muscadine grapes are easier to grow, but are not nearly as popular as bunch grapes. The demand for varietal wine grapes is so strong that even if a bunch grape that is resistant to Pierce's disease and capable of producing the finest wine were developed, it would take decades, if not centuries, to be recognized by the wine market. There are many grape diseases in the South, but Pierce's disease is the main reason European grapes can't grow in most areas of the South. Native grapes, like the Post Oak grape and Mustang grape, are resistant to Pierce's disease, but their quality is poor. Crossing resistant varieties with European varieties has produced hybrids that are resistant to Pierce's disease, such as Blanc du Bois, but low productivity and other disease problems still limit their potential. Regardless, the demand for grapes is high and in many areas of the Southeast, muscadines are much appreciated.

Grapes: Soils and Fertility

Grapes perform best in a loamy, well-drained soil. Obtaining the exact soil pH is not that critical. Bunch grapes do well in soils that have a pH between 6.0 and 8.0.

As the pH approaches 8.0, micro-nutrients such as iron and magnesium become tied up (because insoluble compounds are formed that the plants can't absorb) and deficiency symptoms like interveinal chlorosis can set in. Iron and magnesium deficiency can be corrected by making a foliar application of chelated iron and magnesium or by adjusting the soil pH.

If grapes are grown in a fertile or even semifertile soil, no additional fertilizer will be required. You gauge the fertility needed by the vines' rate of growth. During the development stages (the first 3 years) you should get at least 3 to 4 feet of growth, maybe more. As the vines mature, you want to see a reduction in growth as the plant invests its energy in fruit production.

A good amount of growth would be 24 inches per season. If the vines grow more than this, no fertilizer is needed. If the vine grows less than 24 inches, it may need fertilizer.

When the rate of growth is not enough, a single application of 13–13–13 or 8–8–8, at the rate of one-half to 1 pound per vine in March is usually all that is needed.

Constructing a Grape Trellis

The trellis should be constructed with heavy treated posts. Light-weight trellises will give you nothing but trouble later on, so spend the time and money to build it the right way the first time.

End posts should be solid because they will carry the bulk of the weight. Treated wooden posts, measuring 6 to 8 inches in diameter or a heavy gauge 4-inch metal pipe will work. Brace the end posts using a deadman, screw anchor, or H-end post brace.

A 9-foot end post should be set 3 feet into the ground with 6 feet sticking up to support the wires. Intermediate posts are set every 50 to 80 feet (treated landscape timbers work well as intermediate posts) along the row to give extra support. A 2×2 treated stake or metal T-post is placed at the location of each grape vine (every 8 feet).

High-tension galvanized wire (size 9 to 13 gauge) is usually recommended. You will need 2 wires to support the grape vines and an optional wire to support the drip irrigation line. The irrigation wire should be hung at a height of 18 to 24 inches. The other 2 wires are hung at 4 feet and 6 feet. Once you have completed this step you may plant your vines. A similar structure can be built for muscadines, but the grapes should be planted 20 to 22 feet apart.

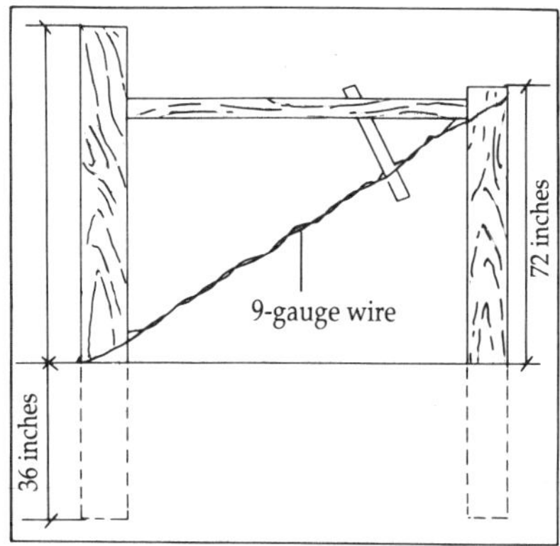

THE "H" END OF END POST BRACING.

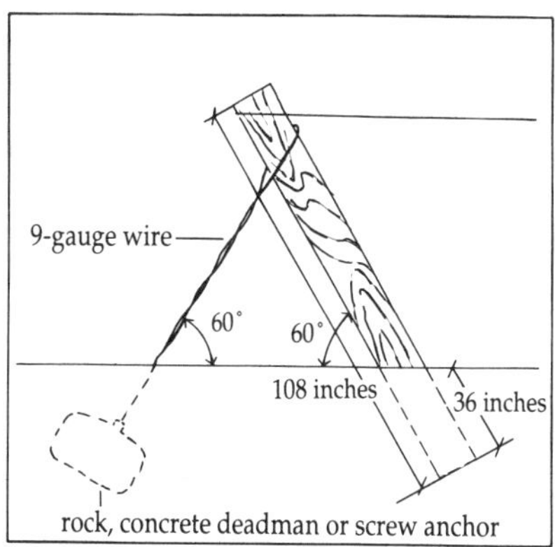

THE INVERTED "V" BRACING SYSTEM FOR END POSTS.

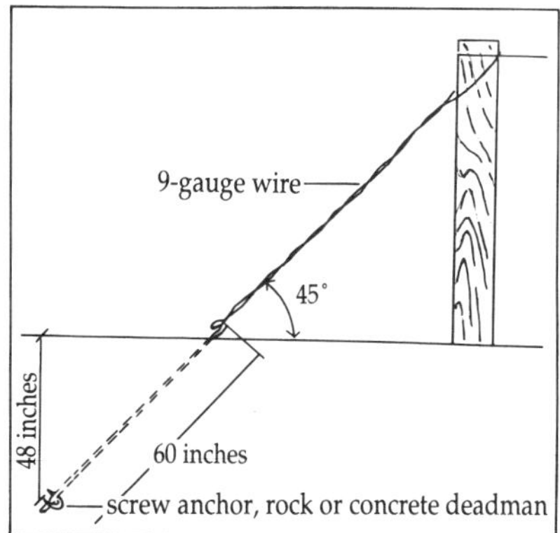

VERTICAL END POST WITH ANCHOR SCREW AND WIRE.

Training and Pruning

Vines should be purchased and planted during the dormant season (December through February). It is best to have the vineyard trellis already constructed and ready to go before planting the vines. Trim off any dead wood and damaged or diseased roots. Plant the vines in existing soil in a location with good drainage.

After planting, trim the vine back to 2 good, healthy buds and tie it to the stake. As the vine grows, the strongest shoot can be trained up the stake to become the main trunk.

At this point, you must decide which training system you plan to use. There are two main systems in use today: the cordon system and the cane system.

Cordon System

As soon as the main trunk reaches the wire located at 4 feet above the ground, the tip should be pinched out to encourage branching. Remove any suckers that develop along the trunk and select 2 lateral (side) shoots to train down the wire. These lateral shoots will become the permanent scaffolds for the life of the vine.

By the end of the fruit-growing season, the main framework should be fairly well developed. The lateral branches should be attached to the wire and trimmed back until they are 4 feet long. Any branches that may have developed on the laterals should be removed at this time.

During the second growing season, select only upright cordons, allow them to grow until the new growth can be attached to the top wire of the trellis. Any fruit that develops during the second season should be removed.

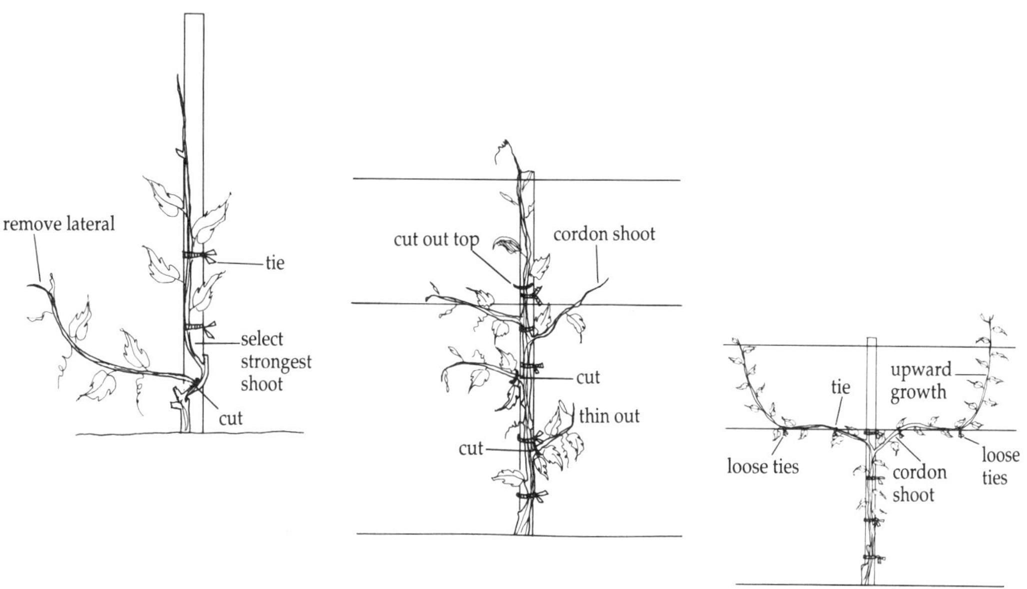

LEFT • SELECT AND TRAIN THE TRUNK SHOOT. MIDDLE • CUT OUT TRUNK SHOOT AND SELECT CORDON SHOOTS BELOW WIRE. RIGHT • TIE THE CORDON SHOOT TO THE CORDON WIRE TO DEVELOP A STRAIGHT CORDON.

By the end of the second season, you should have completed the basic structure of the cordon system. Grapes produce their fruiting canes (cordons) from the healthy buds on last year's wood. Each cane will produce about 2 clusters of grapes and an average healthy vine will only support about 60 to 90 bunches. This means that each year, only 30 to 45 healthy buds should remain after pruning.

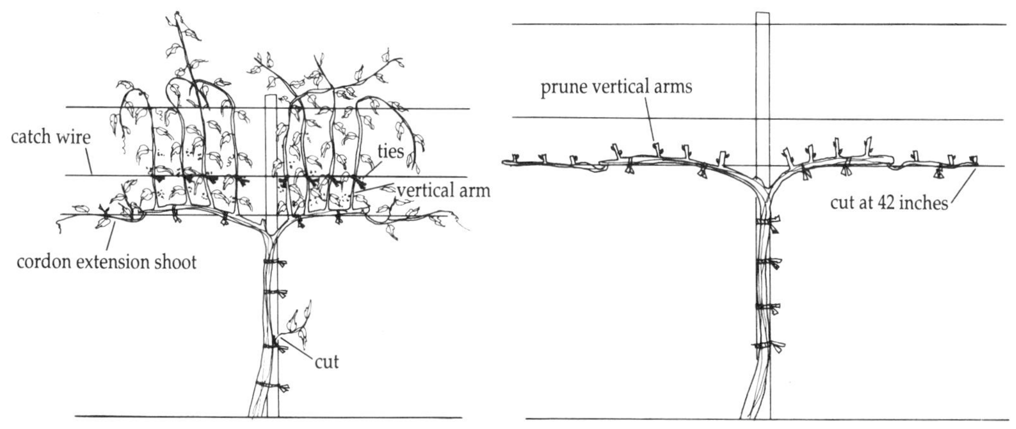

LEFT • TIE VERTICAL ARM SHOOTS TO CATCH WIRE WHEN AT LEAST 18 INCHES LONG. RIGHT • PRUNE THE VERTICAL ARM CANE BACK TO TWO BUDS BEFORE THE FOURTH YEAR'S GROWTH BEGINS.

With the cordon system, you should prune the vines each year, usually in December. Select 15 to 22 upright cordons and prune them back to 2 buds. The grape spurs should be spaced 4 to 6 inches apart along the lateral branches. These grape spurs will support the next season's fruiting canes. When you have finished pruning the vine, all that will remain is the main trunk, two 4-foot-long lateral branches, and 15 to 22 grape spurs with 2 buds each. Now the number of spurs will vary from year to year, based on the rate of growth. A very vigorous vine producing more than 4 feet of new growth can have a few more buds, while a vine producing less than 2 feet of growth should have less buds remaining after pruning. This same pruning system will be used throughout the life of the vine.

Cane System

The cordon system is the most common training system in use today, but some varieties produce better using the cane system. Begin the same way with the cane system as you would with the cordon system. When the vine reaches the bottom wire, it should be tipped to encourage branching. Select 2 lateral branches and train them down the wires. Attach the vines to the trellis with vineyard ties every foot or so. Tie a third upright shoot to the stake and train it toward the top wire. If it gets to the top wire, it too should be tipped and the 2 laterals should be trained down the top wire.

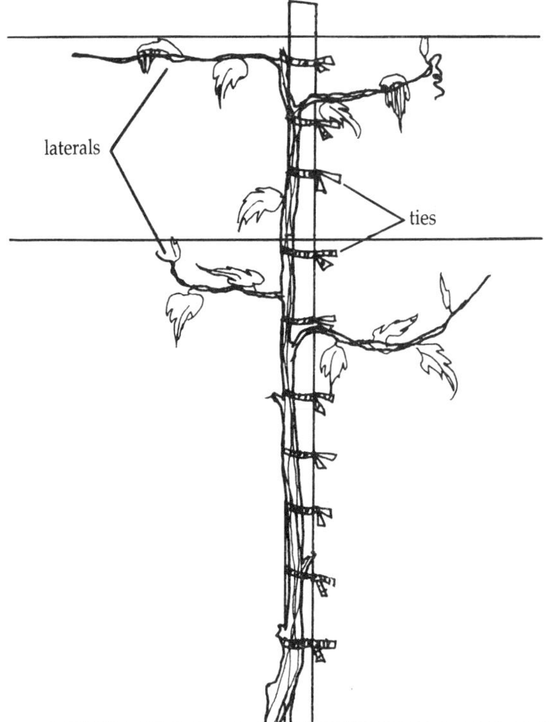

SELECT FOUR LATERAL SHOOTS, TWO AT EACH WIRE AND APPROXIMATELY 6 INCHES BELOW THE WIRE.

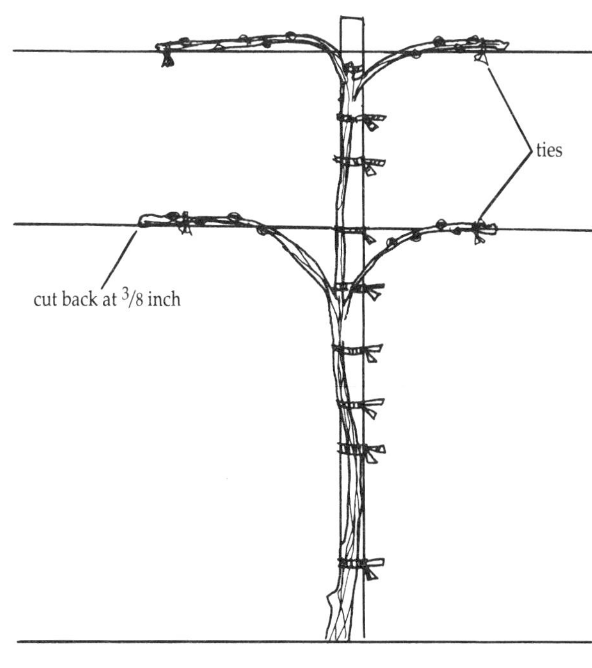

DORMANT PRUNING BEFORE THIRD YEAR'S GROWTH.

By the end of the first growing season, you will ideally have a main trunk to the top wire and 2 to 4 lateral branches. Everything else should be removed. The lateral branches can be cut back, leaving 12- to 18-inch stubs. Remember, do not let the vines produce the second season.

The second year, allow the vines to grow but not to bear. In December, once the vine is dormant, select 4 strong arms (laterals) and attach them to the wires. Near the main trunk, find a renewal cane and prune it back to 2 buds. These spurs will develop into replacement cane for the next season's crop. The 4 laterals should be pruned back, leaving a total of 30 to 45 buds.

Once you have finished pruning the grapes, all that will remain is a main trunk, 4 renewal spurs, and 4 lateral canes with a total of 30 to 45 buds. As with the cordon system, the rate of growth determines how many buds remain after pruning. Each year, you should remove all but 4 of the new canes and 4 renewal spurs.

rutgers plant hardiness zones

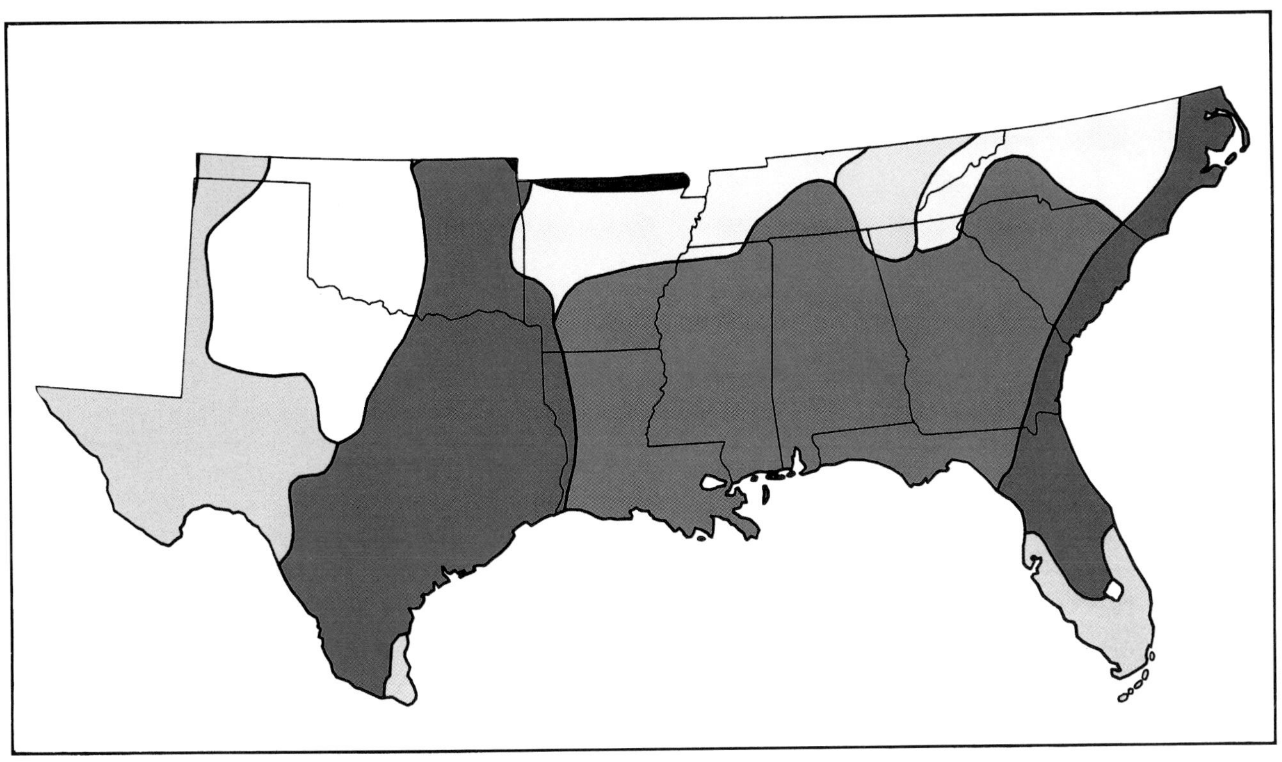

	JANUARY EXTREME MINIMUM TEMPERATURE °F	JULY EXTREME MAXIMUM TEMPERATURE °F	ANNUAL PRECIPITATION (INCHES)	LAST SPRING FROST	FIRST AUTUMN FROST
■	−21.0	106.2	36.3	APR. 24	OCT. 13
■	−16.1	106.9	12.2	APR. 13	OCT. 23
□	−10.5	109.2	21.8	APR. 12	OCT. 25
□	−9.6	105.1	47.0	APR. 09	OCT. 24
□	−9.4	102.0	49.7	APR. 19	OCT. 20
■	0.9	104.7	54.2	MAR. 16	OCT. 31
■	4.3	105.6	39.8	MAR. 10	NOV. 03
□	25.9	99.3	49.2	N/A	N/A

CONCEPT AND CREATION BY DR. ARTHUR T. DEGAETANO AND DR. MARK D. SHULMAN

planning YOUR HOME *orchard*

TOP • *Root sprouts at the base of a tree should be removed.*
LEFT • *Cut off damaged roots before planting the tree.*
BOTTOM, LEFT • *Set the tree at the original soil level or slightly above it.*
BOTTOM, RIGHT • *Cut the tree back 28 to 30 inches immediately after planting.*

apples

LEFT • *Developing apples that are too thick must be thinned to ensure good fruit production.*
BELOW • *Espaliered Anna apple tree.*

Apples trained on a Tatura trellis.

Spreader stakes are used to spread the branches and widen this apple tree's crotch angles.

WEIGHTS ARE USED TO SPREAD THE BRANCHES AND WIDEN CROTCH ANGLES ON THIS APPLE TREE.

APPLES TRAINED ON AN "A" FRAME.

TOP • *DORSETT GOLDEN.*
LEFT • *MOLLIE'S DELICIOUS.*

GALA.

FUJI.

Braeburn.

Starkspur Granny Smith.

TOP • *Starkrimson (Red Delicious).*
MIDDLE • *Akane.*
BOTTOM • *Ozark Gold.*

RIGHT • *CLOTHES PINS ARE USED TO SPREAD THE SHOOTS ON THIS PEAR TREE.*
BELOW • *GOLDEN BOY.*

OAKHILL.

TENNESSEE.

RIGHT • *TURNBULL GIANT.*

Ayers.

Hosui (Asian pear).

Ya Li (Asian pear).

peaches & nectarines

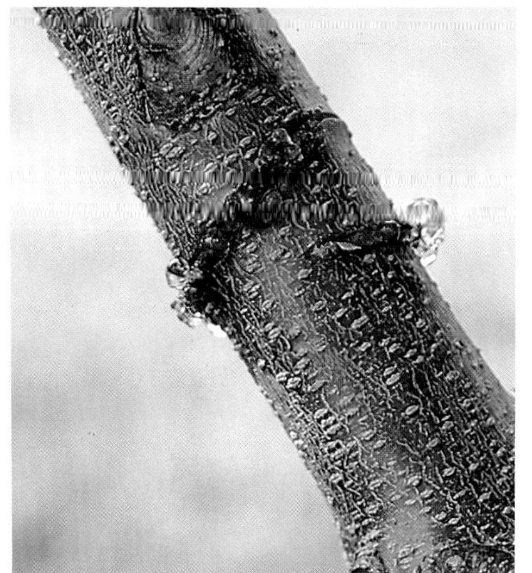

RIGHT • *A GIRDLED PEACH TREE.*
BELOW • *FLORDAKING PEACHES THAT WERE NOT THINNED. NOTE SMALL SIZE AND STRESS ON BRANCH.*

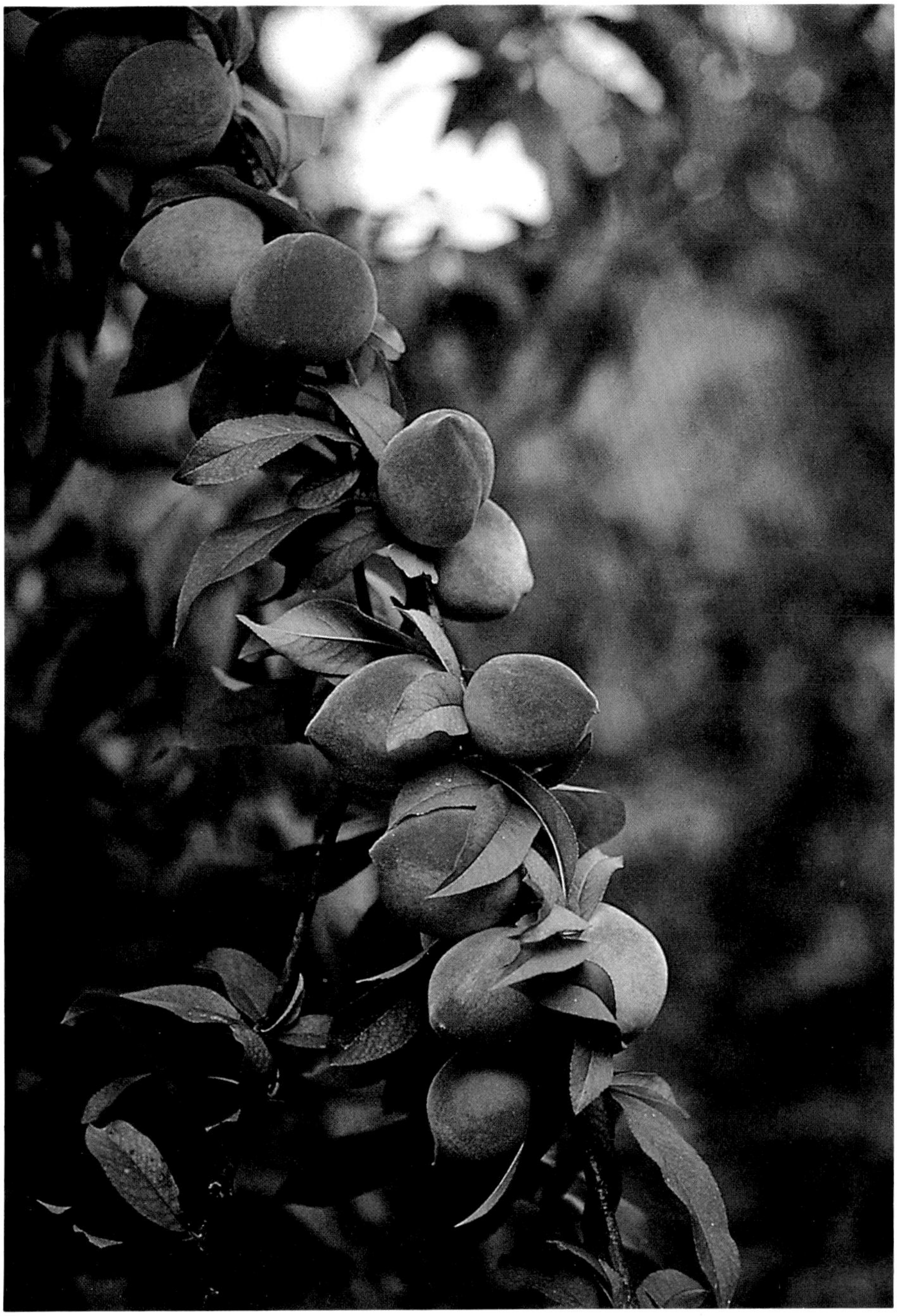

A NECTARINE TREE'S BRANCH BEFORE THINNING.

A NECTARINE TREE'S BRANCH AFTER THINNING.

A peach tree before pruning.

A peach tree after pruning.

La Feliciana peaches.

Texroyal peaches.

Loring peach.

Starlite peach.

LEFT • *RED BARON PEACHES.*

RED GLOBE PEACH.

MAYGLO NECTARINE.

plums, apricots, & cherries

LEFT • *Ozark Premier plum.*
BELOW • *Byron Gold plum.*

Blenheim apricots.

Starking Delicious plum.

berries

Tifblue blueberry.

Brazos blackberry.

Navaho blackberry.

LEFT • *Boysenberry.*
BELOW • *Heritage raspberry.*

LEFT • *PROTECTING NEWLY PLANTED STRAWBERRIES FROM SUMMER HEAT WITH FIBER ROW COVER.*
BELOW • *CHANDLER STRAWBERRY.*

ORLANDO (*SEEDLESS GRAPE*).

Muscadines after pruning.

Muscadine grapes trained on Geneva Double Curtain trellis.

Carlos (muscadine grape).

Black Spanish (bunch grape).

citrus

RIGHT • *SATSUMAS.*
BELOW • *KUMQUATS.*

LEFT • *Alma.*
BELOW • *Celeste.*

SHENG (ASIAN PERSIMMON).

TOP • *Hira tanenashi* (Asian persimmon).
MIDDLE • *Siajo* (Asian persimmon).
BOTTOM • *Suruga* (Asian persimmon).

specialty fruits

RIGHT • *Feijoa.*
BELOW • *Loquat.*

TOP • *POMEGRANATE.*
LEFT • *BANANAS.*

LEFT • *MAYHAWS.*
BELOW • *SILVERHILL ROUND JUJUBE.*

pecans & other nuts

Pistachios in their hulls.

Black walnuts in their hulls.

Pecans in their hulls.

propagating fruits & nuts

LEFT • *Starting to wrap a completed T-bud graft.*
BELOW • *Successful whip-and-tongue graft on a pear tree.*

TOP • *SUCCESSFUL CLEFT GRAFT ON A PEACH TREE.*
RIGHT • *INLAY-BARK ON A PECAN TREE BEGINS GROWTH.*

Flat-headed borer in apple tree trunk.

Bird damage in apples.

Anthracnose fungal disease in grapes.

TOP • *Peach orchard with cotton root rot.*
MIDDLE • *Webworms on pecan tree.*
BOTTOM • *Pear tree with fire blight.*

Plum leaf scorch
a common problem for
southern gardeners.

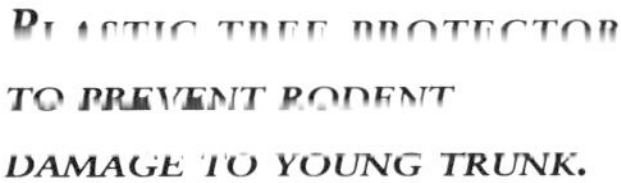

Plastic tree protector
to prevent rodent
damage to young trunk.

Apricot tree with
bacterial canker.

Apple tree with
collar rot.

RIGHT • *Black rot disease in apples.*

Loring peach damaged by sunscald.

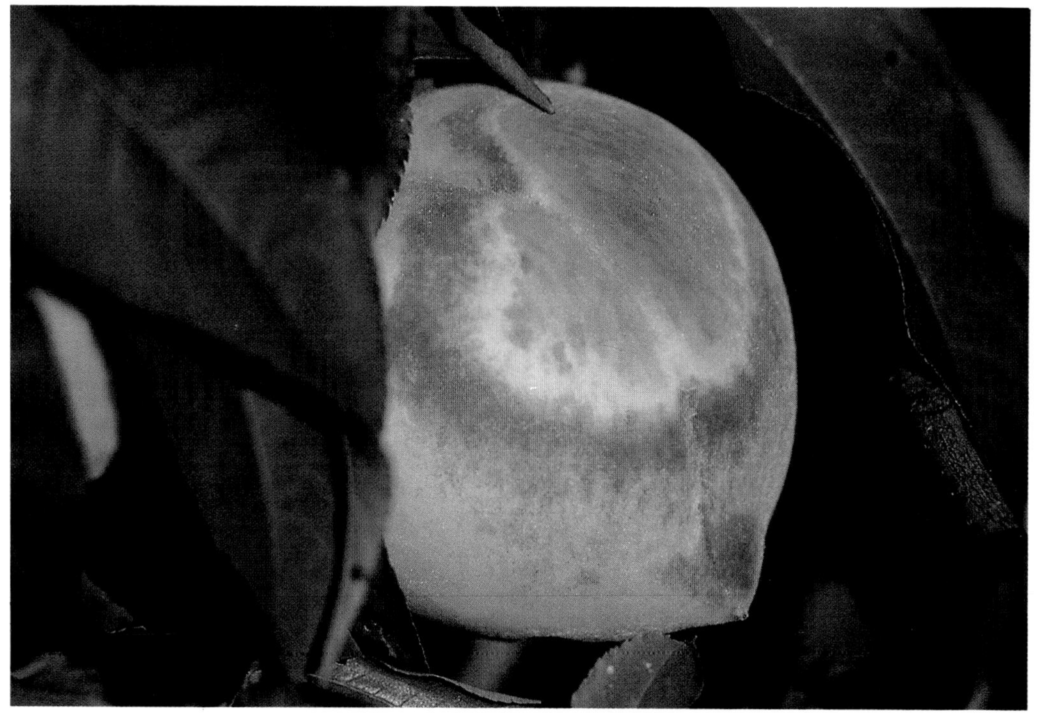

Citrus tree with split bark, caused by winter freeze damage.

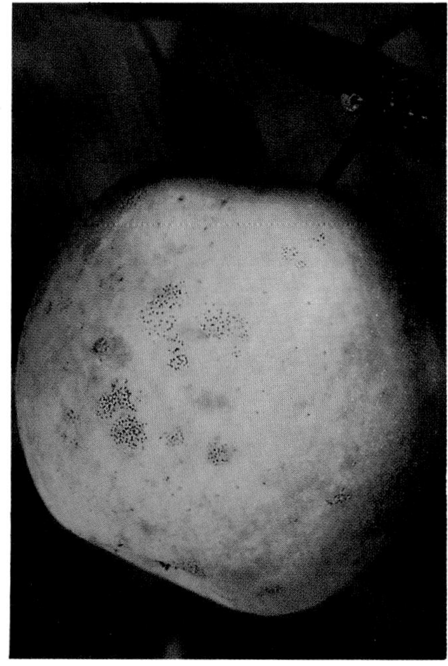

Apple with fly speck fungus.

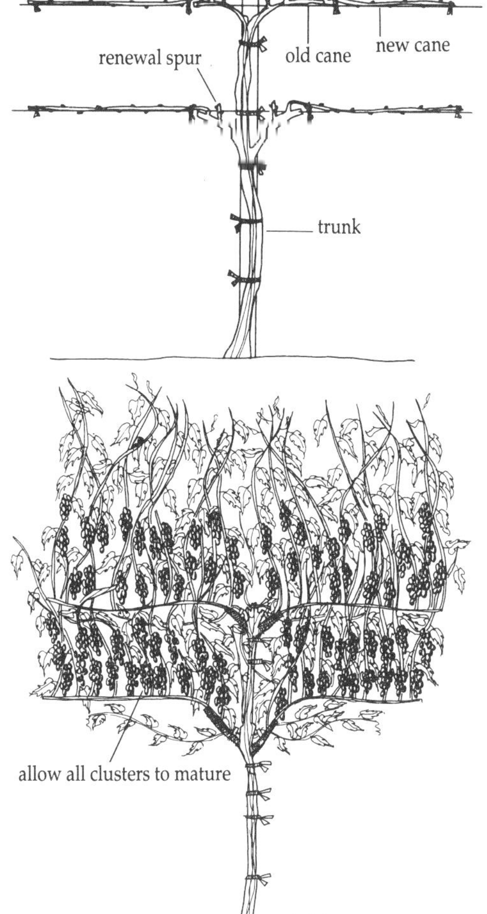

MATURE VINE AFTER CANE PRUNING.

GROWTH AND FRUITING FOLLOWING CANE PRUNING.

Guidelines for Pruning Grapes

1. Prune as soon as the vine is dormant (a few leaves may still remain).
2. Fruit is produced from healthy buds on last year's growth.
3. Vigor can be controlled by pruning.
4. Summer pruning (removal of the top portion of the vines) will also help reduce vigor.
5. Reduce vigor by leaving more fruiting buds.
6. Increase vigor by leaving fewer fruiting buds.
7. Pruning too late (February) can cause the vines to bleed excessively.
8. It is better to prune too much than not enough.

Harvesting

Clusters should be cut, not pulled from the vines. A sharp knife or shears works well. Harvest when the grapes have developed a rich color and have a slight give when squeezed.

Bunch Grape Varieties for the Lower South

Variety	Color	Remarks
Black Spanish (Lenoir)	black	Poor quality but good disease resistance. Like all the varieties in this chart, it is resistant to Pierce's disease though it is susceptible to black rot.
Blanc Du Bois	white	This variety is capable of producing award winning wines, and it is the first such bunch grape variety resistant to Pierce's disease. However, it is susceptible to other diseases—especially anthracnose—and productivity may not be commercially acceptable for pick-your-own operations.
Blue Lake	dark blue	One of the older Florida varieties with adequate quality for jellies and juicing. Productivity is relatively low.
Carman	black	Old variety with medium-sized, compact clusters. Vigorous and disease resistant, but the fruit is only of fair quality.
Champanel	black	Small clusters with large grapes of poor quality. Best if left on the vine until soft ripe—should make bird control even more important though the birds aren't too fond of this one. Good for arbors because it is very vigorous and disease resistant.
Ellen Scott	reddish violet	A Munson hybrid with good production and quality. Relatively unavailable, however.
Favorite	blue-black	Apparently a seedling of Black Spanish with larger grapes and grape clusters. Also slightly better quality.
Fredonia	dark blue	Good quality with spicy flavor, though the grapes have a thick skin. Vines are productive and vigorous though susceptible to downy mildew.
Herbemont	brownish red	Variety with small grapes and tight clusters. Excellent disease resistance and makes a sweet juice. Old variety not readily available.
Lake Emerald	green	This variety has large fruit clusters, but only moderate production. Good disease resistance.
Orlando	white	The first seedless, Pierce's disease-resistant grape! Unfortunately the grapes are the size of buckshot and birds think they're great. Quality is good. Thinning plus application of gibberellic acid shortly after bloom has not proven effective in increasing berry size.
Stover	light green-white	Old Florida variety capable of producing quality wine. Production is low, however.

There are other varieties adapted to the lower South that are resistant to Pierce's disease. Other Munson varieties like Lomanto need to be evaluated. Mississippi varieties like Mississippi Blue and Mississippi Blanc are worth trying. It is also worth noting that most of these varieties will grow in the upper South, but better varieties with less tolerance to Pierce's disease can be grown where this disease is rarely found.

Grape Varieties for the Upper South

Variety	Color	Remarks
Concord	blue-black	Primarily grown for juice and jelly. Grapes have a slightly acidic, wild taste and have a tendency to ripen unevenly. Plants are vigorous but susceptible to black rot.
Mars	red turning blue	Seedless grape with a Concord-like flavor. Good black rot resistance for a seedless grape.
Reliance	coral red	Excellent seedless table grape. Also good juices or jellies. Strong vigorous vines. Susceptible to black rot, but good resistance to anthracnose and mildews.
Saturn	red	High-quality grape similar to Flame Seedless (*vinifera*), but has better disease resistance and cold tolerance.
Seyve-Villard (SV) 5-276	white	French hybrid capable of producing a quality white wine. Plants have good vigor and are highly productive.
SV 12-375 (Villard Blanc)	white	One of the best combinations of European quality and American disease resistance. Produces large clusters on exceptionally vigorous vines.
SV 23-410 (Roucanouf)	white	Good disease resistance and productivity without excessive growth.
Venus	blue-black	Seedless Concord-type grape. Good vigor with good disease resistance. Berries sometimes have partially developed seeds. Best for juice, jellies, or wine.
Verdelet (Seibel 9110)	white	One of the early French hybrids. It produces a yellow gold dessert-quality berry. Can also be used for wine. Partially seedless.

Rootstocks for Bunch Grapes

It is debatable whether rootstocks for bunch grapes work well enough to be worth the effort. Many grapes do quite well with their own roots and have an adequate resistance to the majority of soil-borne pests. The French-American hybrids, for example, will usually benefit from a rootstock that is resistant to pests, including cotton root rot, nematodes, and phylloxera (a small aphidlike insect that attacks the root system). Increased vigor and cold hardiness may also be benefits. Some of these rootstocks include:

- Champanel—resistant to cotton root rot and phylloxera, but susceptible to nematodes. In addition it causes increased vigor that may cause frost damage
- Dog Ridge—best for highly alkaline soils, resistant to nematodes, phylloxera, and cotton root

rot, vigor may cause freeze injury

- La Pryor—similar resistance
- Tampa—Florida variety develped to tolerate sandy soils and nematodes
- Mustang—native Texas species with excellent disease and insect resistance. It has been difficult to propagate, but it is more easily rooted with cuttings from the current season's growth under intermittent mist.

Vinifera (European) grapes have such a limited range within the South because of Pierce's disease that the numerous varieties do not warrant discussion. Unfortunately many nurseries carry these varieties and all appear to be terminally susceptible to Pierce's disease. In an isolated home situation the vines may live for 10 to 15 years before they die and that may be adequate for some homeowners. Most southern growers should resist the temptation to plant *vinifera* varieties such as Cabernet Sauvignon, Chardonnay, Chenin Blanc, Flame Seedless, Perlette, Petite Sirah, Pinot Noir, Thompson Seedless, and Zinfandel.

Muscadine Grapes

Most consumers aren't familiar with the rich flavor of muscadine grapes. It's a cultivated taste, because muscadines literally assault the senses of smell and taste. The berries are sweet, full of complex flavors, and the fragrance is enjoyable. So far all muscadines have some seeds. Fry Seedless is mostly free of seeds, but production has been disappointing. Some of the older varieties had tough skins, but the skin toughness has been reduced through breeding. Someday we should have a seedless muscadine worth planting.

Muscadines produce small clusters instead of big bunches, but they produce many, many clusters and mature vines have the potential to produce 15 tons per acre. The Southeast, notably Mississippi, Georgia, and Florida, have many acres planted in muscadines and virtually all of the other southern states produce some of these grapes commercially. Muscadines have poor storage potential so they are best used for juices, jellies, and wine or for local market and pick-your-own sales.

Another factor to consider when planting muscadines is pollination. Some varieties are self-fertile, which means they produce both male and female flowers while others produce female (pistillate) flowers only. In a single row, every third vine should be a self-fertile type. In a larger planting, every third plant in every 3 rows should be self-fertile. Most of the superior varieties used to be female types, but with today's selection of varieties the majority of a vineyard could be planted with self-fertile varieties. Development of varieties with a dry stem scar has also been very important in recent years. These varieties have much better storage potential.

Muscadine Grapes: Soils and Fertility

Muscadine grapes are native to much of the southeastern United States. This means they are a natural choice for the southern gardener.

Muscadines tolerate damp soil, dry soil, and everything in between. They do seem to prefer a slightly acidic, fertile, and sandy loam soil that is high in organic matter. They don't like very wet or highly alkaline soil. Where soil pH is too high (above 7.5), iron chlorosis can be a serious problem. It can be corrected by regular foliar applications of chelated iron. Where soils are too wet, try raised beds.

Muscadine grapes are native to the southeastern pine forests, where temperatures seldom fall below 10°F and rarely below 0°F. The forest floor is covered with a thick mat of leaves and needles. In cultivation, they still seem to enjoy a thick layer of mulch to help regulate moisture levels and to keep the soil cool through the heat of summer. Unlike other grapes, muscadines enjoy a moderate level of fertility. During the early years, nitrogen is the only nutrient they require.

Fertilizing Muscadines

Fertilizer should be applied one time each in early March, May, and July and placed 12 to 18 inches from vines. Select only one fertilizer for each application.

FERTILIZER	1 YEAR	2 YEARS	3 YEARS
Ammonium Nitrate	¼ cup	½ cup	1 cup
Ammonium Sulfate	⅓ cup	⅔ cup	1½ cups
Cottonseed Meal	2 pounds	4 pounds	8 pounds
Blood Meal	1 cup	2 cups	4 cups
Fish Meal	2 cups	4 cups	8 cups
Sewage Sludge (Sterilized)	5 pounds	10 pounds	15 pounds
Urea Formaldehyde (Slow Release)	½ cup	1 cup	2 cups

Once a vine is 4 years old or older, it should receive 3 to 5 pounds of 8–8–8 or 13–13–13 fertilizer in early March. As soon as you see that fruit has set, an application of nitrogen following the above table for the third year should be applied. Remember, select only 1 of these nitrogen fertilizers each application.

Training and Pruning

Muscadine grapes should be planted during the dormant season (December through February). One- and two-year-old plants are available but two-year-old plants do appear to be more vigorous. No soil preparation is needed for muscadines, but they do benefit from the application of an organic mulch and require good drainage.

There are two main training systems commonly being used to train muscadines. The cordon system for muscadines is similar to the one used on bunch grapes. One of the main differences is the spacing.

Muscadines are much more vigorous and require more space. On the cordon system, the plants are spaced 20 to 25 feet apart in the row and the rows are spaced 10 to 12 feet apart. The other difference is the spur development. With bunch grapes, select a 1-year-old twig and prune it back to the 2 buds every 6 inches along the lateral branch. Muscadines also have spurs every 6 inches, but the spurs are allowed and encouraged to branch until a mass of possibly 6 or 8 spurs are remaining at each spur location. Each year, the spur cluster is pruned back to 4 to 8 subspurs with 2 to 3 buds each. Remember, too, when spur pruning that grapes produce on new growth from buds on last year's wood. Wood that is 2 to 3 years old will not produce like last year's wood.

GENEVA DOUBLE CURTAIN

The other major training system is the modified Geneva Double Curtain. This system utilizes 2 wires spaced about 4 feet apart on the top of 5½- to 6-foot posts. The vines can be planted 15 to 20 feet apart with the rows being 10 to 12 feet apart.

The vines are trained to the top of the trellis and then encouraged to branch, developing a T, where the spurs are to originate. Each year, the vine is pruned back to the lateral, leaving 4 spurs with 2 to 3 buds each. As growth begins in the spring, the strongest shoot on each spur is selected and allowed to grow down its assigned wire. As the vines grow, they will meet the adjacent vine somewhere in the middle. This type of spur pruning is easy to manage and seems to work well for muscadine grapes.

Harvesting

Muscadines are best harvested when fully ripe. You will usually see a color change and the fruit will begin to soften slightly. Because the small clusters rarely ripen all at once, they are harvested by hand or with a catching frame (a light frame covered in fabric), which is hung under the vines as the vines are shaken or bumped to dislodge the fruit. Harvesting will need to be done 2 to 3 times until all the fruit has been removed.

Grape Arbors

Muscadine grapes are very well suited to arbors. They cover well, providing a cool, natural shade that only a living plant can provide. The vines are generally planted at the base of the post supporting the arbor, approximately 15 feet apart. At the top of the arbor, the vine should be tip pruned to develop 2 lateral branches along the top of the structure. These laterals will support the spurs that develop into fruiting canes and cover the top of the arbor.

The top of the arbor should be made of wires rather than wooden lattice. The lattice is more decorative but can make pruning a nightmare because the vines tend to weave in and out of the lattice.

Muscadine Grapes

Variety	Color/ Pollination (S: self-fertile, F: female)	Remarks
African Queen	black, F	Large, very sweet fruit. Uniform mid-season ripening.
Alachua	black, S	Recommended for fresh use. Ripens uniformly and may be harvested mechanically.
Black Beauty	black, F	Fruit size is up to 1¼ inch in diameter and sugar to 24½%.
Carlos	bronze, S	One of the best self-fertile muscadines. Moderately susceptible to Pierce's disease. Quality is excellent.
Darlene	bronze, F	Fruit is a consistent 1¼ inch in size. Also high sugar content with a dry scar.
Dixie	bronze, S	Vigorous plants produce high-quality berries. Mid-season variety.
Doreen	bronze, S	Berries are good for wine or fresh use with over 50% dry stem scars. Plants are vigorous with high yields and good disease resistance.
Farrer	black, F	Fruit produced in large clusters with high sugar content and a dry scar.

Variety	Color/ Pollination (S: self-fertile, F: female)	Remarks
Fry	bronze, F	The fruit of this variety is very large and has excellent flavor. Though it's been around since 1970, it is still popular as a commercial variety. It is mostly for fresh use, jellies, or juice.
Fry, black	black, F	Similar quality in a black grape.
Granny-Val	bronze, S	High yielding with 1¼ inch fruit. Ripens mid- to late season.
Higgins	black, F	Older variety, but still in demand for its high-quality fruit. It is very sweet with low acidity. Not recommended for wine.
Hunt	black, F	Another old variety with high-quality fruit. Excellent for all uses including winemaking.
Ison	black, S	One of the best all-around grapes for fresh use, processing, and wine. Produces large berries in large clusters. Berries ripen uniformly with a dry scar. Sugar content is excellent in this early to mid-season variety.
Janebell	bronze, S	Another large, high-sugar variety with a dry scar. Mid- to late season with good disease resistance.
Janet	bronze, S	Very large berries up to 1¼ inch in diameter. Produces mid-season and has a wet scar.
Jumbo	black, F	Produces one of the largest fruit of any black muscadine. Primarily a home variety as it ripens irregularly over several weeks. Fruit must be fully ripe to be at its peak of quality. Typically poor quality with a nonmelting pulp.
Magnolia	bronze, S	Excellent quality, adapted to commercial plantings, including vineyards. Fruit does pick with a wet stem scar.
Nesbitt	black, S	Very large fruit primarily for fresh use. Has a dry stem scar, high yields, and good disease resistance.
Noble	black, S	Large clusters of medium-sized berries are good for most uses including red wine production.
Pam	bronze, F	Fruit has good color and is produced in long clusters. It is extra large and harvests with a dry scar.
Pineapple	bronze, S	Vigorous, disease-resistant variety with a hint of pineapple flavor.
Regale	black, S	Good wine variety with very heavy yields. Good winter hardiness and ripens early.
Rosa	pinkish red, F	Large variety with good eye appeal and high taste test ratings. Fruit harvests with a wet scar. Good variety for the home and pick-your-own market.

VARIETY	COLOR/ POLLINATION (S: SELF-FERTILE, F: FEMALE)	REMARKS
Senoia	pinkish bronze, S	Fruit is harvested with a dry scar and may be used for an excellent wine. Fruit comes off mid-season and ripens evenly.
Southland	black, S	Good-quality grapes for fresh use or for juices and jellies. Not recommended for wine. Good disease resistance, mid-season ripening.
Sugargate	black, F	Grapes have very high sugar content and are very large, but production is limited.
Sugar Pop	bronze, F	Extra large fruit that pops when eaten. High productivity of fruit with a dry scar.
Summit	bronze, F	Recommended for home and commercial plantings. One of the best varieties considering yield, large size, and quality. Berries also have relatively thin skins.
Supreme	black, F	Extra large, high-sugar variety with a good, palatable skin. Dry scar.
Sweet Jenny	bronze, F	One of the largest fruits, up to 1½ inches in diameter. Very high sugar and good productivity. Produced early to mid-season.
Triumph	bronze, S	Fruit is produced in large clusters and is harvested with a dry stem scar. Berries are thin-skinned, recommended for commercial and home use.
Watergate	bronze, F	Vigorous vines with high-quality, large fruit.
Welder	bronze, S	Excellent-quality fruit is medium-sized and very sweet. Good for fresh use or for winemaking.

citrus 8

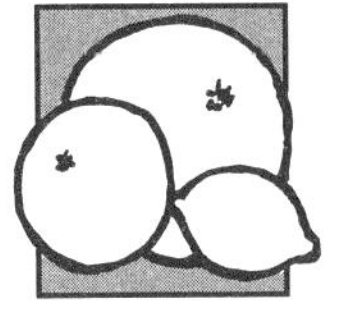

Citrus is one of the most diverse and frustrating fruit crops for the southern grower to work with. Except for Southern California and the tip of Florida, most southern growers often lose an entire crop to freeze damage. Citrus growers (mostly grapefruit producers) in Texas' Rio Grande Valley have suffered devastating losses twice during the 80s. They didn't just lose their crop—most lost their trees as well. Yet climates with warm temperatures during the citrus' maturity phase seem to grow the highest quality grapefruit. At one time there were many acres of satsuma tangerines planted along the upper Gulf Coast. Today only a few scattered plantings remain in southern Louisiana.

However, hardy citrus has been grown north of the Gulf Coast by determined homeowners. Homeowners must be determined because they will have to provide some freeze protection most years. It may be as simple as planting on the south side of the house and dropping a plastic sheet down from the eave or setting up a small electric heater or heat lamp on those few nights when temperatures drop into the low 20s or below. Another possibility would be to grow citrus in a greenhouse. Although setting up a greenhouse may seem like too much work, it doesn't have to be an elaborate structure. In fact, the greenhouse could be open in the summer and covered with plastic in the winter. If you don't mind straining with large pots or whiskey barrels every time a freeze is predicted, you could even grow citrus like the very tender Mexican lime in a container and bring it in every time bad weather threatened.

Another frustrating problem associated with citrus is the unavailability of most varieties. Satsumas (often marketed without the benefit of a variety name), kumquats, and an occasional Ponderosa or Meyer lemon are usually the only available varieties and they are rarely grafted on acceptable rootstocks.

Trifoliate orange is used in most of the upper Gulf Coast. While sour orange is the dominant rootstock used commercially in the Rio Grande Valley, it produces poor plant quality overall. Serious enthusiasts plant rootstocks, usually Flying Dragon trifoliate (it's hardy and dwarfing), and then propagate their own trees with budwood from other citrus enthusiasts. Much of this unavailability is due to quarantines, which prevent the movement of citrus trees across state lines in the South. Although they are inhibiting, these quarantines prevent the transfer of the tristeza virus, citrus canker, and Mediterranean fruit fly infestation to other areas.

Citrus: Soils and Fertility

Citrus grows best in a well-drained, slightly acidic soil. They tolerate sands or clays as long as the drainage is adequate. Soil pH is also less critical. Citrus grows well in soils with pH ranging from 6 to 8.

Trees will usually be purchased as established container-grown, grafted plants. Although we plant most fruit trees during the dormant season, citrus is better planted after the soil has begun to warm in the spring. It is best to give the plants as much time as possible to become established before the winter freezes start.

Citrus should be planted high, with the graft union several inches above the soil line. Citrus are very susceptible to foot rot disease. Planting too deep, having too much moisture around the crown, or having overly wet soil will all contribute to disease problems. Always plant the plants high to keep the roots from staying too wet, but never allow the plants to dry out. A water ring, or well, will help keep the moisture near the roots until the plant becomes established. In most southern soils, nitrogen will be the only nutrient required for healthy, productive growth.

Amount of Fertilizer Applied Monthly from March through August

FERTILIZER	1 YEAR	2 YEARS	3 YEARS
Ammonium Nitrate	¼ cup	½ cup	1 cup
Ammonium Sulfate	½ cup	1 cup	2 cups
Cottonseed Meal	4 pounds	6 pounds	12 pounds
Blood Meal	2 pounds	3 pounds	6 pounds
Fish Meal	2 pounds	3 pounds	6 pounds
Sewage Sludge	10 pounds	15 pounds	20 pounds
Urea Formaldehyde	¼ cup	½ cup	1 cup

A tree is considered mature once it is 4 to 5 years old. Mature bearing trees should receive enough nutrition to make good but not excessive growth.

The application of one of the above fertilizers, applied at the rate suggested for the third year based on the trunk's diameter in inches, should be applied once a year in March. For example, a 3-inch diameter tree would require 3 cups of ammonium nitrate applied in March. When fertilizing, select only one fertilizer for each application.

Training and Pruning

Generally, citrus requires little or no training or pruning. Pruning can actually delay fruit production by reducing the foliage needed to manufacture needed nutrients. Suckers and watersprouts should be broken off as soon as they are noticed and dead or diseased wood should be pruned out. Other than that, not much pruning is needed.

Flowering and Fruit Set

Citrus will usually begin producing light crops the second or third season. Production should gradually increase as the tree grows in size.

Trees usually put on 4 to 5 flushes of new growth per season. In truly tropical climates citrus will produce flowers and fruit on each flush, permitting harvest of fresh fruit all year-round. In most of the South, citrus will only bear fruit on the spring bloom. If off-season (nonspring) bloom and fruit set does occur in temperate climates, it should be removed. Normal fruit and flower drop occurs throughout the season. This fruit drop is to be expected and cannot be prevented.

Freeze Protection

Even in the most mild southern climate, some frost or freeze protection will be required most years. For the deep South, freeze protection will involve banking mulch or soil up and around the graft union each winter to protect it from freeze injury. More protection will be required the farther you are from the coast. Don't let your location prevent you from growing citrus if that is what you want to grow.

Many people construct makeshift greenhouses over their trees each winter by draping sheets of plastic over frames made of 2×4s or PVC pipe with 1 or 2 150-watt light bulbs or a small heater in the structure to keep the winter chill away.

Container Culture

Growing citrus in containers is another way of growing them in areas where winters are too severe. Most citrus adapt well to container cultivation. Flying dragon or trifoliate rootstock will help dwarf the tree, making it easier to handle and increasing its hardiness.

KEYS TO SUCCESSFUL CONTAINER CULTURE

1. Select a container large enough to accommodate the plant.
2. Use a soilless potting media.
3. Make sure the container has drain holes.
4. Locate container in full or nearly full sun.
5. Keep soil evenly moist but be careful not to overwater.
6. Apply a soluble fertilizer (2 times a month) during the growing season.
7. Only prune to maintain size and eliminate dead or diseased growth.
8. Don't expect the yields that are obtained from trees grown in the ground.

Citrus for the South

Variety	Cold Tolerance	Remarks
Mandarins	22° to 28°F	This is a large group, which includes satsumas (the most commonly planted citrus in the lower South) and tangerines. Kimbrough, Owari, and Silverhill satsumas are sometimes available. Kawano wase, Vermillion 2, Armstrong Early, Obawase, and Ishi Kawa Unshu are other satsumas to look for. Other mandarins include Pong Koa (hardy with excellent flavor), Dancy tangerine, Changsha tangerine, Ponkan honey orange, Fairchild, and Sunburst tangerine.
Kumquats	20° to 24°F, especially if grafted on trifoliate rootstock	Meiwa is the preferred variety. It is round with few seeds and it is much sweeter than Nagami. Nagami is an elongated fruit—the one most commonly found at the grocery market.
Grapefruits	26° to 28°F	Bloomsweet is a slipskin white-fleshed grapefruit that is relatively hardy. Henderson is the most cold-hardy red variety. Rio Red and Ray Ruby are excellent red varieties that are less cold hardy.
Sour Fruits	20° to 28°F	Hardiness varies greatly within this group from the very tender Mexican lime to very hardy Thomasville Citrangequat (also a good rootstock). Lemonquat and limequat are intermediate and will

Variety	Cold Tolerance	Remarks
continued		need some protection along the Gulf Coast. Species types like Ichang lemon and Citrus taiwanica are hardy but the fruit is marginal. Actually, the sour orange often used as a rootstock makes a good sour juice though the fruit is rather seedy. Ponderosa lemon, with its huge fruit, and Meyer lemon, with more normal-sized fruit, are often available though both need frost protection and have fruit that has a resiny flavor. The homeowner wanting an attractive tree with small, ornamental orange fruit would do well to look for the Thomasville Citrangequat. The fruit is sour, slipskin, and very good for lemonade-type drinks.

figs 9

The fig is a traditional southern fruit—easy to grow—though its existence is not entirely trouble free. Hard winters often damage fruiting wood, especially on the Celeste variety, which bears almost entirely on last year's growth. Varieties with an open eye at the end of the fruit are subject to souring from the dried fruit beetle. Hot, dry weather often causes the fruit to shrivel and get hard. And even if all goes right, birds, raccoons, opossums, nematodes, and other varmints often get the figs before the grower does. Regardless, they still produce one of the easiest to grow, the most nutritious, and the most delicious crops. They need mulching annually, measured and thorough watering when it's dry, and a net to keep the varmints from harvesting the crop. As far as spraying is concerned, figs almost have to be grown organically because very few pesticides can be used on them.

Figs: Soils and Fertility

Figs are very tolerant of soils but grow best in a deep clay loam soil. Figs can be grown successfully on very light sandy soils but nematodes (microscopic round worms that feed on the root system) can be a serious problem. Figs are the nematode's favorite host.

Adding organic matter at planting time will help control the nematodes. The organic matter also provides the nutrients and moisture retention figs need. A heavy layer of mulch, 8 to 12 inches thick, will allow the fig to grow and produce where nematodes are a problem because it improves plant growth, promotes soil moisture retention, and maintains a moderate soil temperature.

Figs require a tremendous amount of water and mulches hold the moisture in the soil. Additional water, however, must be applied during periods of drought to allow for healthy growth and fruit development. Summer fruit drop is a serious problem with figs. Lack of water and nematodes are the main causes for this drop. Be sure to watch for plant stress and apply water when needed.

Figs should not be fertilized in most southern soils. Too much fertilizer can cause fruit splitting and increase the chance of frost injury. The breakdown of the organic mulch should provide all of the nutrients the fig tree will need.

Pruning and Training

Figs produce best with little or no pruning. Two main training systems are used: The single-trunk system, in which trees are trained to have 1 main trunk and 2 vase-shaped branch structures, should only be used in the very deep South where freezing weather is not a problem. The other system, the multi-trunked bush, is by far the most popular and the best for southern growers. This system keeps the crop more accessible and makes the trees less vulnerable (than single-trunk trees) to severe killing freezes.

With either system, pruning and training is generally not required. Each year, the trees can be thinned a little to prevent the accumulation of dense unproductive twig growth.

When old trees become too large to manage easily, they can be reduced in size by pruning ⅓ to ½ of the large, tall branches back to a lower branch. This process should be done each year for 2 or 3 years until the size is reduced. This 2- to 3-year process will allow you to continue harvesting a crop each year while bringing the fig tree into the desired boundaries. For multi-trunked bushes, remove a few canes each year to prevent overcrowding.

Fruit Thinning and Harvesting

Along the Gulf Coast, we grow closed-eye figs that produce parthenocarpic fruit (fruit produced without pollination). Parthenocarpic fruit are very sensitive to stress. Thinning is not required because overproduction causes stress and the tree thins itself.

Figs should be harvested as soon as they become ripe. You will notice a change in color and the fruit will become soft. You should wear gloves and protective clothing because many people have allergic reactions to the sap or latex that the plant exudes.

Propagation

Figs can be easily propagated with stem cuttings. In December collect 6- to 8-inch terminal shoots from vigorous 1-year-old wood. Small diameter, weak cuttings make inferior plants and should be avoided. Tie the cuttings in small bundles and place them in a trench with the cut end sticking up (cuttings are upside down). Cover the cuttings with 2 to 4 inches of soil and wait for the development of callus on the cut end. In April, remove the cuttings from the callus bed and place them right side up in a well-drained soil with about 2 inches sticking out of the soil. The cuttings will root and be ready to move to a permanent location by the first dormant season.

Frost Protection

Figs can suffer damage if temperatures fall below 15°F. Plant your trees in a protected area or provide protection if temperatures routinely fall below 15°F. In northern parts of the Gulf Coast, figs can be grown if they are protected during the winter by a frame covered in plastic and filled with leaves (for insulation). In the southern regions, a thick layer of mulch or soil banked up over the crown of the plant is all that figs require.

Figs for the South

Variety	Harvest/Color	Remarks
Alma	late June light yellow	Fair quality, fruit has a drop of "honey" in the eye, reducing damage from the fruit beetle.
Brown Turkey	June brownish maroon	High-quality variety even though it has an open eye.
Celeste	June and July purplish brown	Still probably the best-quality fig grown in the South. It has a complex sweetness and leaves a pleasant aftertaste. It also has a closed eye.

Variety	Harvest/Color	Remarks
continued		Unfortunately it is somewhat susceptible to cold and normally bears on last year's wood. A hard freeze or overzealous pruning can destroy the crop. Prune only ⅓ of last year's growth. If trees become overgrown, prune them back in stages over 2 to 3 years.
Excel	August yellow with amber pulp	Large, productive California variety. Resists splitting and adapted to container growing.
Flanders	July and August violet-striped and white-flecked, amber pulp	Vigorous variety. Developed by Dr. Condit in California and reportedly doing well in the South. Productive and resistant to splitting.
Green Ischia (Verte)	July and August green with red flesh	Good-quality fruit but the tree is only moderately productive. Eye is partially closed so the fruit beetle is not too damaging and the green color may make it less attractive to birds.
Magnolia	July and August reddish brown with pink flesh	Grown primarily as a fig for preserves. The fruit is large but has an open eye and thus is susceptible to the dried fruit beetle. Relatively hardy and bears good crops on new growth so it can be pruned heavily.
Nardine	July and August	Another Dr. Condit hybrid.
Panache	August yellow with green stripes, pink flesh	Needs a long season. Best for fresh use.
Tena	August and September light green, pink flesh	Heavy producer, good for fresh or dried use. Can be grown in large pots.
Texas Everbearing	July and August brown to purple, amber flesh	Large fig with a closed eye. Best for preserves. Produces on current season's growth.
Yvonne	August and September light yellow with freckles	Another Dr. Condit variety—sweet, vigorous, and productive.

10 persimmons

This ancient fruit was introduced into the United States in the nineteenth century and is emerging as a crop with a great deal of potential for southern growers. The South has a mild climate that allows us to grow many of the nonastringent varieties that would freeze in the North before the fruit matured. The nonastringent varieties are sweet and non-puckering but still crisp and typically appealing to those that try them for the first time. Astringent varieties (puckering until ripe) are gelatinous when ripe though very tasty and have a range of complex flavors including hints of cinnamon, watermelon, pumpkin, and others. Some astringent varieties develop seeds and dark flesh and become nonastringent when they are pollinated. These are termed pollination-variant types. Unless varieties that are known to produce a number of male flowers are included in the planting, these varieties will remain astringent. Production and demand for this type of persimmon has primarily been limited to the Orient.

Freezing the ripe fruits is a good way to store them. They can be removed, partially thawed, and eaten with a spoon like an all-natural freezer pop. Whether astringent or nonastringent, the closer the fruit is to tree ripe when picked the better its quality will be when ripened in storage.

Native American persimmons are not to be totally ignored; there are actually quite a few varieties. John Ricks is one of the best known and one of the largest. All are astringent, which is important because most of us have eaten a wild fruit that has made us pucker up. Perhaps that's why there is a certain reluctance to recognize the persimmon as a fruit crop with serious potential. Regardless, there is an increasing demand for this fruit. Maybe the native persimmons will gain a following as well.

Persimmons: Soils and Fertility

Persimmons, like most fruit, prefer a slightly acidic (pH of 6.0 to 6.5), well-drained fertile soil. The persimmon is tolerant of varying soil types and actually does better than other fruit crops in heavy clay soil. Just remember, like most fruit, they don't grow as well in extremely wet or poorly drained soil.

Persimmons live very long and make a nice landscape tree. Their fall color and decorative fruit make them a worthwhile addition to the landscape even if you don't like their fruit.

Persimmons have been studied extensively in Japan and New Zealand, where they've determined that nitrogen is needed to induce flowering and is generally the most important element for successful growth and good fruit production. Potassium is also important; it promotes shoot growth. Phosphorus is least required but does enhance fruit color. A typical lawn fertilizer like 15–5–10 or 21–7–14 or something similar would make an excellent fertilizer for persimmons. Magnesium is also an important element. A lack of magnesium will usually result in stunted plants or blackened leaf tips. Two or three tablespoons of Epsom salt ($MgSO_4$) sprinkled around the tree each year will usually solve this problem.

Fertilizer should be placed around the trees in March (before growth begins), in late May, and again in August. Whenever fertilizing, place the fertilizer several feet away from the tree and thoroughly water the soil.

Fertilizer Applications

TREE AGE	MARCH	LATE MAY	AUGUST
1	½ pound	¼ pound	¼ pound
2	1 pound	½ pound	½ pound
3	1½ pounds	¾ pound	¾ pound
4	2 pounds	1 pound	1 pound
5 to 7	3 pounds	1½ pounds	1½ pounds
7 to 10	5 pounds	2½ pounds	2½ pounds

These fertilizer rates are for a 15–5–10, a 21–7–14, or a similar fertilizer.

Training and Pruning

The tree should be planted during the dormant season (December through February). At planting time the tree should be cut back one-third to one-half of the tree height.

Most persimmons are trained using a modified central leader system. For information on using this system, see Chapter 2.

The palmette system is growing in popularity because it encourages higher tree density, which produces greater yields in a tree's early years. This system can be trained on a trellis, trained as an espalier on a fence or wall, or grown freestanding in rows. The trees are spaced 15 feet apart in rows spaced 10 feet apart or about 290 trees to the acre.

A main trunk is selected and trained straight up. Every 2 to 2½ feet, a limb is selected and trained at a 45° angle. If trained on a support, the limbs are attached where they cross the wires.

Once the tree begins producing a crop regularly, you should watch for a late season or second-season flush of growth. This is usually a result of high fertility, excessive fruit thinning, or mild climatic conditions. The second flush doesn't usually produce fruit well and is generally pruned out in late summer.

Flowering, Pollination, and Fruit Thinning

Persimmons have one of the most interesting and varied flower structures. Many persimmon varieties produce only female flowers; though some produce male and female flowers on the same tree, and others produce perfect (hermaphroditic) flowers that contain the male and female parts in the same flower.

Persimmons are one of the few fruits that can produce their fruit parthenocarpically (without pollination and devoid of seeds). When pollen is present, persimmon trees will normally set fruit and seeds will be present. Many astringent varieties become nonastringent when seeds are present.

Pollinating persimmons can be valuable because it increases the quality and reduces fruit drop: pollinated fruit is much less likely to drop than parthenocarpic fruit. Some varieties, such as Fuyu, are much better if pollinated because they have a serious problem with fruit drop if they are not.

Excessive fruit drop can be attributed to a number of things. Lack of pollination is a common cause. Other things that can contribute to the problem are insufficient sunlight for the fruit, excess vegetative growth, and an overly heavy fruit load. Water stress, although it may have a role in fruit drop, does not appear to be as important as previously believed. Fruit drop, due to drought, should not occur until the tree is stressed to the point of defoliation.

The calyx (leafy structure attached to the fruit) is important to the fruits' health and development. Scientists don't completely understand the calyx's function, but they know it is involved in gas exchange and has a large effect on fruit growth and size.

Each flowering shoot will produce from 2 to 4 flowers (fruit). If all these flowers produce fruit, the tree will be overloaded. Thinning is critical to tree health and helps ensure years of production. Generally, persimmons should be thinned to 1 to 2 fruit per shoot. The fruit with the largest calyx will develop the largest fruit. Also, the basal flowers (flowers nearest the base of the shoot) will be the largest. This means, while you're thinning, select basal fruit with a large well-developed calyx.

Harvesting

Persimmons are very well adapted to the southern climate. The high fall temperatures are needed for the nonastringent varieties to lose all of their astringency. When fall temperatures are cool, these varieties may not lose their astringency.

Nonastringent varieties are by far the most popular in this country. If you grow astringent varieties, the pucker can be removed by spraying the mature, orange, and firm fruit with 35% to 40% ethyl alcohol and placing in a sealed container for 10 days at around 69°F. The fruit will remain firm for several days.

Persimmons are harvested from September to December, depending on the variety. Nonastringent varieties can be picked when they are a bright orange to orange-red color but still firm. They can be eaten when firm or soft.

Astringent varieties, on the other hand, must be eaten while soft unless treated as explained above. These varieties achieve the best quality when allowed to soften on the tree. However, you may have to fight the birds and varmints if you want to harvest the persimmons. Astringent varieties can be harvested when they are firm and highly colored. Place the fruit at room temperature in a sealed paper bag and they will soften in a few days.

Asian Persimmons for the South

Variety	Astringent (A) or Nonastringent (N), Pollination variant (PV)	Ripe/Color	Remarks
Chocolate	A, PV	September orange with dark, flecked brown flesh	Considered one of the best flavored; also very productive. Acorn-shaped.
Fuyu	N	October and November orange with light orange flesh	The standard by which nonastringent varieties are judged. The crisp flesh is sweet with complex flavors and the fruit can be eaten over a long period of time. It is also a variety with

Variety	Astringent (A) or Nonastringent (N), Pollination variant (PV)	Ripe/Color	Remarks
continued			much identity confusion. There are also many Fuyu seedling varieties—probably much of the source of confusion. The fruit has a flattened tomato shape and requires thinning to develop good size.
Fuyu, Giant (Hana Fuyu)	N	October and November orange with reddish orange flesh	This Fuyu type is almost half again as large as regular Fuyu and not as flattened.
Giombo	A	November and December light orange with orange flesh	This variety produces large, cone-shaped fruit, which may weigh up to 1 pound. Tops in quality.
Great Wall	A	September orange with orange flesh	Produces a rather small but early fruit with a square, flattened shape. Very cold hardy.
Hachiya	A	October and November orange with orange flesh	This is one of the most widely planted astringent varieties. It produces large, acorn-shaped fruit on a vigorous, spreading tree. This makes an attractive landscape tree and, like most persimmons, it has bright orange-bronze fall color. In the upper South it is not reliably hardy nor productive.
Hanagosho	N	November orange with orange flesh	Good quality but matures late. Fruit is round and conical in shape. Produces a small number of male flowers.
Hira tanenashi	A	September and October orange with orange flesh	Medium-sized fruit, flattened and usually seedless with a rather thick skin. Ripens over a long period and astringency may be hard to remove just by storing the fruit.
Honan Red	A	October and November reddish orange	Relatively small-fruited Chinese variety. Shape is long and conical.

Variety	Astringent (A) or Nonastringent (N), Pollination variant (PV)	Ripe/Color	Remarks
Ichikikei Jiro	N	September orange with orange flesh	The fruit is large, flat, and of very good quality. Tree is somewhat dwarf.
Izu	N	August and September orange with orange flesh	Good-quality, medium-sized fruit. One of the earliest nonastringent varieties. The sugar content (15% to 17% soluble solids) is lower when compared to later varieties like Suruga (soluble solids over 20%).
Jiro	N	October orange	Similar to Fuyu but larger. Trees are very productive.
Maru	A, PV	September orange-red with dark reddish brown flesh	Not well known outside of California but considered a gourmet variety. Low chilling, probably best adapted to the lower South.
Nishumura Wase	A, PV	August orange	Must be fully seeded before it becomes nonastringent. Produces a number of male flowers.
Siajo	A	September and October yellowish orange with orange flesh	This is an excellent variety for both the commercial grower and for the home landscape. It is a vigorous, upright tree producing large crops of elongated, acorn-shaped fruit. When fully ripe they are of very high quality. Can be eaten fresh or dried.
Sheng	A	October orange with orange flesh	The fruit is flattened, 4-lobed, and large in size. The tree is open, spreading, and somewhat dwarf.
Shogatsu	N	October and November orange	This variety produces sweet, medium-sized fruit. But its main contribution may be producing male flowers where seeded fruit is desired in other interplanted varieties.
Suruga	N	November and December orange-red fruit with orange flesh	This is one of the latest ripening nonastringent varieties. The fruit is often very large and is delicious while still crisp. This

Variety	Astringent (A) or Nonastringent (N), Pollination variant (PV)	Ripe/Color	Remarks
continued			should be one of the main varieties planted in the lower South, along with Fuyu and Izu as companion nonastringent varieties, in addition to Saijo, Giombo, and Hira-tanashi as astringent varieties.
Tamopan	A	November and December reddish orange with orange flesh	One of the older varieties with a distinctive caplike belt on the fruit. Only fair quality.
Tanenashi	A	September and October light yellow to orange with orange flesh	This is one of the most commoly offered varieties. Unfortunately it is also one of the worst to drop fruit when under stress. If the acorn-shaped fruit matures, it is of poor quality with a pasty texture.

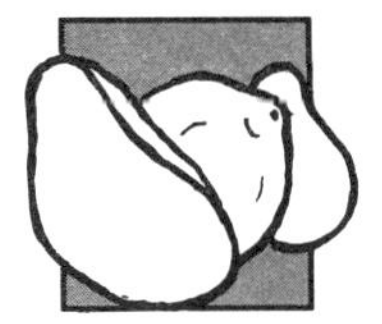

11 specialty fruits

Standard fruits such as peaches, apples, and pears seem difficult enough to grow. So why do growers even consider cultivating exotic fruits? Perhaps it's explained by the old adage, "Variety is the spice of life," because new and unusual produce is very popular in today's market. While most exotic fruits will be easiest to grow from the Gulf Coast south, some, like the jujube, can be grown throughout the South. The determined grower can always resort to a greenhouse for the tropicals.

Exotic Fruits for the Gulf Coast and South

FEIJOA (Pineapple Guava)

This plant will actually grow north of the Gulf Coast. It's reported to be able to survive 5°F, but a lot of its success depends on the variety and how much cold preconditioning it gets before the first hard freeze. The New Zealand varieties Mammoth and Triumph seem to be especially cold-sensitive. The green skin is bitter and tough so they need to be peeled, or just cut in quarters lengthwise, so the fleshy part can be eaten. It has a tropical taste—with a hint of pineapple and many other tropical flavors. The fruit is both sweet and tart. It's not only good fresh, but it can be cooked or used for jams and jellies.

However, the feijoa may not be a reliable producer; heat stress may cause much of the fruit to drop. So far, standard landscape varieties have been the best producers. These varieties are also very attractive as large evergreen shrubs or small multitrunked trees in a landscape. Several California varieties are being tested—Coolidge, Trask, and Nazemetz—that have carried a few fruit to maturity. They haven't proven to be any better or larger than the landscape types. All feijoa's flower petals can be eaten because they are fleshy, white, and tropical tasting. Add some to a fruit salad for a fresh, new taste. Even if this plant doesn't become a dependable producer, it is a pest-free and attractive addition to any landscape.

LOQUAT

This plant is about as hardy as the feijoa, but has an additional problem or two. The main problem is that it blooms in the fall. Unless you have a mild winter or live in the Rio Grande Valley, southern Florida, or southern California, the fruit (which should ripen in the spring) will freeze. The loquat is also very susceptible to bacterial fire blight. Anyone trying to grow pears knows how serious this problem can be. So why try? Because the fruit is so good.

Most of the loquat trees growing in landscapes produce small, seedy fruit. But there are a number of improved varieties—Advance and Champagne, for example. These varieties produce much larger fruit that have more flesh in relation to their large seeds. However, the common landscape variety of loquat is still good to use for jams or jellies. Try it combined with strawberries (they mature about the same time and complement the loquat). They can be a bit too sour to eat fresh. The loquat is also an attractive small-specimen tree if it does not develop blackened limbs caused by fire blight. When this happens, prune out the dead limbs 12 to 18 inches below the blackened tissue, dipping your pruning shears in a 10% household bleach solution for 10 seconds between each cut.

PASSION FRUIT

Most of the cultivated *Passifloras* aren't hardy in the majority of southern growing regions. The native Maypop (*P. incarnata*) is very hardy; in fact it's a weed. The fruit must be mushy ripe before it is good. The hybrid variety Incense produces gorgeous dark purple flowers, but isn't known for its fruit. The rest of the varieties can only be grown in the tropics or in a greenhouse.

POMEGRANATE

This shrub is grown today mostly for its beautiful orange flowers, but it was once more commonly planted for its leathery orange fruit filled with juicy pulp. The ornamental varieties produce double the flowers and rarely bear fruit. Unfortunately, the fruiting varieties often don't fruit either. Lack of cross-pollination may be a problem or poor pollination due to the high humidity in most southern growing areas may be the culprit. The juicy interior can be eaten fresh (the numerous seeds are crunchy and rather good), the juice can be extracted (the flavor has hints of strawberry and raspberry) or used to make wine. Varieties are not numerous; the most common one is Wonderful. Fleishman is a comparatively new variety that was developed in California.

JELLY PALM (*Butia capitata*)

This slow-growing, feather-leaf palm is common from the upper Gulf Coast south. Homeowners often ask if it is edible. The bright orange-yellow fruits about the size of a Ping-Pong ball are edible even though the flesh is kind of stringy and there's a small coconutlike seed inside. The pulp is another of those tropical tasting, but hard-to-describe delicacies. They're good fresh and they also make great jelly.

BANANA

Bananas are never going to grow well in most of the South. No doubt, some varieties are hardier than others, but even the hardiest will need a greenhouse when temperatures drop below the mid-20s. Suppose you get one of these fruit stalks next spring. What do you do next? Not much. When the flower stalk stops producing little green bananas, the end contains only male flowers and you might as well cut them off. The entire stalk can be cut and ripened in a warm room in the house after the ridges on the fruit begin to round off and the fruit begins to develop some yellow color. Some of the hardier varieties include Raja Puri, Dwarf Lady Finger, and Dwarf Jamaican Red.

OTHER EXOTIC FRUITS

Someone always wants to grow papayas, mangoes, kiwis, dates, lemons, cherimoya, white sapote, or some other fruit that is unlikely to survive in the South. Unless you have a conservatory at your disposal, forget it. Even if you have a conservatory you'll need to keep the cotton swabs handy—pollination is a problem, too. **Papayas** can be grown for fun, more or less as an annual. In the tropical South they may survive to bear mature fruit. Try to get the Hawaiian types, which have both male and female flowers on the same plant. If you don't you may raise a crop of male papayas (not much to eat) or a crop of females (equally poor for eating).

The **kiwi** has been a big disappointment. The plants live for a few years, but reports of fruit production have been scarce. It seems they either don't get enough chilling hours or they break dormancy too early. The hardy kiwis sound promising, but they don't like Southern summers.

Undoubtedly, a few **lemons** have been raised in the lower South, but hardier citrus like **satsumas** and **kumquats** are easier to grow. But even satsumas and kumquats do best when planted on the south side of the house where you can drop a sheet of plastic over them from the eave and stick in a light bulb to provide heat for those few cold nights we have each year. **Mangoes** and **sapotes** don't even like to be chilled, let alone frozen.

Exotic Fruits North of the Gulf Coast

MAYHAW

Many people think this fruit could be the next popular choice for southern fruit growers. This is a fruit that can be grown in virtually all of the South with the possible exception of areas west of Houston, Texas. Mayhaws could even be grown in more areas throughout the South with the use of an alkaline soil-tolerant rootstock.

The mayhaw fruit is strictly for processing. It's too sour for fresh consumption. Unlike some hawthorns with dry, mealy fruit texture, its fruit is juicy and large and ranges in size from ½ to 1 inch in diameter.

There are two primary species of mayhaw. *Crataegus opaca* with yellow-red to orange fruit that is slightly irregular in shape (larger at the top) and *Crataegus aestivalis* with shiny red, uniformly shaped fruit. Varieties have been selected from both species. Opacas include: Super Spur, Warren Opaca, T.O. Warren Superberry, Mason, and Highway. *Aestivalis* varieties include: Big Red, Heavy, and Big V. None of these varieties is likely to be found at your local nursery. Sherwood's Greenhouses (see the list of fruit and nut catalogs in the appendices) propagates several varieties on Parsely Hawthorn rootstock, but in areas where heavy clay soils or even slightly alkaline soils exist these trees may exhibit iron chlorosis. Fortunately mayhaws seem to be happy on just about any tree species hawthorn rootstock. Native mayhaws, green haw, or any others that are adapted to your area should work. Membership in the Southern Fruit Fellowship (see the Appendices) help you locate growers that will share graftwood. A whip-and-tongue graft used in late winter is one of the main techniques used to propagate mayhaws.

Contrary to popular belief, mayhaws do best on good upland soils. Although they can survive in low flooded areas, this is due to a lack of competition from other tree species that crowd them out in better areas. Commercial plantings should be located on these good soils and given the same level of insect, disease, and weed control that would be provided for any other fruit crop. It appears that a minimum of pests would be attracted under such conditions, but if you plant enough of anything, some pest will find it and become established when the crop is growing under monoculture conditions. Hawthorn rust (similar to cedar-apple rust) has been one of the main problems. Resistant varieties would be the best solution, but fungicides have been used with some success. Aphids, scale insects, and wormy fruit are other potential problems.

Plants should be spaced a minimum of 25 feet apart in the row; rows should be 25 to 30 feet apart. Relatively little pruning is required once a 3- to 5-foot long trunk devoid of branches has developed. All mayhaws appear to be self-fertile, so planting pollinator varieties isn't necessary.

The fruit is harvested by shaking the trees over tarps. A commercial operation could adapt a smaller version of the pecan shaker to do the job. This is one of the most appealing features of this fruit—it is already well adapted to mechanical harvesting. The mayhaw also makes such good jelly, syrup, and other products that it may likely become the new popular fruit of the South. At the very least it is a beautiful, medium-sized landscape tree that offers an excellent fruit as well as striking white flowers.

JUJUBE

This exotic fruit should grow in most areas of the South. It's a nice landscape plant except that most varieties have a few thorns and tend to root sucker. The jujube has beautiful glossy foliage and makes a nice specimen tree. The fruit is about the size of a date and, in fact, is called the Chinese or red date when cooked in a heavy syrup and then dried. When eaten fresh the jujube is like a sweet, dry apple (somewhat mealy). Some varieties are better than others. A favorite is Silverhill Round. Sherwood is also good. The most readily available varieties, Li and Lang, are also good. They are best for eating when they are still half green.

PAWPAW

These trees are hardy and can withstand subzero temperatures, but they do like sandy soil, plenty of water, and a little afternoon shade. The genus *Asimina* grows in soils from Florida to Michigan. Northern cultivars haven't grown well in the South. The 3- to 5-inch yellow fruits hang in clusters and have yellow-orange flesh. It has been described as having a banana custard flavor. Growers interested in this fruit will have to plant seedlings from southern seed sources (see appendices). Although a good pawpaw makes its difficult cultivation worthwhile the success of these seedlings is inconsistent, so expect poor performance.

GUMI (*Elaeagnus multiflora*)

This attractive, small tree is related to the Russian Olive and Silverthorn. It grows best in east Texas, Louisiana, and further east. Unlike the Silverthorn, this plant is deciduous, but it produces metallic red berries in the late spring. They're beautiful and the birds like them; they also make good jelly.

12 pecans & other nuts

The pecan is North America's greatest contribution to the world's nut crops. Pecans are in demand worldwide and can be cultivated in a large part of the South. Yet pecans grown in the South still suffer from diseases, insects, weeds, and varmints like squirrels and crows. Variety selection with pecans is much more critical than it is with short-term fruit crops such as peaches. Even though large trees can be topworked by grafting to new varieties, the process is so painstaking that the grower may be stuck with an inferior variety for a long time.

Home gardeners planting a pecan in their landscapes should consider that the tree will become very large and difficult to spray. It isn't practical for homeowners to purchase adequate spray equipment. Even if homeowners hire a professional pest control operator to do the job, they have to consider whether they want to submit their neighbors to pesticide spray drift at least three or four times a year. The only alternative is to select varieties that are extremely resistant to diseases like pecan scab fungus and to accept that some insect damage, which will destroy most of the crop many years, will occur. Regardless, the pecan can be a beautiful specimen in a large and spacious landscape. The development of nontoxic vegetable oil sprays (such as citrus oil) that can reduce aphid populations does offer some hope. These are the pests that excrete copious amounts of honeydew that covers cars, kids, lawns, shrubs, and smaller trees and that causes a black sooty mold growth in later stages. Research to develop other low-toxicity pesticides that control pecan pests with little danger to people, pets, beneficial insects, and the environment in general is currently under way.

Pecans: Soil and Fertility

The pecan is best adapted to rich, alluvial soils. These are the deep, fertile soils adjacent to streams and rivers. Alluvial soils are formed over millions of years as the top soil that has eroded upstream is deposited along the banks of these streams on the way to the ocean. However, to say that any creek or river bottom is a good place to plant pecans is false. Pecans have specific soil requirements. Only soils with the best drainage should be considered for pecans.

The soil should be a deep (30 to 36 inches minimum) well-drained sandy loam to sandy clay loam with a porous subsoil. Soil pH is less of a factor with pecans. Although a slightly acidic soil (6.0 to 6.5 pH) is ideal, pecans seem to tolerate alkaline soils fairly well and lime can be added to highly acidic soils to achieve the desired pH.

Although pecans tolerate occasional flooding, areas that flood frequently (especially during the fall) should be avoided. A fall flood can float the entire crop downstream.

Pecans get big, so allow plenty of space (35 feet × 35 feet minimum, 50 feet ×

50 feet preferred) when planning your orchard. Avoid planting trees like peaches, plums, nectarines, and apricots near pecan trees because they are sensitive to sprays containing zinc or copper.

Pecans are heavy feeders and don't compete well with weeds. Plan to maintain a clean basin several feet around the tree during the first 5 years to allow for maximum use of water and nutrients.

Young-grafted pecan trees (5 to 8 feet tall) should be planted in the dormant season (December through February). I prefer to plant the trees a little high and mound soil up around the roots. No fertilizers should be used at planting time, but a zinc spray should be applied as soon as the buds begin to swell. If the tree has produced 18 inches of terminal growth by the end of May, apply a ½ pound of ammonium nitrate or a similar nitrogen fertilizer 18 to 24 inches away from the trunk. Any trees producing less than 18 inches of growth by the end of May should not be fertilized until the second year.

Zinc is an important element in cultivating pecans, especially during the early years. Zinc is required for proper cell elongation. Pecan trees have difficulty absorbing zinc through the roots, especially in soils with higher pHs, so even where the soil contains zinc, the trees must be sprayed every 2 to 4 weeks with NZN or zinc sulfate from April (bud break) until the end of June. When zinc sprays are not used, the trees can be stunted and very slow to come into production.

Starting the second year, pecans should be fertilized aggressively. Monthly applications of a nitrogen fertilizer should be applied at or near the drip line starting in March and continuing through June. Use only one fertilizer for each application. Nitrogen is the only necessary nutrient in soils where most pecans are grown, but a soil test should be done to see if any other nutrients are needed. Plan to continue spraying your trees with zinc until they are too large to spray.

Amount of Fertilizer Applied Monthly from March through June

FERTILIZER	1 YEAR	2 YEARS	3 YEARS	4 TO 15 YEARS
Ammonium Nitrate	⅓ pound	⅔ pound	1½ pounds	1½ pounds*
Ammonium Sulfate	½ pound	1 pound	2 pounds	2 pounds*
Cottonseed Meal	2 pounds	4 pounds	8 pounds	8 pounds*
Blood Meal	1 pound	2 pounds	4 pounds	4 pounds*
Fish Meal	1 pound	2 pounds	4 pounds	4 pounds*
Sewage Sludge (Sterilized)	1½ pounds	3 pounds	6 pounds	6 pounds*
Urea Formaldehyde (Slow Release)	⅓ pound	⅔ pound	1½ pounds	1½ pounds

*AMOUNT OF SPRAY APPLIED PER INCH OF TRUNK DIAMETER.
NOTE: SELECT ONLY ONE.

Once the tree is 15 years old or older, broadcast a split application of 25 to 50 pounds of ammonium sulfate (total for the season) under the trees in March and again in May. You will have to mow the areas where grass is allowed to grow under the trees, because that much nitrogen will cause it to grow vigorously.

Water is critical for good pecan growth and production. A mature pecan tree will require 150 gallons per day during periods of maximum stress (June through August). The minimum amount of rainfall per week is 1 inch and 2 inches per week is ideal. When rain is insufficient, be prepared to water. A slow trickle or drip system is better than using sprinklers, but be sure to water regardless of the method.

TREE AGE	APRIL	MAY	JUNE	JULY	AUGUST	SEPTEMBER
1 Year	7	7	14	28	28	14
2 Years	14	14	28	56	56	28
3 Years	28	28	56	112	112	56
4 Years	56	56	112	240	240	56

Water Requirements (in Gallons per Week) for Pecans Grown in Well-Drained Soils

Training and Pruning

Pecans are trained using the central leader training system. Just after the tree is planted it should be pruned back to one-third or one-half of its size. Try to cut the trunk back to a bud scar. By early summer, you should have a number of shoots developing. Select the straightest, most healthy upright shoot to become the central leader, or main trunk. All other upright shoots should be removed at this time to funnel all of the tree's energy into the remaining leader. Any horizontal shoots can be kept to help with photosynthesis and increase trunk diameter. The "trashy trunk" method of pruning allows these branches to remain until they are 1 inch or more in diameter. The main reason for "trashy trunk" pruning is to help increase the trunk diameter.

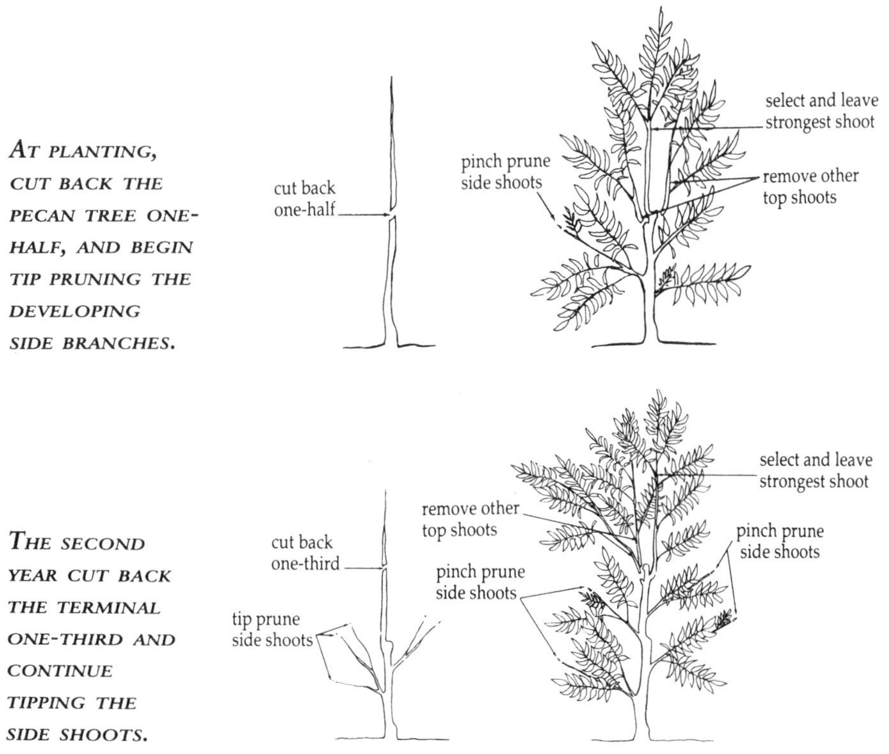

At planting, cut back the pecan tree one-half, and begin tip pruning the developing side branches.

The second year cut back the terminal one-third and continue tipping the side shoots.

At the end of the first growing season, you should have a strong main trunk with several trashy horizontal shoots. When the tree is dormant, tip all of the side shoots and cut back the new growth on the main trunk (central leader) to one-third of its previous size. In early summer, select the dominant shoot and remove all of the other vertical shoots. Weak horizontal branches should be left alone.

This process of cutting back the terminal by one-third and selecting the main trunk is continued until the tree is too tall to reach. Remember to tip prune the trashy branches along the trunk. Narrow crotches should be eliminated whenever they are noticed.

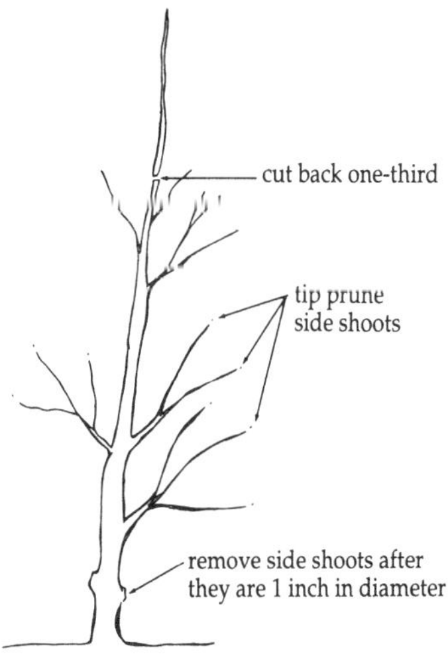

The third and fourth year, during the dormant season, cut back the terminal one-third, select and tip the well-placed side shoots and remove any lower branches larger than 1 inch in diameter.

As the tree matures, select permanant scaffold branches at a height of 6 to 8 feet. You should select scaffold branches that have wide crotch angles and are evenly spaced around the tree. As the "trashy trunk" branches reach 1 inch or more in diameter, they can be cut back to the branch collar.

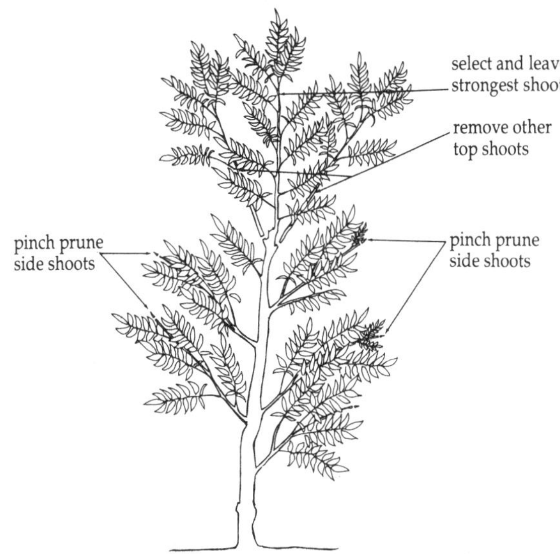

Select shoots for training and cut back pecan tree in May and June during the tree's third and fourth years.

As the scaffold branches develop, they should be tip pruned to encourage branching. Multiple branches arising from one point (crowfeet) should be thinned until only 2 branches remain. A well-trained, mature tree should have 1 strong main trunk, with scaffold branches radiating from it, without crowfeet or weak crotches.

Rejuvenating Old Trees

Many people find themselves with an old nonbearing pecan tree that they want to bring back into production. Depending on the overall health of the tree, this process can take 1 or 2 seasons or more to rejuvenate.

STEPS FOR REJUVENATING

1. Clean area around the tree, eliminating competition from weeds and other vegetation.
2. Remove all dead and diseased wood.
3. Fertilize, using recommendations for mature trees.
4. Evaluate the nut crop. This is the time to decide whether grafting with an improved variety is warranted. If you decide to graft the tree, grow it for 1 season under good fertility before you start. A very weak tree may die when stressed by grafting.
5. Place the tree under a good watering program.
6. If practical, the tree will benefit from applications of foliar zinc and insect and disease pesticides.
7. Continue a program of good care from this point forward.
8. Pecans live a long time under good management. A fifty-year-old tree is still a youngster!

Harvesting and Storage

Pecans should be harvested as early as possible for optimum quality and appearance. Commercial pecans are shaken from the tree as soon as the shuck splits. The home pecan grower can use long poles to help knock the pecans from the tree. Early harvested pecans have more astringent flavor, but it will be lost during the curing process.

Most pecans are green when first harvested so curing is required to achieve the maximum quality. Home curing can be accomplished by drying the pecans at room temperature with 65% to 70% humidity for 2 to 3 weeks. Commercially, the kernel moisture is removed by circulating hot (140°F) dry air around the nuts for several hours or days.

Once you have finished curing the pecans, they are ready for processing. Numerous commercial shellers are available to help with this chore. Pecans are easier to shell and have a higher percentage of halves if they are conditioned by soaking in hot water (185°F) for 3 to 5 minutes, dried, and allowed to rest for 12 to 24 hours before shelling.

Storage Life for Pecans Held at Various Temperatures

TEMPERATURE	*IN SHELL (MONTHS)*	*SHELLED (MONTHS)*
70°F	4	3
50°F	9	6
32°F	19	12
0°F	24	24

Variety	Pollen Release (early: protandrous, late: protogynous)	Harvest (early: late September; late: October to November) Kernel Percentage/ Nuts per Pound	Remarks
Caddo	early	early 50% 60 to 70	One of the most scab-resistant varieties. Average production of small football-shaped nuts.
Candy	late	early 48% 66	Produces small but very high quality nuts. Good disease resistance.
Cape Fear	early	mid-season 52% 50 to 55	Good disease resistance and better than average kernel. Shell is resistant to cracking during harvest, but trees may begin to produce lower-quality nuts after 15 years or more.
Cheyenne	early	mid-season 55% to 60% 50	This is an early bearing, precocious variety. As a result, the tree is also comparatively small and adapted to high-density plantings/home landscapes. Cheyenne also has a light-colored, high-quality kernel. Reported to be especially susceptible to aphids.
Choctaw	late	mid-season 55% to 60% 35 to 40	Popular as a home variety, Choctaw has a tendency to split during harvest. It has good scab resistance and an attractive kernel.
Desirable	early	early 52% to 55% 40	Early and consistent producer. Desirable is still considered one of the best commercial varieties for the Southeast. It does, however, tend to have limb breakage.
Elliot	late	early 50% 75 to 80	Considered one of the most disease-resistant varieties for the Southeast. It produces small but very high-quality, light-colored kernels. Trees are slow to begin bearing—taking 12 years or more—but produce consistent crops. Good for home use and the kernels are in demand by shellers.
Forkert	late	mid-season 60% to 64% 50	High-quality kernels and good disease resistance are this variety's chief attributes.

Variety	Pollen Release (early: protandrous, late: protogynous)	Harvest (early: late September; late: October to November) Kernel Percentage/ Nuts per Pound	Remarks
continued			Though popular in some areas of the Southeast, it is not well known.
Gloria Grande	late	mid-season 47% 47	This is a commercial variety popular in South Carolina but less widely known in other areas of the South. Its large size and thick shell make it less susceptible to bird damage. It produces consistent crops when mature and has good scab resistance and good crotch angles.
Graking	late	mid-season 54% 40	Like most of O.S. Gray's varieties, this one has fallen by the wayside. It may be worth redeeming for its large size and good scab resistance. GraPark Giant is another O.S. Gray variety worth considering.
Houma (tested as 58-4-61)	early	very early 55% 55	This variety has excellent scab resistance and matures very early. It has been a consistent producer and has a significantly higher yield than Desirable. Early maturity also has the advantages of early harvest and reduced predator damage.
Jackson	early but comes as close to being self-fertile as any variety because pollination overlaps with receptivity.	mid-season 60% 42	This is a large pecan with large dorsal and ventral grooves, causing it to be less likely to hold off-flavored punky material. Overall it has high quality and good scab resistance. Yields are about half of what good commercial varieties produce, so this is primarily a variety for the home grower.
Jubilee	late	early 51% 40 to 50	Reported to have outstanding resistance to scab, good quality, and a high percentage of halves when shelled. It also has been a reliable producer even in bad years.

Variety	Pollen Release (early: protandrous, late: protogynous)	Harvest (early: late September; late: October to November) Kernel Percentage/ Nuts per Pound	Remarks
Kernodle	late	late 60% 63	Another variety with potential for the homeowner looking for extreme disease resistance or for the commercial grower selling to the shelling industry.
Kiowa	late	mid-season 55% to 60% 40 to 50	This is a Mahan × Odom cross with good disease resistance and large size. It tends to produce narrow-angled crotches. The tree is also precocious.
Mahan	late	mid-season 55% to 60% 35 to 50	Worth mentioning only because it is the parent of so many USDA varieties. It is large and has healthy foliage and good tree form, but the nuts often fill poorly as the trees age. Planting of this variety is no longer recommended.
Maramec	late	early 54% 56	This variety is an Oklahoma State University release. It appears to be a consistent producer with good scab resistance worthy of trial, especially in the upper South.
Melrose	late	mid-season 55% 55	This variety has excellent resistance to the pecan scab fungus. It also produces a high-quality nut with open kernel grooves that do not retain packing materials. The nuts are somewhat pointed at both ends but should be good for both the homeowner and the grower.
Moreland	late	mid-season 55% 55 to 60	This is a chance seedling discovered in Louisiana with good disease resistance. It has average precocity and high-quality kernels. Tendency for alternate bearing and to suffer some phylloxera damage.
Oconee (tested as 56-7-72)	early	mid-season 54% 48	This variety was released because of its large size, good production, and high-quality, easily cracked kernel. It has

Variety	Pollen Release (early: protandrous, late: protogynous)	Harvest (early: late September; late: October to November) Kernel Percentage/ Nuts per Pound	Remarks
			only adequate scab resistance, so a good disease spray program will be necessary. It has shown a tendency to alternate bearing after 10 years of production.
Osage (tested as 48-15-3)	early	early 55% 81	This is a small pecan best suited to the upper South. It is precocious, potentially heavy yielding and has a high-quality kernel that easily shells out in halves.
Owens	early	mid-season 48% 50	This variety produces large thick-shelled nuts. The trees have good scab resistance. Because it is a protandrous variety, it may be of value as a pollinator for the mostly protogynous varieties.
Pawnee	early	early 55% to 60% 55 to 60	Precocious, large, good-quality pecan. Potential for high yields with some disease resistance and apparent aphid resistance. Recommended for high-density plantings.
Podsednik	early	late 50% 22 to 30	Typical of extremely large pecans, it is more of a curiosity than a variety worth planting. The nuts will be large but relatively scarce.
Schley	late	mid-season 60% 50	This is an old and very high-quality pecan variety, but it has a deserved reputation for poor production. Disease resistance is average to good.
Shawnee	late	early 55% to 60% 55	This variety has been somewhat neglected. It has an excellent quality kernel and good disease resistance. It matures early.
Sumner	late	mid-season 50% to 55% 55 to 60	This is a precocious variety with medium-sized nuts, good disease resistance, and excellent quality.

Variety	Pollen Release (early: protandrous, late: protogynous)	Harvest (early: late September; late: October to November) Kernel Percentage/ Nuts per Pound	Remarks
Surprise	early	mid-season 49% 38 to 45	Variety seedling from Alabama. Good scab resistance and consistent production even in bad years.
Western (Western Schley)	early	mid-season 60% 55	Productive, high-quality pecan but very susceptible to pecan scab and other diseases. Does best when planted west of San Antonio.
Wichita	late	mid-season 55% to 60% 60	A high-quality, variety, disease-susceptible for Western climates only. Good production.

Other Nuts

WALNUTS (English, Carpathian, and others)

About 90% of English walnuts are grown in California and enjoy an advantage in climate there as well as in marketing. Regardless, it is tempting to try growing English walnuts even if they are generally inferior to the pecan. Dr. Loy Shreve of the Texas Agriculture Extension Service has done much to search for cultivars adapted to the South. Many of these are currently being evaluated in Texas, primarily in the Uvalde area.

Dr. Shreve has collected many of the best varieties from Romania, Czechoslovakia, Hungary, Poland, Russia, Italy, and China. The varieties he has acquired have been subjected to decades of disease pressure in these countries and many have good resistance to walnut anthracnose (*Gnomonia leptostyla*) and bacterial blight (*Xanthomonas juglandis*). One of Dr. Shreve's main contributions in the production of English walnuts has been demonstrating that the English walnut will grow very well on *Juglans microcarpa*, a small black walnut native to Texas. Other rootstocks produced trees that were extremely chlorotic in the alkaline soils of Central and West Texas. In areas of the South with acidic soils, the Eastern black walnut (*Juglans nigra*) is the preferred rootstock. It may be some time before varieties adapted to the South can be recommended with confidence, but several nurseries (see the Appendices) offer English walnuts.

EASTERN BLACK WALNUT

This is a crop that is valued more for its beautiful wood than for its nuts. Whereas a good pecan variety will be 55% to 60% kernel and an English walnut will be 40%, a good black walnut variety may be 30% or slightly better—and the kernel is hard to get at. In fact, the hard shells are valued for metal cleaning and they are even used in oil well drilling. The genetic potential exists to develop better black walnuts with good disease resistance and productivity, but breeding nut varieties is a long-term, expensive process.

Anthracnose (*Gnomonia leptostyla*) is the major disease of this crop. It causes early fall leaf drop, which results in poor kernel filling and a tendency to bear alternate years. Other characteristics that need improvement include lateral bud fruitfulness, spring freeze susceptibility, precocity, productivity, and nut quality.

The black walnut kernel has a strong, though pleasant, flavor and is high in oil and protein. Commercially, they have probably been used more for ice cream flavoring than for anything else though they are good in cookies, cakes, and other foods.

The Thomas variety is the best known, but is generally considered inferior today even though few other varieties are propagated. Kwik-Krop is available from Starks and is an early-bearing variety with good-quality nuts. Surprise is a heavy-bearing variety with a 35% kernel, but is has brittle wood and is difficult to find. The variety Football II is a good, straight-growing timber tree and produces high-quality nuts that are 29% to 32% kernel. It also will be difficult to find. Sparks #147 is in the same category. Nolan River Nursery (see the Appendices) would be a good place to start looking if you are interested in black walnuts.

HAZELNUTS (Filberts)

The European species probably won't be happy in many areas of the South (most production is in the Pacific Northwest) but there are hazelnuts that are native to areas of the South. For example, hazelnuts native to the Carolinas may be adapted to much of the upper South.

CHESTNUTS

Chestnut blight virtually wiped out the production of American chestnuts after its accidental introduction into this country in 1904. The Chinese chestnut is highly resistant to this disease but produces an inferior nut. Hybrid varieties however, like the Dunstan series offer some potential for U.S. production of this valuable crop. In recent years the chestnut weevil and the Oriental chestnut gall wasp have threatened production of even blight-resistant varieties.

PISTACHIOS

Growers in West Texas, New Mexico, and Arizona could produce pistachios. These nuts do best in a dry climate with 1000 chilling hours and good water for irrigation. Female trees, such as Kerman or Joley, that produce nuts require pollinator trees, like Chico, to produce. Trees are spaced 11 to 17 feet apart within rows and rows are spaced 22 to 30 feet apart. One male tree is needed to pollinate every 10 to 12 female trees.

propagating fruits & nuts 13

Even the grower planning a small commercial operation doesn't necessarily need to know how to propagate fruits and nuts. But this know-how can come in handy and be fun and rewarding. Propagation techniques vary with the age of the plant. If you are topworking seedling rootstocks for an apple, pear, or peach tree, you will need to do some form of chip budding or T-budding. If the understock is a larger tree with woody bark, then the technique would more likely be cleft grafting or bark grafting. Blackberries are propagated by root cuttings, bunch grapes are propagated by stem cuttings (or they are grafted to rootstocks propagated this way), and other fruit crops like the muscadine grapes are propagated by layering. If the propagation technique is asexual, be aware that there are plant patent laws that may protect the originator's right to license a variety.

Sexual propagation—planting from seed—is primarily used to produce rootstock. The chance of a seedling being better than existing varieties is said to be one in ten-thousand. Fortunately, this hasn't stopped enthusiasts from planting their own peaches, pecans, or other seeds on occasion. Many of our most prized commercial varieties are chance seedlings that some grower had the wisdom to propagate asexually. Though it's possible to grow your own rootstock, ordering from commercial specialists that produce thousands of rootstocks (from seedlings or asexually in stooling beds) is usually the best source when you're getting started.

Pecan rootstocks may be worth growing for some producers, though they are inexpensive and available from commercial sources. It's best to select good seed from a large-size variety in the fall when it is freshly harvested. Choctaw, for example, is reported to be a good variety for seedling production. Though not absolutely necessary, pecans are often soaked in water for several days, especially if they have not been harvested recently. Each day the water is poured off to leach out inhibitors and to separate poor seed, which will quickly float to the top.

Unless you have access to a bulldozer with a U-shaped digging blade, it's best to plant the seeds in 55 gallon drums filled with a loose soil mix enhanced with approximately 5 pounds of slow-release fertilizer per cubic yard. Drill 4- to 6 ½-inch drainage holes in the side of the barrels near the bottom.

Plant approximately 50 pecans 2 to 3 inches deep, and expect most of the germination to occur in the spring when temperatures warm up. In the lower South, it's probably best to store the pecans in damp peat moss in a refrigerator at 35° to 37°F until February or March to prevent fall germination and the possible loss of the tender rootstocks. Some growers also plant in deep plastic growing containers to allow the tap root to grow uninhibited for a season or two.

Seedlings grown in barrels are easy to remove the next fall/winter planting season. Water the soil thoroughly and simply pull them out of the loose soil medium. The taproot should have developed without distortion. Set them out with the tap root straight in the hole and the plant level at 1 to 2 inches high. Don't put a bunch of organic matter in the bottom of the hole because it will become waterlogged and may kill the tree. Use of slow-release fertilizer tablets in the top half of the hole is a good idea because they're not likely to burn tender roots.

Recently, it has been shown that woody plants destined for container production benefit from air pruning of the roots during their early development. The technique, quite simply, is to plant the seeds in quart-size milk containers with only two ¼-inch cross straps across the bottom and grow these containerized plants on a bench with an expanded metal covering. Thus when the roots grow to the bottom of the container, they are air pruned and quickly develop a dense, fibrous root system. Specially designed plastic containers have been developed for this purpose; although used commonly, milk containers with the bottom cut out don't hold up very well. Pecan seedlings may also benefit from even larger containers. By the end of the first growing season you should have strong seedlings ready for the field.

Fruit seeds—for apples, pears, peaches, plums, and others—need a cold, moist treatment known as stratification. This treatment can be achieved naturally by planting the seeds outdoors in the fall in seedbeds. Come spring, about 50% of the seed will probably come up. Plant breeders get a little more serious. They carefully crack the seeds out of the pit (in the case of peach and plum), stratify the seeds in damp peat moss at 35° to 37°F for 60 to 90 days, then plant the seeds in the greenhouse. Seed treated this way often begins to develop roots in the cold storage. It is suspected that the first seeds to sprout, while being stratified, will be lower chilling fruit producers because the seedlings broke dormancy early. Most growers will never bother to grow their own rootstocks or get involved in breeding new varieties, but almost everyone wants to know how to plant a few seeds from a good batch of fruit, even if the chances aren't too high that any of them will be a commercial success.

Terms Home Growers Need to Know

Understanding the following terms and definitions associated with propagation techniques is the first step in learning about these methods:

Asexual—Propagation other than by seeds. Includes cuttings, budding, grafting, and most tissue culture techniques.

Bark slipping (slip)—A growing stage that occurs after dormancy and throughout most of the growing season in which the bark pulls away easily from the cambium. Dry weather conditions or other stress factors may prevent slipping during the summer.

Bench graft—Grafting seedling rootstocks indoors during the dormant season. These grafts are then stored in damp peat moss to allow callusing before they are planted in the spring.

Budding tape—Usually a flexible, white tape without adhesive. Budding tape is made of rubber and is designed to break down soon after bud growth begins so it won't girdle the tree. A number of products have been devised to hold in and seal the bud. Their function is to prevent moisture loss while holding the cambium tissues in contact.

Budstick—Current season's growth with plump, mature buds in the leaf axils (angle between leaf petiole and stem).

Callus tissue—Undifferentiated growth tissue that develops around wounded areas caused by grafting, budding, pruning, or some sort of injury to the tissue.

Cambium—A layer of rapidly dividing cell tissue, located just under the bark.

Clone—An asexually propagated variety identical to the mother plant.

Rootstock—A seedling or clonal plant used to develop the root system. Usually selected for hardiness, pest resistance, or dwarf characteristics.
Scion—A term synonymous with graftstick. A budstick serves a similar purpose, except individual buds are removed from it.
Stratify—To store seeds in a cold, moist condition. This treatment substitutes for the natural, moist chilling conditions that these seeds would normally receive in nature and serves to break the dormancy of many seeds.
Tissue culture—A laboratory procedure that uses small pieces of meristematic (actively growing) tissue to culture callus tissue, from which an intact plant can eventually be developed. This is a technique that rapidly multiplies plant numbers, but so far its use has been limited to the production of some rootstocks.

Cuttings and Layering

Propagation by cuttings is not used with many fruit or nut crops but one exception is the blackberry. It propagates readily from root cuttings, 4 to 6 inches long. Juvenile pear growth (young, vigorous shoots in the semihardwood stage) will also root to some extent, but the technique is hardly practical.

Bunch grapes are typically grown from cuttings. One-year-old wood, pruned out during the dormant season, is cut into 12 to 18-inch lengths and wrapped in bundles by variety. These can be stored upside down in damp peat moss in the refrigerator to promote callusing for 6 to 8 weeks or until they can even be stuck into a planting row. It would be best to plant them first in a nursery row, removing the ones that root after one season and planting them in a permanent location—or you may end up with some skips. Very often these cuttings will be taken from a rootstock variety and the production variety will be chip budded or bark grafted on a year or two later. The top or bottom of a grape cutting can be very hard to distinguish, so try to keep the cuttings pointed in the right direction within the bundles from the beginning. When in doubt, look for the old leaf scars and a bud close by. The leaf scar is on the bottom end. Though muscadines won't root easily from dormant wood cuttings, they can be rooted from semihardwood cuttings taken in late spring and summer and rooted under intermittent mist in the greenhouse.

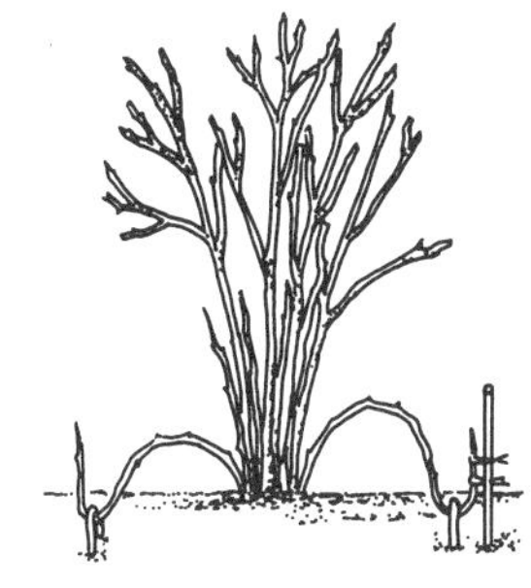
Layering technique.

Layering has been used to a large extent as a propagation technique for muscadine grapes. Long shoots are pegged down and after a growing season, roots on the new plants will have formed and can be cut off and transplanted.

Budding Techniques

T-budding was used for many years as the primary technique for producing varieties of apples, pears, peaches, plums, and other fruits that have thin seedling bark. It is still a successful method, but nurseries are shifting to chip budding as the primary technique for propagating fruit trees. It is believed to produce straighter trees, stronger unions, and a higher percentage of "takes." It also allows for a slightly longer propagation window since the bark need not slip as readily as is required for T-budding. The majority of chip budding will still be done in the early spring and fall, however. Both techniques are limited to rootstocks and branches ¼ to 1 inch in diameter.

Budsticks are normally collected fresh within a few hours or days of their use. The leaves are often removed, leaving a small section of leaf petiole as a handle, though good results have been achieved with the leaf intact. The leaf quickly dries up but moisture and nutrients may be absorbed into the bud tissue as it heals. Commercially, these leaves or petioles are a nuisance to accomplished budders. Working in teams of two, they may propagate a row of 1,500 to 2,000 trees per day. Budsticks may be stored for weeks, or even months when wrapped in damp paper towels, placed in plastic bags, and held in the refrigerator.

CHIP BUDDING

A smooth section is located on seedling rootstock about ¼ inch in diameter, 6 to 8 inches above the soil line. The first cut forms the bottom lip on the stock. It should be about ⅛ inch deep at a 20° angle. The second cut is started 1¼ inches above the first cut and should have an inverted U-shaped shoulder that intersects the first cut. Many propagators tend to cut out an A-shaped piece.

The second cut intersects with the first cut, so the piece can be removed from stock.

Matching cut, around bud, is made on the budstick.

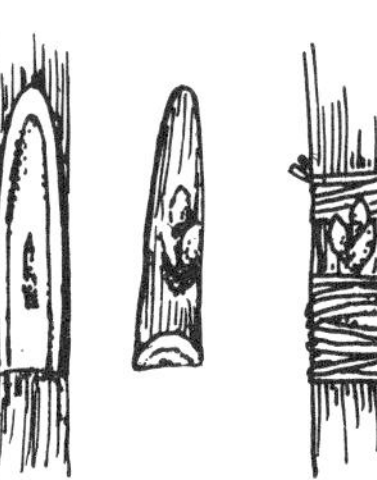

Placing the bud on the stock.

This piece is discarded and a similar cut is made on the budstick. The sliver of wood from the budstick (with a good, plump bud) is then inserted into the notch cut in the rootstock. Since the piece of wood cut from the budstick may not be of exactly the same width, it is important to line up the cambium tissues on at least one side. Thus, the budstick may be situated to one side rather than being centered in the cut.

Practice should help propagators minimize the difference in the two cuts and create almost matching cuts on the stock and budstick. It is critical that the length of the bud piece matches and does not overlap or, particularly, so that it doesn't leave a gap of cut surface at the top of the cut on the stock.

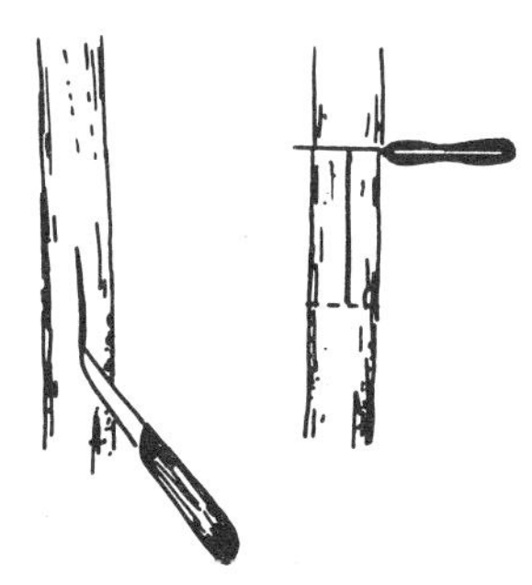

Making the T-shaped cut.

The bud can be secured using several materials. The main objective is to hold it firmly against the stock and prevent moisture loss. Standard budding tape or budding strips are often used to hold the bud in place and polyethylene tape can be used to hold in moisture. A new material called parafilm, developed for laboratory use, is simple to stretch over the bud. When overlapped, it forms a seal that holds in moisture while allowing gases to permeate. This product is available from laboratory suppliers. It is fairly expensive but only a ½- to ¾-inch piece is used per bud. Removing the paper covering is laborious at times, so it has not been received with much enthusiasm by commercial growers. Instead they use a ½-inch clear plastic tape (no adhesive) instead of parafilm to wrap buds, removing it 3 to 4 weeks after setting the bud. Commercially, most chip budding is done in late summer or fall. The buds are forced out the next spring (at bud swell) by cutting off the stock ¼ inch above the bud.

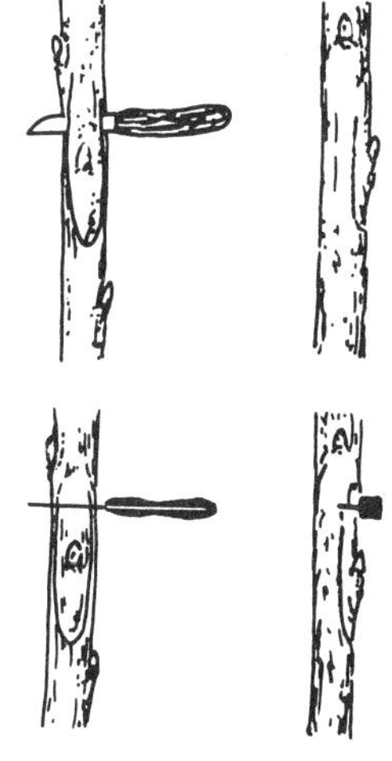

Removing the bud.

T-BUDDING

T-budding accomplishes essentially the same thing as chip budding. A T-shaped cut is made in the bark and the flaps are carefully teased back to accept a bud. A well-developed bud is taken from a budstick by slicing under the bud approximately ⅛ inch above and below it. Usually the small sliver of wood adhering to the inner surface is carefully removed by loosening it along its length. This leaves only a thin strip of bark with a bud. Once the bud has been nestled into the T-shaped cut, it is tied with budding strips or tape (usually leaving the bud uncovered) to secure the bud to the stock.

Budsticks cut for T-budding in the spring should have mature buds in the leaf axils. For this reason, it is commonly referred to as June budding. However, it may be accomplished over a long season, as long as good growing conditions occur. This will allow the bark of the rootstock to slip (pull away from the cambium). Dormant buds can even be applied earlier in the spring if taken from budsticks stored in the refrigerator and wrapped in damp paper towels and placed in plastic bags. Certainly, buds can be applied all summer and into the fall, unless the bark tightens up due to drought and heat stress. Buds applied in September and in later fall usually are not forced out by cutting back the stock until spring.

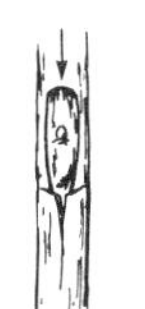

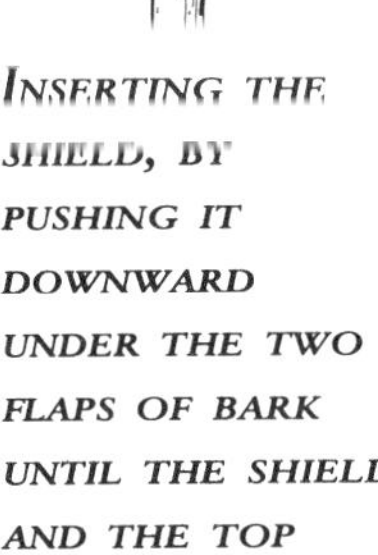

Inserting the shield, by pushing it downward under the two flaps of bark until the shield and the top of the stock line up.

PATCH BUDDING

Another budding technique is often referred to as the patch bud. This process has primarily been used on pecans. While it works with pecans and other seedling trees with thick bark, it is mostly of value to the commercial pecan nurseryowner whose primary concern is producing grafted trees for the homeowner.

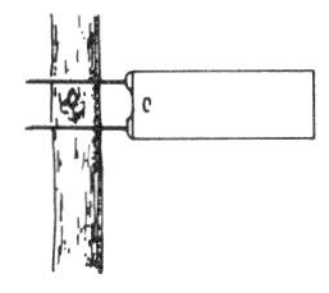

Preparing the bud, by using a double-bladed knife to cut a patch with a bud in the middle of it.

Patch budding does not work well for commercial pecan growers because they have developed a preference for seedling trees which are grown to a height of 10 to 12 feet and are topworked with the inlay bark graft. Also, patch budding requires the use of a twin-bladed knife that is fairly expensive, so unless the grower anticipates that he will use this technique a lot, it is probably best left to the nurseryowner.

Most information on patch budding suggests that it can be used in the spring and from late summer to fall (once new buds have matured in the leaf axils). Spring patch budding is dependent on the use of dormant budwood, which must be taken out of the refrigerator and seasoned at room temperature for several days so that the bark will slip. In reality, this is hard to do so most patch budding is accomplished in the late summer and fall.

Readying the stock for fitting the patch.

Seedling trees or shoots, ⅜ to 1½ inches in diameter, are best for patch budding. Fresh budwood is collected and wrapped in damp paper towels, then stored in plastic bags. The bags can then be stored in an ice chest with a small amount of ice in the bottom. Unlike budwood collected for T-budding, the entire leaf petiole is removed.

First, the double-bladed knife is used to make horizontal cuts half of the way around the rootstock, 6 to 8 inches above the ground.

Next go to the budstick, which should have been cut from new growth and should be ½ to 1 inch in diameter, and make a similar cut by rolling the budwood over the double-bladed knife.

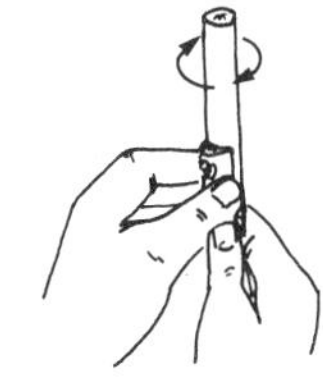

Removing the bud patch.

There should be a healthy bud in the center of the section. Return to the rootstock and with a single-bladed knife make one vertical cut. Carefully raise the bark with the tip of the knife. Then, remove the patch from the budstick with 2 vertical cuts. Carefully lift up the bark and remove it. Try not to touch the inside surface because it contains the cambial (growth) tissue that may be injured by the oils and other natural contaminants on your hands. In fact, this is a good rule to remember for any grafting or budding technique.

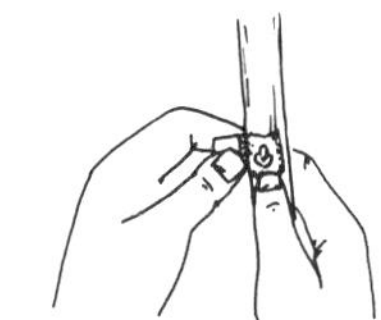

Fitting the bud patch on the stock.

Grip the sides of the bud shield and lift it out. If necessary hold the single-bladed knife against the inner surface, to keep from dropping the bud. The bud shield is placed next to the vertical cut made on the stock. The remaining flap is pulled back and torn or cut so that the bud shield will fit in the hole.

Grafting (white budding) tape is used to wrap the bud beginning below the shield area and continuing above it. The bud is left exposed, however covering it with parafilm would be beneficial. Clear tape, used in chip budding, works well and would be used to cover the entire bud. It should be removed after 3 to 4 weeks. Using this technique, buds would normally be forced the following spring by cutting off the stock several inches above the bud.

Grafting

Grafting basically involves the use of more woody tissue. Except for the inlay-bark graft and the whip-and-tongue (splice) graft, grafting is usually done to correct some mistake. For example, cleft grafting is done to topwork a variety that has not been successful. The inlay-bark graft is commonly used to topwork seedling pecans after they've developed a substantial trunk. The whip-and-tongue graft can be used to bench graft small seedlings during the dormant season or to graft seedlings in the field.

WHIP-AND-TONGUE GRAFT

This is a dormant-season graft. It can be used in the field usually in January or February or as a bench graft as soon as dormant rootstocks and scion wood are available. The bench graft is done in the comfort of the workshop and the grafted trees are stored in damp peat moss at 40° to 50°F until the wounds callus (about 2 months) and then can be planted.

This propagation technique is primarily limited to seedlings or limbs ¼ to ¾ inch in diameter. Since it requires a long smooth cut, it is important to use a sharp grafting knife, although this graft has undoubtedly been accomplished with a sharp pocket knife many times. Utility knives are inexpensive and make excellent whip-and-tongue grafting knives. Wipe off the oil coating before using and keep a sharp blade in the handle at all times. A grafting knife works best because it is only beveled on one side and produces a smoother cut. Good knives, like the German Tina knives, are expensive and may have to be ordered from one of the suppliers listed in the Appendices. Regardless of the expense, it is a good investment, because these knives will hold a sharp edge much longer than common stainless steel pocket knives.

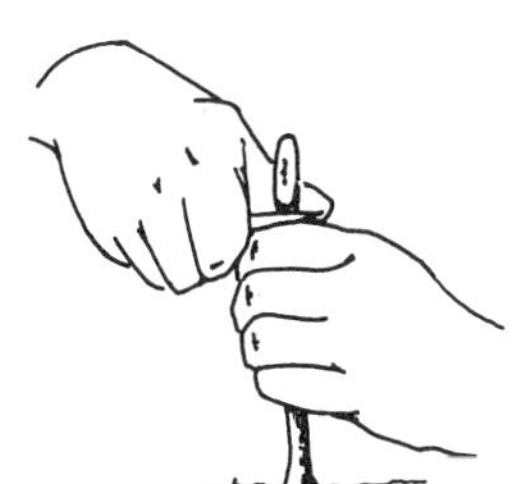

MAKING THE UPWARD CUT ON THE ROOTSTOCK.

This graft is executed by making the first cut on the rootstock 6 to 8 inches above ground level (or above roots when bench grafting). It should be a straight, sloping cut, 1½ to 2 inches long.

A similar cut is made on the scion (graftstick from an improved variety). To make the tongue cut, start ⅓ of the way down from the tip of the slanting cut and try to make a straight cut, ⅔ of the length of the slanting cut.

Be careful not to split the wood. An extremely sharp knife with a ridged blade

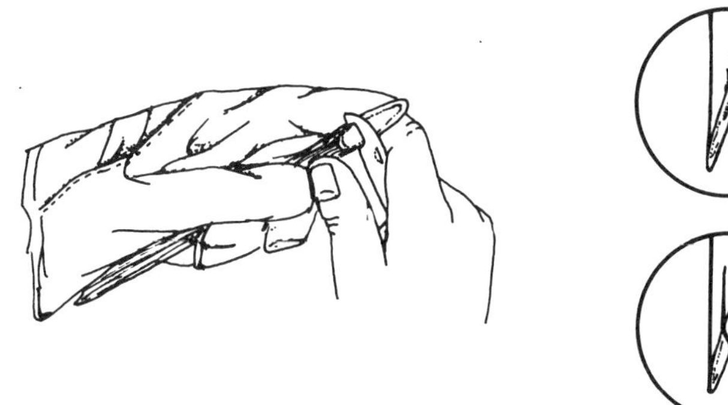

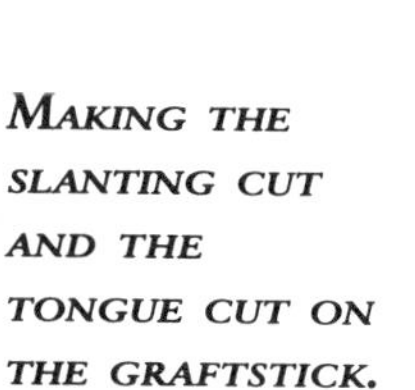

MAKING THE SLANTING CUT AND THE TONGUE CUT ON THE GRAFTSTICK.

will make the execution of any grafting technique much easier. A similar tongue cut is made on both the stock and scion.

Now, match the two pieces together interlocking the tongue cuts. Do this carefully to avoid splitting the wood on either piece. Pressing the top portion of the cut surfaces against each other (not touching the fresh cuts with your fingers) should help open the cuts and allow the union to occur. When orienting the scion with the stock, make sure that one edge is lined up rather than setting the scion in the middle. Often the scion is slightly smaller in diameter, but it's important that at least one section of both cambial tissues match. Even if the match isn't perfect—your first attempts may produce upper portions that overlap—the graft will often take, provided that the cut tissue on one side heals before growth begins in the spring.

FITTING THE GRAFTSTICK AND ROOTSTOCK TOGETHER.

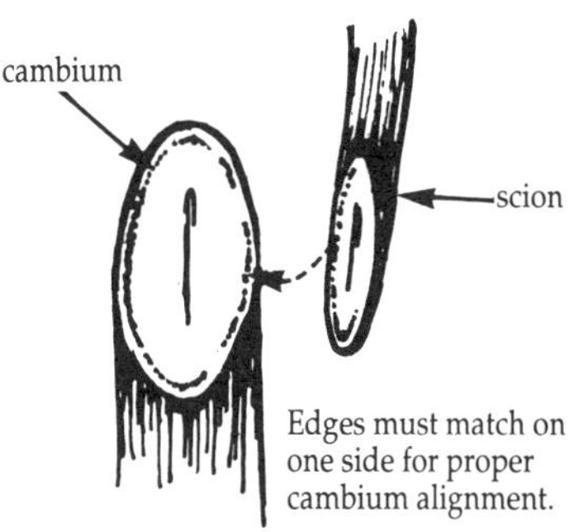

LINE UP GRAFTSTICK AND ROOTSTOCK ALONG ONE EDGE INSTEAD OF IN THE MIDDLE.

Wrap a whip-and-tongue graft done in the field with budding tape, beginning ½ to 1 inch below the cuts and extending the same distance above the cuts. Flexible budding tape can be secured by lapping it under the final wrap and pulling it tight. A little extra pull and it should break, leaving about 1 inch of loose tape.

After growth starts in the spring, cut off the tape to prevent girdling. Bench grafts can be secured similarly, but rubber budding strips are adequate because the graft will be allowed to heal (callus) under moist, storage conditions. Budding tape could also be used for the bench graft.

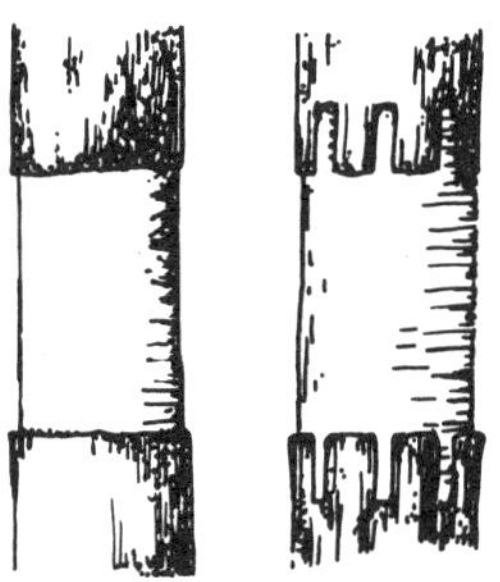

PREPARE THE STOCK.

BRIDGE, INARCH, AND CLEFT GRAFTS

Bridge grafting and inarch grafting are generally used in an emergency to save a valuable tree. The bridge graft is used to reconnect cambial tissue separated by a damaged section of bark, which occurred as a result of rodent damage, tractor blight, or other injury. Sloping cuts are made on each end of scions, about 2 inches long, and a ½-inch chisel cut is made on the back side. These scions should have been collected while dormant and kept in cold storage, as described for the inlay bark graft. (Of course they must also be from a similar species.) Spring (April or May) is the best time to attempt this graft; in fact, that's when it's most often needed to repair damage caused by rodents during the winter.

The damaged area on the tree should be trimmed and slots should be cut in the bark to receive the slanting cuts on the scions. Be sure to orient the scions properly (right side up). When fitted into the slots, they should bow slightly. Wire nails or staples, as described for inlay bark grafting, are used to secure the scions. These scions are usually spaced every 3 to 4 inches around the damaged area. The unions should be painted with grafting wax or with one of the new grafting paints.

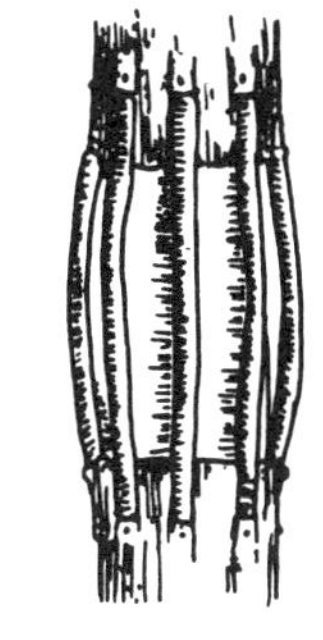

FITTING THE SCIONS INTO THE PREPARED SLOTS.

The inarch graft is similar to the bridge graft, except that seedling trees are planted every 6 inches around the base of the tree to be saved. The inarch graft is used when a tree's root system has been damaged or diseased and needs a new, possibly pest-resistant, root system. The seedlings develop such root systems and are then grafted into the existing trunk tissue. The seedlings should be planted in the winter and the grafting should be done in April or May.

The cut on the top of the seedling is made about 6 inches long with a ½-inch chisel cut on the back side. Place the cut scion surface (actually a seedling with roots attached) against the trunk of the damaged tree and make vertical cuts along each side down to the wood. Connect the base of these cuts with a horizontal cut, lift up the flap and cut most of it off. The cut surface of the scion should fit neatly in this channel with the tip inserted snugly under the small flap at the top. Use 4 to 6 small nails to secure the scion in the channel. Finish by sealing the entire graft with grafting wax.

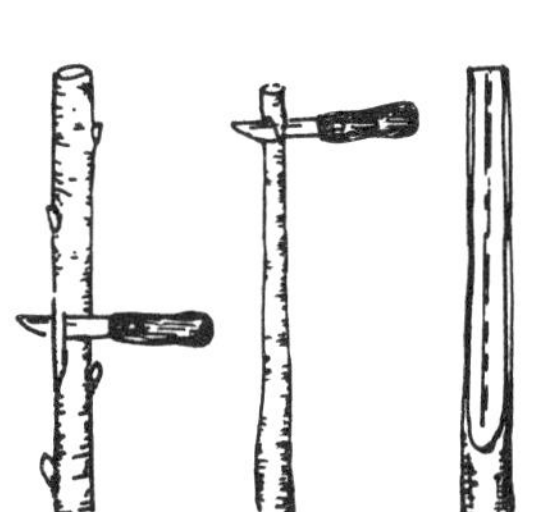

Preparing the seedling.

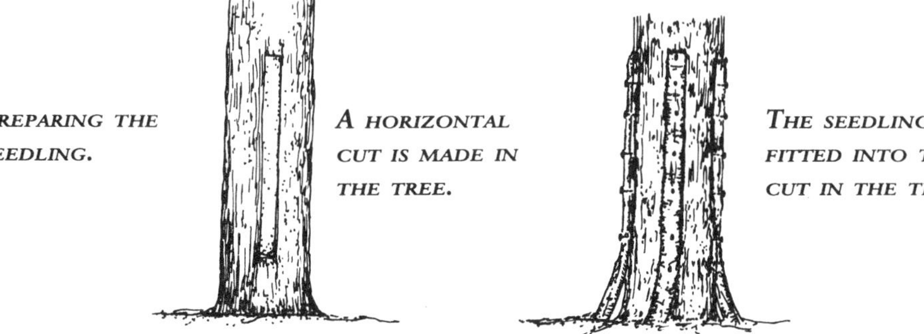

A horizontal cut is made in the tree.

The seedling is fitted into the cut in the tree.

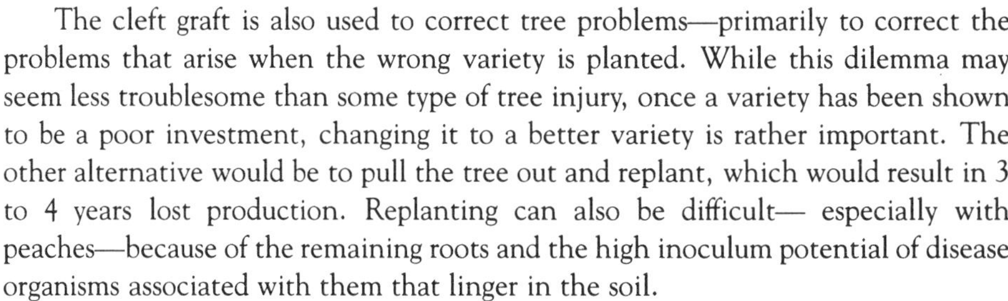

The cleft graft is also used to correct tree problems—primarily to correct the problems that arise when the wrong variety is planted. While this dilemma may seem less troublesome than some type of tree injury, once a variety has been shown to be a poor investment, changing it to a better variety is rather important. The other alternative would be to pull the tree out and replant, which would result in 3 to 4 years lost production. Replanting can also be difficult— especially with peaches—because of the remaining roots and the high inoculum potential of disease organisms associated with them that linger in the soil.

Splitting the wood.

Cleft grafts are used when the stock is 1 to 4 inches in diameter. Usually, one scaffold is left intact as a "nurse" limb for the first season to provide some shade for the tender bark and to slow the growth of scions. Even with this nurse limb, scion growth may require tipping back and bracing to prevent wind damage.

The best time to use this graft is late winter or just before the buds begin to swell. If dormant scions are available, you may try the graft later (several weeks into the growing season or through May), but the high sap pressure generated during this early growth phase may reduce the percentage of successful grafts. During the prime season, while the stock is still dormant, graftwood (scions) should also be dormant. They may be collected as needed or they can be wrapped in damp paper towels and stored in plastic bags. Store them in the refrigerator, removing a few as needed for grafting. Fortunately, these scions will tolerate several days of shipping and are often distributed this way. The comparatively cool weather during this time of year, no doubt, prevents the cambium in these scions from becoming active.

Hold the split open so the scions can be inserted.

A special tool is used for cleft grafting and purchasing one is advisable if you plan to use this technique a lot. If you think you'll only do a few cleft grafts, then a thick-bladed butcher knife or machete and a screwdriver will suffice. First cut out the top with a pruning saw. As always, be careful not to severely damage the bark. If a section strips off, recut the stock. Make the cut where you have a smooth section 6 to 8 inches long, free of limbs or knots below the cut. Otherwise the wood may not split uniformly.

Center the knife blade or cleft-grafting tool and split the wood 2 to 3 inches deep by pounding on the tool with a hammer. Remove the blade and open the cleft with a large screwdriver or the end of the cleft-grafting tool.

Two scions are used for the cleft graft. The basal end of the scion is cut to form a sloping wedge, about 2 inches long, that is wider on the outside edge. The inside edge should not be cut too thin however, as this would allow unnecessary air space between the wood surfaces.

The wedge-shaped scion is inserted into the cleft with the two cambium surfaces matching. The scions should be held firmly in place; healing will occur before growth begins in the spring. Carefully remove the wedge and look to see that the scions are in line so that their cambium tissue matches with the stock's cambium tissue. Remember, the bark on the rootstock is much thicker, so the cambium will be deeper.

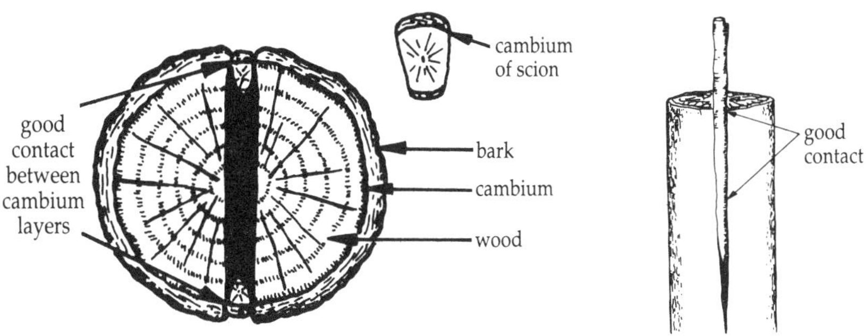

GOOD CONTACT BETWEEN THE CAMBIUM LAYERS OF THE STOCK AND THE SCIONS.

Be sure that the buds on the scion are pointing up. If the scion is inserted upside down, buds may temporarily sprout but the graft will ultimately fail.

The graft can be sealed with grafting wax or grafting paint, but the aluminum-foil-and-plastic-bag technique, used in inlay bark grafting, will work fine.

The stock in this graft usually has a large root system and will push the scions rapidly. Once growth is 18 inches long, it is advisable to pinch out the terminals. Should both scions take, the outside scion should be retained and the inner one should be removed to simplify aftercare. Bracing may be required (a 2 × 2 or wooden stake nailed to the opposite scion works well), or scion growth can be overlapped and tied, causing a natural inarch graft to occur and strengthen the tissues. This makes for a rather unusual looking growth. The tree will be cumbersome to prune, but the strength gained is significant.

INLAY BARK GRAFT

This propagation technique has been used to graft thousands of acres of improved pecans. It is one of the easiest to do, provided a few basic requirements are followed. Homeowners can successfully graft a seedling tree on their first attempt about as readily as the seasoned professional can topwork an entire orchard.

The first requirement is to store dormant graftwood (scions). Even this step may not be necessary if the beginner can find a place to buy the scions in the spring (from April to June), when most of the grafting is done. Scions should, of course, be selected from improved varieties that the grower wishes to propagate. Scionwood should come from straight, one-year-old growth that is ¼ to ½ inch in diameter. Scions larger in diameter work better on large-diameter cuts in the tree to be grafted. For example, if you plan to graft a tree that is 1½ inches across, a scion similar in size will be adequate while the larger scion will be harder to position flat against the stock because of the small stock's greater curvature. Large scions seem to grow more vigorously when they are used on larger stocks. Young, vigorous trees or trees that have been pruned back severely produce the best graftwood.

Sticks are cut in lengths of 6 to 18 inches. Six inches is a good size for the scion. Some propagators like to have ready-made scions when they start working trees. Smaller scions should have ¼ inch of their ends sealed with wax, grafting paint, or natural orange shellac before storage. The advantage to larger sticks is that there are fewer cut surfaces to dry out and sealing really isn't necessary. Ideally, each 6-inch scion should have at least 2 to 3 healthy buds. Tie the sticks in conveniently sized bundles and label each bundle.

The scions are then packed in damp paper towels, sphagnum moss, or newspapers and placed in plastic bags. It is important that the packing material not be too wet. It will need to be checked while in storage to ensure that the packing material hasn't dried out. Store the scions in the refrigerator at 34° to 45°F until needed, once the bark begins to slip in April. Then take out only what will be needed for each grafting session and keep the scions on ice. Remove a small portion as needed for use in the field.

The inlay-bark graft is best used on the central trunk of the tree, 7 to 8 feet above the ground, where the trunk is 1½ to 4 inches in diameter. Look for a relatively flat surface on the trunk, facing into the direction of the prevailing summer winds: this is usually facing southeast or southwest. Cut off about 3 to 4 feet of the terminal growth.

The technique can also be used on side branches when topworking a tree. However, this is a difficult and long-term process requiring several years of aftercare to remove suckers and excessive shoot growth. For this reason, topworking is often left to the professional. While a few side branches can be grafted to establish a new variety, it is important to keep the grafts from being shaded by removing limbs above them. If you put a scion on a side limb, be sure to place it on the top side.

After the trunk or limb has been removed with a pruning saw, trim the rough-cut surface with a knife until it is smooth. Serious pecan grafters like to have two knives—one for these rough cuts and one to cut scions. If the limb cracks and strips off bark when falling, or if a single smooth cut was not made, it is best to recut the stub below the tear or below the jagged cut.

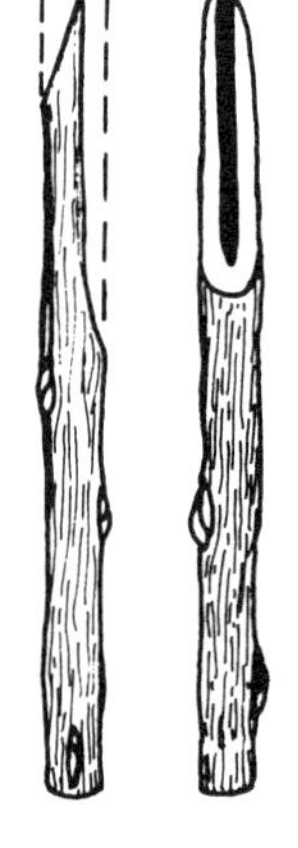

Chisel cut on scion.

Next a smooth shield-shaped piece is cut into the bark to prepare an area for the scion to fit. Try to remove the rough bark down to the point where it becomes white, but leave as much thickness of the white bark above the cambium as possible. If you cut too deep and remove a section of the white bark to the cambium, recut the stub and start over.

The scion cut starts 1½ to 2 inches from the base, just below and opposite of the lowest bud you plan to save. This cut shouldn't be attempted with one stroke, but with a number of whittling cuts. Cut in at a fairly steep angle to create somewhat of a shoulder and then cut straight out to the end of the scion. The length of this cut should be smooth and straight. Propagators often check for this by laying the grafting knife blade along the cut surface. Some propagators prefer a 2½- to 4-inch cut. This is because they believe that the more exposed cambial tissue will heal better. Of course, this requires a longer scion and more skill to make this longer yet smooth and even cut. After making the long cut, a short ½-inch chisel cut is made on the opposite side. This allows the scion to slip easily into the inlay cuts.

The cut surface of the scion is placed against the prepared shield and a cut is made first along the right side of the scion. Try to follow the edge of the scion closely. This is where you first appreciate the importance of straight scions. Beginners tend to angle their blades, cutting a channel too narrow for the scion to fit in. As you cut, make sure that the knife blade is perpendicular to the stock. This cut should be made through the bark to the cambium. Don't worry about cutting too deep. The hard wood inside the cambium tissue will prevent an excessively deep cut.

Keeping the scion in place, carefully move your hand around and make a similar cut on the other side of the scion. These cuts should stop about ¼ inch above the chisel cut.

Remove the scion and carefully start peeling the flap down about ¼ inch. It should now be possible to push the scion into the inlay cut, stopping at the shoulder. This may cause slight tearing where the base of the scion fits, but this area is where the most rapid healing occurs.

The scion can be secured in several ways. The traditional technique is to use ½- to ¾-inch wire nails. First, a ½-inch nail is used to close the flap just above the chisel cut. Most of the flap is cut off above the nail and a second ¾-inch nail is hammered in closer to the top of the inlay. A staple gun can also be used. In this case, 2 ⁹⁄₁₆-inch, flat-tipped staples are put through the intact flap, into the scion and the woody tissue below. It is important to avoid using chisel-tipped staples because they tend to split the scion. Some people use a complete wrap of plastic tape to secure the scion, but this is impractical because it must be removed shortly after spring growth begins to prevent girdling.

An 8- to 12-inch square piece of aluminum foil is used to reflect heat. Make a tear 3 to 4 inches long in the center of the foil and wrap it around the top of the stock with shiny side of the foil out.

Cut the tip out of a plastic bag and slip it carefully down over the scion. Tie the bag at the scion first with budding tape and then again lower on the stock, near the base of the bag. A small hole can be pricked in the bag just above the last tie to drain excess moisture. If the tip of the scion has not already been sealed, it is a good idea to put a drop of white wood glue on it, so it won't dry out.

Buds should begin to swell within 2 weeks. If growth hasn't begun within 4 weeks, you probably need to start over. After 6 to 12 inches of new growth it's best to remove the plastic bag, especially in humid climates. When the growth is 18 inches long, break out the tip to prevent the development of a 5- to 6-foot long wind-susceptible whip. It may also be necessary to brace the new growth with a 2 × 2, nailed opposite the graft. Place a piece of foam insulation between the graft shoot and the brace and tie the two together with 1-inch plastic tape.

This usually isn't needed before August, when hurricane winds can occur. Be sure to remove or adjust the tape next season to prevent girdling.

FOUR-FLAP GRAFT

The four-flap graft is somewhat slow to execute. Simply stated, it entails placing healthy cambium tissues in contact with each other and sealing them to prevent drying. Another name for this graft is the "banana graft." It has been used primarily on small pecan rootstocks up to 1 inch in diameter.

The bark must be slipping in order to perform this graft. Thus, the best success with this method has been in April and May. However, with good growing conditions, the four-flap graft can be used through June or as long as the stored, dormant graftwood remains viable. This graft works best when the rootstock and scion are the same diameter or when the scion is slightly larger.

The prepared rootstock.

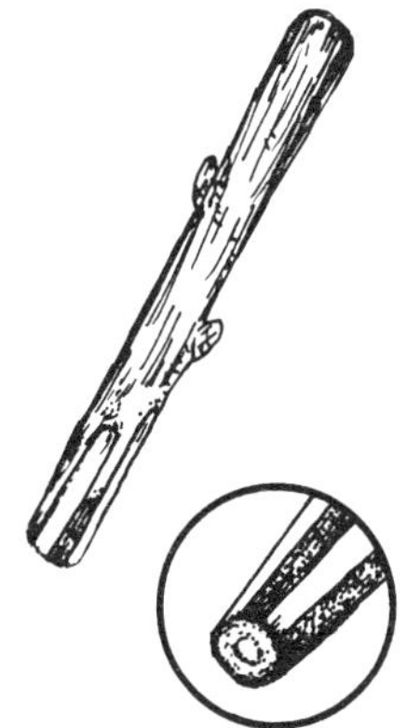

The prepared scion.

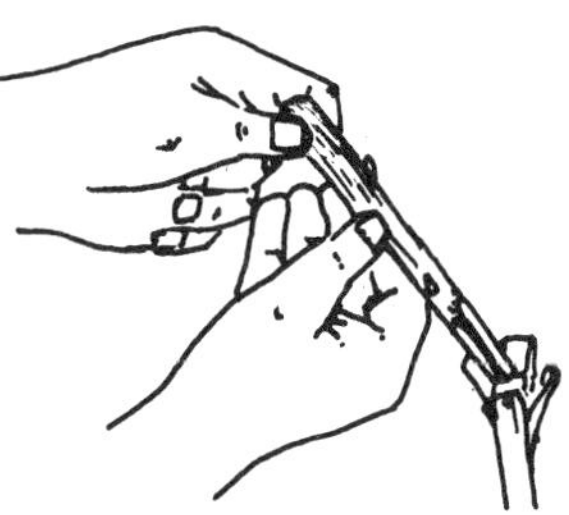

Inserting the scion into the rootstock.

Begin by cutting off the stock at a diameter slightly smaller than the scion. It should be cut straight across with scissor-type pruning shears. If possible, leave several nurse branches below the cut. The nurse branches should be cut back to 6 inches. They will keep the trees growing vigorously without competing with the growth of the scion.

Make four vertical cuts down the bark on the rootstock. These should be spaced evenly, be perpendicular to the wood and measure about 1½ inches long. Wrap a small rubber band several times around the rootstock and roll it down several inches below the cuts.

To determine where to begin these cuts, rock your knife across the top of the cut surface, making a cross that extends into the top portion of the bark. Use these marks as a starting point to begin the vertical cuts.

Cut any wax or other sealant off of the base of the scion and make 4 vertical cuts, 1½ to 2 inches long, just through the bark and down to white wood. The objective is to make a square peg from a round one. Narrow slivers of bark should remain between each cut surface.

Carefully pull the 4 flaps down on the stock. Try not to handle the inner surface of the bark. Using scissor-type pruners, cut out the central core (the banana). If you have assistance, this will be easy; if not, you may cut off or damage one of the flaps. If this happens, start over with a fresh cut on the stock.

Insert the cut end of the scion into the four flaps, aligning the cut surfaces with the flaps. Then, roll up the rubber band to hold the flaps in place. Make sure the remaining strips of bark left on the scion match with the flap edges. This is where the healing will take place.

If the cut surfaces of the scion extend above the flaps, cut off a portion of the bottom of the scion so that the flaps just cover the scion cuts or extend slightly above the cuts.

Start below the cuts on the stock and wrap the graft with budding tape, being careful to prevent the scion from twisting. If a rubber band is used to hold the flaps around the scion, it can simply be covered in the process. A small piece of aluminum foil should be wrapped around the taped area to reflect heat. A plastic bag can be used as a cover to prevent the graft from drying out. Simply tear or cut the corner out of a small sandwich bag and slip this over the scion. Tie the top of the bag above the graft and the bottom of the bag below the graft, securing the foil too. If the tip end of the scion has not already been sealed, coat it with a small amount of wood glue or a similar product.

Shoots that develop below the graft should be tipped back to prevent them from overgrowing the scion. Since the scion is normally in a terminal position, once it begins strong growth it should dominate the growth below it. This is a very strong graft union, so bracing will not usually be necessary. After shoots 4 to 6 inches long have developed on the scion, the plastic bag and wrapping tape can be removed. In an arid climate, it may be best to leave the bag on an additional 4 to 6 weeks. When properly executed, this graft creates a large area of contact between the cambium tissue of the stock and the scion, resulting in strong, rapid growth with a high survival rate.

14 pest & disease control IN THE HOME orchard

When you decide to grow fruit trees, you have to expect a few pest problems. A good orchard manager must be prepared to identify the pest and take action when necessary. Most important, correct identification is essential in making the right orchard management decisions. There's no point in applying costly pesticides to kill beneficial insects or an inconsequential amount of pests.

For too long we have approached pest management with an arsenal of pesticides, applied with little concern for the long-term environmental effects. This shotgun approach to pest control, although effective in the short term, is not the most efficient or cost-effective method of solving a pest problem.

Pesticides, both organic and chemical, are valuable tools to the southern fruit grower, and when used properly can improve the quality of the fruit we grow; many of the fruits we grow in the South could not be grown successfully without the use of pesticides. Even though chemicals must be applied with care, proper use of labeled pesticides is safe and may make fruit safer to eat by eliminating contamination from fungi and insects. Because pesticide regulations are different in every state, growers should contact their state's agriculture extension office (see the Appendices) to obtain a spray schedule for their area. The following spray recommendation chart was developed by the Texas Agricultural Extension Service and is representative of the charts developed for most of the southern states.

Sample Homeowner's spray schedule for pecans

Timing	Pest	Pesticide	Rate / 1 gal. water[1]	Remarks
	INSECTS			
Dormant season (winter)	scale insects phylloxera	97% oil emulsion	¼ pt	Spray tree trunks and branches thoroughly.
	NUTRITIONAL			
Budbreak (just as the buds begin to split and show green color) Terminal bud growth should be 2 inches in length.	rosette	Zinc sulfate 36% WP or Zinc nitrate 6-17% liquid	2 tsp 2 tsp	Zinc sprays are essential for early season pecan growth. Early frequent applications will give the best response. Elemental zinc is toxic to most plants other than pecans and grapes, therefore, avoid drift to protect from phytotoxicity. If drift is a possibility, use NZN. Do not use any zinc product at higher than labeled rates since foliage burn can result. When applying more than one zinc spray in 2 weeks, reduce rate by one-half. Never spray young trees that are not actively growing.
	INSECTS			
	phylloxera	Malathion® 50% EC (Several formulations)	2 tsp	If dormant oil was not used, then treat trees where a history of phylloxera damage indicates a need for control.
	DISEASES			
	scab and other foliage and nut diseases	Benomyl 50% DF (Several formulations) or Thiophanate-methyl (Topsin-M® 70% WP)	½ - 1 Tbs ½ - 1 Tbs	
	NUTRITIONAL			
Prepollination (when leaves are one-third grown and before pollen is shed) mid-April	rosette	Same as bud-break		

[1]Due to variation in concentration of pesticides in different products, refer to label for specific rate per 1 gallon spray solution.

Timing	Pest	Pesticide	Rate / 1 gal. water[1]	Remarks
	DISEASES			
	scab and other foliage diseases	Same as bud-break		
	INSECTS			
	fall webworm walnut caterpillar	Bacillus thuringiensis (Several formulations)	Refer to label	Repeat sprays as pest problem reoccurs.
		or		
		Diazinon® 25% EC (Several formulations)	2 tsp	
		or		
		Malathion® 50% EC (Several formulations)	2½ tsp	
		or		
		Carbaryl (Sevin® 50% WP)	2 Tbs	
	NUTRITIONAL			
Pollination (when case-bearer eggs appear on tips of nutlets) May	rosette	Same as bud-break		
	INSECTS			
	pecan nut casebearer	Same as pre-pollination		Apply in late April or during May (consult your county extension agent for precise local timing).
	DISEASES			
	scab and other foliage and nut diseases	Same as bud-break		
	INSECTS			
Second generation case-bearer (42 days after first case-bearer spray)	pecan nut casebearer	Same as pre-pollination		
	aphids	Diazinon® 25% EC (Several formulations)	2 tsp	Treat yellow aphids where an average of 20 per compound leaf are found or when excessive honeydew is produced.
		or		
		Malathion® 50% EC	2½ tsp	

WP = wettable powder, EC = emulsifiable concentrate, DF = Dry Flowable

TIMING	PEST	PESTICIDE	RATE / 1 GAL. WATER[1]	REMARKS
continued		(Several formulations) or Dimethoate (Cygon 267® 30.5% EC)	0.5 Tbs	
	DISEASES			
	scab and other foliage and nut diseases	Same as bud-break		May be required during extended periods of high humidity.
	DISEASES			
Water stage (when water collects inside nut) - mid- to late July	scab and other foliage and nut diseases	Same as bud-break		Treat where there is a history of disease problems and during high humidity.
	DISEASES			
Half-shell hardening - mid- to late August	scab and other foliage and nut diseases	Same as bud-break		
	INSECTS			
	aphids	Same as for aphids listed above		Treat yellow aphids when an average of 10 per compound leaf are found or when excessive honeydew is produced and aphid populations persist.
	hickory shuckworm	Diazinon® 25% EC or Sevin ® 50% WP	2 tsp 2 Tbs	
	pecan weevil	Carbaryl (Sevin® 50% WP)	2 to 3 Tbs	Treat areas with a history of pecan weevil infestation. One to three treatments at 10- to 14-day intervals are needed for heavy weevil infestations.

[1]*DUE TO VARIATION IN CONCENTRATION OF PESTICIDES IN DIFFERENT PRODUCTS, REFER TO LABEL FOR SPECIFIC RATE PER 1 GALLON SPRAY SOLUTION.*

Refer to the charts in this chapter to aid you in identifying pest problems correctly so you can take the necessary pest control measures. When selecting pesticides, always start with the safest products first. It's also important to realize that sometimes no control is the best pest control.

Bird Control

Birds can be a beautiful garden friend or an adversary to the fruit grower. The most effective bird control is a physical barrier, such as netting. Bird netting is about the only sure control, but it is difficult to use and requires a lot of labor to set up and take down.

There are a number of ways to reduce the damage without getting rid of the birds. Unfortunately pest problems are always worse in an urban environment, where there is a shortage of fresh fruit even for birds.

A number of products guaranteed to get rid of birds work with some limited success. Plastic hawks, rubber snakes, scare eyes (beach balls with flashy colors and shiny spots), flash tape (shiny tape twisted through the tree), noisemakers, carbide cannons, and scarecrows are all designed to scare the birds away. They all work to some extent, but they must be moved around frequently to keep the birds off guard. The best strategy is to use a number of scare devices in combination.

Fruit growers often wonder why birds peck a small hole in the fruit, leaving the rest on the tree to rot. A number of naturalists believe birds are after the moisture in the fruit, not the fruit iself. One way to accommodate this need without sacrificing your fruit is to leave water out for the birds. Try everything you can to get rid of the birds and then be prepared to share with the ones that persist.

VARMINTS

This group of pests includes a number of animals—squirrels, rabbits, raccoons, opossums, mice, and rats. These animals can damage the tree trunk by chewing on the bark. They will also break limbs and, of course, eat the fruit. Control can be achieved in a number of ways, including live traps, electric fences, and guns (if you live outside city limits and the animal in question is in season).

DEER

Deer can completely devastate a grower's plantings. They not only eat the fruit and foliage, they can also destroy young trees and cause severe damage to mature ones. Installing an 8-foot-high deer-proof fence the most effective way to keep deer out of your orchard. Electric fences, if maintained, are also very effective. Some research data even indicates that deer can be repelled by hanging bars of scented soap in the trees. Human hair, obtained from your local barber shop, put in the legs of ladies' hosiery and hung from the tree's branches will give short-term results, as will spraying the area with a solution of 1 dozen eggs and 1 gallon of water.

General Pest and Disease Problems

Symptoms	Possible Causes	Comments and Remedies
Premature fruit drop.	Natural thinning	Most trees produce more fruit than they need and thin themselves naturally.
	Spring frost	Frost often kills developing fruits or flower buds.
	Poor pollination	Tree may require other trees nearby to pollinate it; be careful not to kill bees with insecticides.
	Environmental stress	Drought, cold, or heat can cause fruit drop.
	Disease stress	See controls under specific diseases.

Symptoms	Possible Causes	Comments and Remedies
	Use of Sevin insecticide	Sevin causes some fruit thinning if used within 40 days of fruit set.
	insects	Identification is critical to safe, effective pest control.
Poor fruit development (small number of fruit on tree).	Poor pollination	Tree may require other trees nearby to pollinate it; be careful not to kill bees with insecticides.
	Biennial or alternate bearing	Apples, pears, and pecans can overbear one year and produce few fruit the next year if not properly thinned.
	Improper pruning	Do not prune off fruit-bearing wood during the dormant season. For proper instructions on pruning see Chapter 1.
	Frost injury	
Fruit too small.	Failure to prune	Peaches, nectarines, plums, and apples tend to produce many small fruits if not pruned or thinned properly.
	Poor soil fertility	Run a soil test and begin a fertilizer program.
Many small twigs broken off.	Squirrel damage	Squirrels girdle branches, which then die back and fall off of tree.
	Environmental stress	Drought or waterlogging can cause limbs to die and break off.
	Mechanical injury	
	Disease or insect damage	See following chart on specific diseases.
	Holes in limbs and trunks with tunneling beneath	Borer damage. Use registered insecticides.
Large areas of split bark; no decay evident.	Freeze cracks (Usually occurring on southwest sides of tree's trunk and major limbs.)	Freezes can split tree trunks if sap in trunk expands. Use tree wrap or latex paint to protect bark from sun and extreme temperatures.
	Sunscald (Usually affects tops of tree's limbs.)	Thin-barked trees (young ones, for example) split when exposed to intense sunlight. Use tree wrap or block sun with a board on bright days.
	Mechanical injury (lawnmower, for example)	Dig up grass around trunk and replace with mulch to avoid mowing too closely to base of tree.
	Lightning injury	
Large areas of split bark; decay evident in wood.	Secondary decay of any of the wounds described above	No adequate controls; remove loose bark and water and fertilize tree when necessary.
Gray-white powdery growth on leaves; leaves and fruit may be distorted.	Powdery mildew (fungal disease)	Use registered fungicide.

Symptoms	Possible Causes	Comments and Remedies
Black, sooty growth on leaves, stems, and/or fruit.	Sooty mold (fungus that grows on honeydew—substance secreted by aphids and other insects)	Identify insect. Then control with registered insecticide.
		Identify specific insect and treat with registered insecticide.
Brown dead areas on leaf margins.	Leaf scorch, caused insufficient transport of water to leaves	Water tree heavily during dry periods. Scorch is usually caused by hot, dry weather. A root rot or another root damage may also be involved.
	Leaf burn, possibly caused by overfertilizing	Do not overapply commercial, highly soluble fertilizers.
	Cold injury	Do not fertilize late in season.
Tree wilted possibly with light green- to yellow-colored foliage.	Dry soil	Water heavily during drought.
	Root rot (fungal disease)	Improve drainage.
	Root knot or root-feeding nematodes	Submit soil sample for nematode analysis.
	Various fungal, bacterial, or viral diseases	Identify disease problem or submit a sample for laboratory diagnosis.
	Water-logged soil	Improve drainage.
Interveinal yellowing of leaves; no wilting apparent.	Nutrient or mineral deficiency	Run a soil test.
	Herbicide injury	Avoid applying herbicide too close to the tree.
	Water-logged soil, resulting in poor transport of nutrients to leaves	Improve drainage.
Large, corky galls at base of tree and on roots.	Crown gall (bacterial disease)	Some galls can be pruned out, but it is best to consult an arborist. Trees may live for many years in spite of galls.
Young leaves curled and distorted; cluster of insects on underside of leaves.	Aphids	Use registered insecticide; thorough coverage of underside of leaves is necessary.
Silk tents in branch crotches.	Tent caterpillar	Physically remove tents or use registered insecticide when caterpillars are small.
Silk tents on ends of branches.	Fall webworm	Physically remove fall webworm or use registered insecticide when caterpillars are small.

Symptoms	Possible Causes	Comments and Remedies
Crescent-shaped scars on fruit; whitish, legless grubs with brown heads present.	Plum curculio	Use registered insecticide on a regular schedule.
Leaves with tiny white spots, often dirty with webbing.	Spider mites	Use registered miticide.
Bark encrusted with tiny, slightly raised bumps; apples may have red spots with white centers.	San Jose or peach scale	Use registered insecticide.

Pest and Disease Problems with Apples and Pears

Symptoms	Possible Causes	Comments and Remedies
Leaf spots with light tan centers and brown borders; large rotten spots with black pimplelike structures appear on fruit. Cankers with black pimplelike structures may appear on twigs.	Black rot (fungal disease)	Prune out dead wood, maintain tree health, use approved fungicide.
Olive-brown velvety spots on leaves and young fruit; fruit spots develop into brown corky lesions and mature fruit is distorted.	Scab (fungal disease)	Use registered fungicide.
Bright yellow spots with orange or black centers on leaves; orange spots with small cuplike structures on fruit.	Rust (fungal disease)	Do not plant cedar trees, which are alternate hosts of the fungus, in the area; use registered fungicide.
Sunken, light brown circular spots with salmon-colored specks (spore masses) on fruit; apple tastes bitter; sunken lesions may appear on branches.	Bitter rot (fungal disease)	Use registered fungicide spray program; prune out dead branches (fungicide not necessary if pruning is done).
Circular clusters of tiny black specks and small sooty smudges on fruit.	Fly speck and sooty blotch (two fungal diseases that commonly occur together)	Use registered fungicide; does not affect fruit taste or quality.
Sunken, dark green lesions with a feathery pattern on fruit.	Quince rust (fungal disease)	Use registered fungicide.
Spots on fruit that do not fit previous descriptions.	Corking, a physiological problem associated with certain varieties	Submit sample for laboratory diagnosis.

Symptoms	Possible Causes	Comments and Remedies
White, funguslike residue on the bark.	San Jose scale	Most golden types are susceptible; use registered insecticide.
Misshapened, dimpled fruit.	Stink bugs	Use registered insecticide.
Bark on young branches is rough and pimpled; tissue beneath bark has brown spots.	Measles, believed to be a nutrient imbalance	Run a soil test.
White, cottony insect mass.	Wooly apple aphid	Use resistant rootstocks; spray with registered insecticide.
Sunken, black or wine-colored cankers on young twigs, larger branches or trunk; leaves wilt, curl and cling to twigs; shoot tips may be curved into "shepherd's crook."	Fire blight (bacterial disease)	Prune out affected branches. Use streptomycin antibiotic or copper containing bactericide during bloom. Remove suckers as they appear because they are very susceptible to fire blight. Do not plant apples near pears, which are highly susceptible to fire blight; grow resistant varieties.
Black sooty coating on upper surface of leaves.	Sooty mold (fungal disease)	Control insects that secrete honeydew (aphids, scale, whitefly).
Tree breaks off at graft union during strong winds.	Poorly constructed graft or branch Virus infection of graft union	No control available. No control available.
Pink-white worms bore into blossoms on end of apple; clusters of round, brown frass pellets (larval droppings) inside fruit.	Codling moth	Use registered insecticide.
Apples dimpled with faint brown streaks in the flesh.	Apple maggot	Use registered insecticide.
Bark comes loose from trunk near ground level or graft union.	Flathead borers	Paint trunk with latex paint in June or July. Use registered insecticide.

Pest and Disease Problems with Stone Fruits, Apricots, Cherries, Peaches, Plums, and Nectarines

Symptoms	Possible Causes	Comments and Remedies
Small, angular leaf spots (1/16 to 1/8 inches long) confined between veins; spots are green, then purple, then brown; small, circular, depressed spots with watersoaked margins on fruit; sunken cankers may appear on twigs.	Bacterial spot	Spray with registered copper-containing fungicide in late winter. Plant resistant varieties. **Do not use copper fungicides during growing season.**

Symptoms	Possible Causes	Comments and Remedies
Small, olive-green spots on young fruit; spots eventually turn brown and velvety; similar spots on leaves.	Scab (fungal disease)	Use registered fungicide when petal fall and shuck split occurs. Does not affect fruit quality.
Purple spots appear on upper surfaces of cherry leaves; leaves become shotholed and turn yellow; fruit may also be spotted.	Cherry leaf spot (fungal disease)	Plant resistant cherry varieties; use registered fungicide.
	Shothole fungus	Use registered fungicide.
Peach or nectarine leaves puckered, thickened, and curled from time they first appear in spring; leaves red or orange at first but turn yellow; shoots swollen and stunted.	Peach leaf curl (fungal disease on peaches and nectarines)	Use registered fungicide in late winter.
Blossoms and young twigs wilt and decay during bloom; sunken cankers with gummy ooze develop on twigs; circular spots, which develop tufts of gray spores during moist weather, form on fruit.	Brown rot (fungal disease common to all stone fruit)	Use registered fungicide once a week and one day before picking. Remove all affected fruit on tree and on ground. Prune to allow good air circulation.
Sunken cankers on twigs, larger branches, and/or trunk; leaves above canker wilt.	Cytospora canker (fungal disease)	Prune out cankers.
Swellings that split the bark appear on plum or branches and later turn coal black; leaves may wilt above swellings.	Black knot (fungal disease of plum and cherry only)	Use registered fungicide. Prune out affected twigs at least 4 inches below knots. Destroy wild plum and wild cherry trees in the area.
Shoot tips stunted; leaves yellow and curled upward; severe defoliation.	Nutrient or mineral deficiency	Run a soil test.
New growth at tip of twig wilts and dies; maturing fruit may contain ½-inch long pinkish worms.	Oriental fruit moth	Use registered insecticide to prevent damage.
Gum oozes from holes at base of trunk or lower branch crotches; sawdust may be evident.	Peach tree borers	Use registered insecticide on bark only.
Gum oozes from cuts, buds, and injured areas of bark.	Bacterial canker	Clean pruning tools between each tree; avoid summer pruning.
	Normal sap production	No control needed.

Symptoms	Possible Causes	Comments and Remedies
Many small round holes in twigs and branches.	Shothole borer	Remove and destroy all dead or dying wood; use registered insecticide to protect healthy trees.
Tiny, white, flat insects encrusting bark.	White peach scale	Use a dormant oil spray or treat with registered insecticide when eggs are hatching during the growing season.

Pest and Disease Problems with Pecans

Symptoms	Possible Causes	Comments and Remedies
Leaves curled and distorted, honeydew sooty mold; leaves chlorotic and may shed.	Aphids	Use registered insecticide.
Premature nut fall with frass (larval droppings) on the nuts.	Pecan nut casebearer	Use registered insecticide.
Silk tents on ends of branches.	Fall webworm	Use registered insecticide. Remove webs.
Silk tents in branch crotches.	Tent caterpillars	Remove tents; treat with registered insecticide.
Red-headed larva feeding in nuts.	Weevils	Use registered insecticides.
Small, crinkled, rosetted leaves and shoots.	Zinc deficiency	Use foliar zinc sprays.
White powdery fungus growth on nuts.	Powdery mildew (fungus disease)	Use registered fungicide.
Small, olive-colored spots on twigs and underside of leaves; tiny black dots on shucks enlarge to form black lesions; nuts drop prematurely.	Scab (fungal disease)	Use pecan fungicide spray program; plant resistant varieties.
Downy or frosty-looking spots appear on lower leaf surfaces; later greenish yellow spots are evident on both leaf surfaces.	Downy spot (fungal disease)	Use pecan fungicide spray program.
Reddish brown, irregular spots with grayish concentric rings on leaves.	Brown leaf spot (fungal leaf spot)	Use pecan fungicide spray program.
Empty nut shell.	"Pops"—a problem whose cause is unknown	Environmental stress or poor pollination are thought to be causes; no controls are known.

Symptoms	Possible Causes	Comments and Remedies
Feeding punctures to kernels; black blotches on kernels.	Plant bugs	Plant resistant varieties.
Small, cream-colored worms in immature nuts or in the green shucks after shells have hardened.	Hickory shuckworm	Clean up and destroy fallen nuts to eliminate over-wintering larvae.

Pest and Disease Problems with Walnuts (English and Black)

Symptoms	Possible Causes	Comments and Remedies
Darkened areas on hulls, leaves, and twigs.	Walnut blight (bacterial)	Spray with copper-based fungicides. Plant resistant varieties.
Spotting on the leaves and twigs.	Anthracnose (fungal)	Plant resistant varieties.

Note: Walnuts suffer from many of the same leaf-feeding insects that attack pecans.

Pest and Disease Problems with Other Small Fruits

Symptoms	Possible Causes	Comments and Remedies
Grayish white, moldy growth on leaves.	Powdery mildew fungal disease	Use fungicide program.
Galls at base of plant, on roots, and on canes; plants stunted.	Crown gall (bacterial disease)	Prune out galled canes; no chemicals will control this disease. Clean tools after pruning to prevent spread of disease.
Plants wilt; leaves may turn yellow.	Dry soil	Supply water.
	Water-logged soil	Plant in well-drained area.
	Cotton root rot (fungal disease)	No effective control.
	Root rot (fungal disease)	Plant in well-drained soil.
	Root knot (nematode problem)	Check roots for knots; fumigate soil; rotate to a noninfected site.
Green and yellow mosaic or mottle pattern on leaves; plants may be stunted.	Virus disease (any of several)	Purchase certified virus-free plants; prune out affected canes; if more than 20% of canes are infected, remove entire planting; control aphids with registered insecticide; remove nearby related wild plants (such as wild brambles).
Leaves rolled or tied together; small caterpillars feeding inside.	Leafrollers	Use registered insecticide.
Leaves distorted, wilting; accumulation of honeydew; cluster of insects on underside of leaves.	Aphids	Use registered insecticide.

Pest and Disease Problems with Blueberries

Symptoms	Possible Causes	Comments and Remedies
Plants stunted and discolored.	Soil pH too high	Blueberries require acid pH; run a soil test.
	Nutrient deficiency	Run a soil test.
	Virus diseases	Submit sample for laboratory diagnosis.
	Poor quality water	Do a water analysis.
Berries turn reddish or tan color as they ripen and become shriveled and hard; blossoms turn brown and wither; centers of new leaves are black.	Mummy berry (fungal disease).	Use registered fungicide.
Branches die back; cankers may be evident externally; internal discoloration not reddish brown.		Common in spring.
Ripe berries too soft.	Blueberry maggot	Use registered insecticide on a regular schedule.
Terminal leaves roll and turn brown.	Blueberry leaf tiers	Prune out and use recommended insecticides.

Pest and Disease Problems with Brambles (Blackberries and Raspberries)

Symptoms	Possible Causes	Comments and Remedies
Plants wilt; leaves turn yellow at bottom.	Dry soil	Supply water.
	Water-logged soil	Improve drainage.
	Root knot (nematode problem)	Rotate to a noninfected site; fumigate soil.
Ripening berries covered with tufts of gray, green, white, or black moldy growth.	Fungal fruit rot (any of several)	Use registered fungicide; pick berries regularly and immediately.
White or tan spots with purple borders appear on canes; canes die.	Anthracnose (fungal disease)	Use registered fungicide in early spring and fall; prune out old canes.
Leaves curl downward; leaves smaller than normal; internodes shorter than normal.	Leaf curl (virus disease)	No control; destroy plant.
	Aphids	Look for clusters of small gray insects on underside of leaves; control with registered insecticide.
	Herbicide injury	Find source of herbicide and eliminate.
Blisterlike reddish orange pustules develop on lower leaf surfaces.	Rust disease (fungal disease)	Plant resistant varieties; remove and destroy affected plants; remove nearby wild brambles.

Symptoms	Possible Causes	Comments and Remedies
Insects feeding inside cane. Cane looks like a snake that swallowed a rabbit.	Cane borer	Practice sanitary pruning; destroy infested canes.
Multiple shoots (rosetting or "Witches Broom") from buds infected on last year's primocanes; developing flowers are pinkish and elongated; fruit does not form and leaves may develop from the sepals.	Rosette or Double blossom (fungal)	Plant resistant varieties (Humble and trailing types), established from root cuttings; sanitary pruning and spray (with registered fungicides) during bloom.

Pest and Disease Problems with Grapes

Symptoms	Possible Causes	Comments and Remedies
Brown spots with dark borders on leaves; grapes turn black, shrivel up like raisins and remain attached to stem.	Black rot (fungal disease)	Use registered fungicide. Plant resistant varieties.
Brown leaf spots.	Fungal leaf spot (any of several)	Use registered fungicide.
Small yellow spots appear on upper leaf surfaces; white, cottony growth forms on underside of spots.	Downy mildew (fungal disease)	Use registered fungicide.
Canes die back; dark lesions on canes.	Phomopsis dieback (fungal disease)	Use registered fungicide.
Leaf resembles a fan; main veins are drawn together and teeth along margins are elongated.	Fan leaf (virus disease)	Remove affected plants.
	Herbicide injury	If symptoms occur in spring when lawn herbicides are being applied, herbicide injury is a likely cause. Do not apply lawn herbicides in hot weather; wait to apply herbicides until wind has died down.
Plants stunted, leaf margins turn brick red.	Pierce's Disease (Mycoplasm)	Plant resistant varieties; no chemical control.
White powdery fungal growth.	Powdery mildew	Use registered fungicide.
Small, green seedless grapes are intermingled with ripe grapes in the clusters.	Shot berry, caused by environmental stress or poor pollination	No control available.

Symptoms	Possible Causes	Comments and Remedies
Grapes and/or leaves webbed together; some grapes collapsed.	Grape berry moth	Use registered insecticide.
	Grape leaf folder	Use registered insecticide.
Small, rough galls the size of a small pea on the underside of leaves; swellings on roots.	Grape phylloxera (insect)	Plant resistant varieties; no chemical controls.
Insects found in canes.	Apple twig borer	Use registered insecticide.
Galls on roots; plants stunted.	Root knot nematodes	Fumigate.
Fruit and leaves have gray spots with dark halos.	Anthracnose (fungal disease)	Use registered fungicide.

Pest and Disease Problems with Strawberries

Symptoms	Possible Causes	Comments and Remedies
Small spots with white or tan centers and reddish brown borders on leaves.	Mycosphaerella leaf spot (fungal disease)	Plant resistant varieties; use registered fungicide.
Purplish or brown spots on leaves, not covered in previous descriptions.	Fungal or bacterial leaf spot (any of several)	Submit sample for laboratory diagnosis.
White or gray crusty material covering leaves, stems, and/or fruit.	Chemical injury	
	Slime mold (fungus)	Slime molds grow on plant surfaces during wet weather and disappear again in dry weather; no need for control.
Gray, fuzzy mold on fruit especially during wet periods.	Gray mold (fungal disease)	Use registered fungicide.
Plants wilt; leaves may turn brown at margins; roots and crowns discolored when cut open.	Red steele (fungal disease)	If many plants show symptoms, replant in another area; plant in well-drained area.
	Nematode injury	Plant resistant varieties (certified).
		Fumigate soil.
Fruit is hard and leathery with brown spots.	Leather rot (fungal disease)	Mulch; rotate if infection is severe.
	Environmental stress	Poor growing conditions can cause berries to become dry and hard.
Fruit is soft with brown spots.	Fungal or bacterial fruit rot (any of several)	Mulch; use strawberry fungicides.
	Pill bugs and slugs	Use commercial baits.

Symptoms	Possible Causes	Comments and Remedies
Malformed berries; looks like several berries have grown together.	Fascination—a response to environmental conditions	Common in certain varieties in fall and spring.
Berries seedy at tips.	Insect injury	Use strawberry insecticide spray program.
	Mites	Use registered miticide.
	Frost injury	Protect plants from frost by mulching.
	Nutrient deficiency	Run a soil test.
Flower buds droop, turn brown, and may drop on ground.	Strawberry weevil	Use registered insecticide.
Elongated black lesions, reddish brown crown rot.	Anthracnose	Reduce the fertility.

Pest and Disease Problems with Persimmons

Symptoms	Possible Causes	Comments and Remedies
Curling and cupping of the terminal leaves.	Persimmon psylla	Apply registered insecticides during the spring.
Brown leaf spots.	Fungal leaf spot (any of several)	Use registered fungicides only if severe.
Wilting and death of the top; eventual tree death.	Persimmon wilt	Prevent suckering and remove root sprouts. Do not locate near infected native persimmons.

Pest and Disease Problems with Figs

Symptoms	Possible Causes	Comments and Remedies
Shriveled, leathery fruit, which may drop.	Hot weather stress	Mulch trees and water thoroughly.
Sour, decaying fruit.	Fruit beetle	Plant varieties that have closed eyes.

These diagnostic charts offer general information on pesticide recommendations. It is imperative that growers follow pesticide spray schedules available from the cooperative extension service in their states. Very often specific pesticide uses are approved within a single state. County offices of the extension services are available almost everywhere. If there isn't an office in your area, contact the land grant university in your state to obtain fruit and nut spray schedules.

planning 15

PICK-YOUR-OWN & SMALL-ACREAGE orchards

Growers who plan to establish a small operation to sell at a roadside stand or to produce brokers or who decide to plant a small pick-your-own (PYO) orchard have much more at stake than the small-scale gardener. How do you determine what and how much to plant, how to promote, whether to diversify, and whether to buy or lease? The questions go on and on. That's why it's most important to develop a plan.

Lots of people envision a small farm as a great place to retire. Producing a crop is extremely satisfying. It's the kind of reward that makes up for a little extra hard work. However, you must realize that maintaining a horticultural operation is a labor-intensive endeavor.

The PYO saves a lot in labor expenses but growers must open their farms to a bunch of strangers—most of whom will be friendly, considerate customers. Unfortunately, a few will eat their weight in fruit while at the farm, waste fruit, damage plants, and let their children run wild.

Any commercial planting that you plan to harvest yourself will require a large, semiskilled work force during the harvest season. It may be difficult to assemble a work crew for short-term jobs and you may have to do considerable training to ensure that your trees aren't damaged and that the fruit is picked at the prime stage for harvest. Roadside markets need to be located on a well-traveled road. If you plan to sell to produce brokers or directly to a grocery chain you will need to work out the details well in advance of production. More than a few orchards have started out as PYOs only to change to self-harvested orchards after a few years of dealing with the public.

Whatever system you decide on, make a plan. A 1-acre planting will keep you plenty busy and supply supplementary income. A 5-acre planting will barely support a small family. Caring for 10 to 40 acres with help from some permanent employees is a full-time job. While an acre may be tended with minimal equipment, a significant investment in equipment must be made to tend a 5- to 10-acre block. As a result, 20 acres is usually considered a minimal commercial size to justify the necessary investment and time.

One of the hardest decisions will be deciding what to plant and how much of each. Assuming you plan to start small and be cautious the first year, you might plant 1 acre of fruit crops. Strawberries will produce the first spring if planted in the fall so, even though they can be difficult to grow, they are a good choice for the first year, especially for a pick-your-own operation. Blackberries will produce 14 to 16 months after a winter planting and the planting will last for many years, unlike strawberries which will be plowed under each summer. Peaches and plums will take 3 to 4 years to begin producing marketable crops, but they are always in demand. You will probably want to include a ½ acre of peaches in this initial planting. Plums are more risky because of their susceptibility to bacterial diseases like bacterial canker and leaf scorch. Other optional crops would include apples (this may be a main crop in some areas), pears, and Asian persimmons. Orchards planted in the upper South will do quite well with apples while it will be difficult to grow low-chilling varieties, like Anna and Dorsett Golden, in the lower South.

An additional ¼ acre could be planted to vegetables. If you have access to a farmer's market then you could buy some of your vegetables from a wholesaler for retail sales at the market. However, you may want to market most of the vegetables as pick-your-own crops because people like to harvest their own tomatoes, squash, and green beans. Your customer's kids will get a kick out of digging potatoes. You may want to sell other crops like sweet corn in a retail arena because many people don't know when corn is ripe to pick.

Specialty vegetables could also be an option, depending on your clientele. Luffa or sponge gourds (edible when small), cucuzza gourds (*Lagenaria* species), fuzzy gourd, bitter melon, and Asian eggplants are some of the specialty crops for the spring and summer season. Premium melons like the French Charentais (cantaloupe type) or seedless watermelons should be a big hit though they may mature after the fruit crops and require a special advertising effort to draw customers back. They could also be marketed directly or sold to a broker.

Cut flowers will also sell well—especially the early ones that come off with the fruit crops. Gladiolus, larkspur, cornflowers, and dianthus (including annual carnations) would be popular early in the season. If you've planned to offer crops throughout the summer and into the fall, then zinnias, gomphrena (one of the everlastings that could be marketed year-round), and montbretia (an orange, summer-flowering, gladiolus relative) would be available to sell along with these later crops.

If you will be selling fall crops, like Asian persimmons, then cool season vegetables like Chinese cabbage, Pac Choi, broccoli, cauliflower, daikon (Asian radish), lettuce, and radicchio (one of the salad chicories) may be appropriate. The greatest challenge is to tailor the crops you grow to your clientele. Don't be afraid to try a new crop if you are willing to promote it; you could become the sole source for a new fruit or vegetable for several years or until other growers catch up.

The second year, add an additional acre of fruit crops. Plant more peaches and blackberries—or strawberries, if you've been successful growing them—and persimmons. Also plant another ¼ to ¾ acres of vegetable and flower crops. You should have some idea of which crops were most popular last year.

It may be a good idea to remain small for the next few years but by the fourth year you should decide whether to remain small or expand. Most important, look at the economics of what you have been doing. If your clientele has been steadily increasing and you often sell out of produce, then you should consider expanding your operation. That is, of course, if you can manage expenses and make a profit while expanding. It's also important to consider your quality of life because the satisfaction of producing a good crop won't be enough of a reward if the pressures of dealing with the public and paying off the bank are too much. We can't control the weather, so ask yourself what you would do if a freeze or flood destroyed your production for a season, what contingency plans could you make, and would you have enough reserve cash to get by for a few months or even for a season? Because these emergencies can occur, an operation with a large retail market offers the best security—you can always buy good produce elsewhere to stock your roadside market until you can get back into production after a disaster.

The PYO orchard's main attribute is its labor savings. Most clients also find that it is fun. Visiting the PYO can be an outing or even a picnic; it's a time for your customer's kids to get out and play—assuming that you've provided the facilities. Chances are good that the experience will make them want to come back, even if it is easier to go to the grocery store. The produce doesn't even have to be much of a bargain. Most PYO orchards charge close to retail price. After all, not only does the customer get to pick the best, most fresh produce, but they also get to experience the fun of the harvest.

Choosing to market pick-your-own produce will have an affect on which crops you should grow. Some fruits, like strawberries and peaches, are commonly frozen or made into jelly, so sales of large quantities to individual customers is likely. Other fruits, such as grapes and citrus, are more commonly bought in smaller quantities and therefore may not be as well suited to a pick-your-own marketing plan. The same is true for vegetable crops.

Just remember you are relying on unskilled labor. Transport them to the field and point out the ripest fruit. If you don't make the effort to get your clients started, they will wander through the orchard or fields picking green fruit until they find the ripe fruit. Then they will dump the green fruit and start over. Some of your income will immediately begin to decompose on the orchard floor. It is wise to give your customers instructions for picking fruit before they go to the field. Some of this information can be repeated on signs in the field. Be sure to provide picking containers and bags—very few customers will remember to bring them. Some sort of concession stand is absolutely necessary. Shaded water and rest facilities are also a good idea. You will also need to provide temporary toilets, especially during the harvest season.

There are some basic business policies the PYO grower should use. Charging for produce by the pound rather than by volume is the best method, so you will need accurate scales. Most PYO growers have found that it is better to keep prices high—at retail levels or even higher—and spend more time and money on advertising. (Once you lower your prices it's hard to go back up.) You will have to grow high-quality produce and do a lot of promotion, especially when you're getting started. Once people find out about the quality of your fruits and vegetables new customers will learn about your operation from others, similar to the way the restaurant industry operates.

Your PYO must be at a convenient location. Being located on a major highway is ideal, but if you are a few miles off of the highway and you produce high-quality fruit people will find you, provided you give them a little help. More than half of your customers are likely to come from 25 miles or less. Although it is imperative that you plant on good agricultural land, it may be even more important that you are located close to a large population center. The following promotion ideas apply mostly to the PYO farming operation, but some of them can also be used to promote roadside stand marketing.

- Try to get free coverage in local newspapers and on radio and TV. Good fruit and the fun people will have harvesting it is a legitimate story. Send the local media a box of fruit, pictures, and any promotional material you may have.
- Advertise. Small, local papers will probably be the best medium to use. Advertising in larger papers and on radio may be the next move. Don't

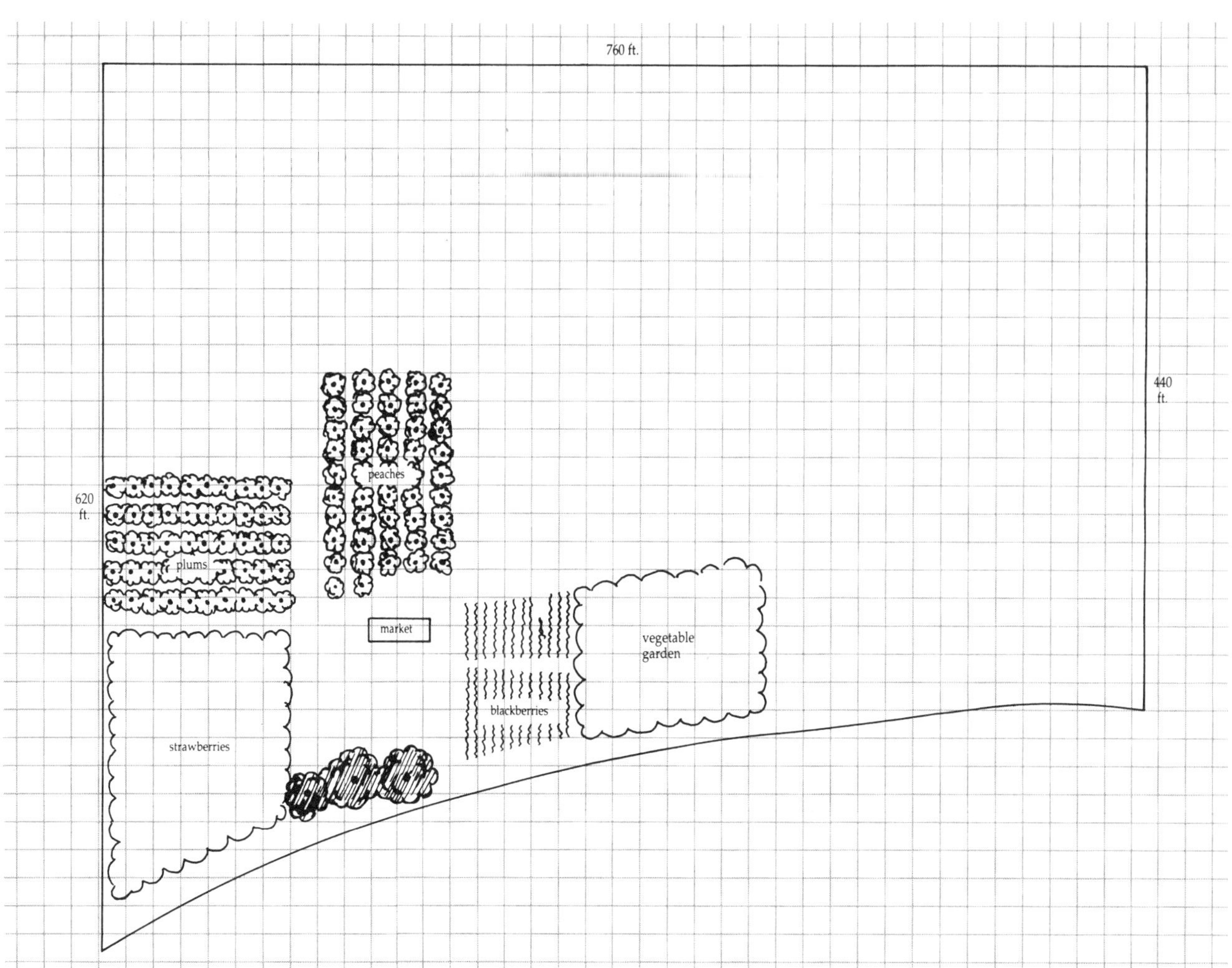

Plan for a 10-acre pick-your-own orchard. Initial planting of ½ acre peaches, ½ acre plums, ½ acre blackberries, ½ acre vegetables, and ¾ strawberries.

overdo it. You don't want more people at the farm than you have produce to satisfy.

- Put up attractive signs. Use billboards if possible, but be sure that they are done professionally. Slapping some paint on a piece of plywood may discourage potential customers or suggest that you've made a similar effort in growing your produce. Also put up smaller, directional signs along the route. Customers that have been lost in the woods for several hours will automatically be disgruntled by the time they find you.
- Put a lecture together and make sure to include slides. Garden clubs, civic clubs, and service clubs (such as Rotary) are anxious to hear from new speakers.
- Offer educational tours for elementary schools. The kids will get excited about seeing the developing fruit and will probably encourage their parents to bring them back.
- Set up a message machine on a special PYO number to tell people what produce is available and how to get to the farm.
- Have postcards ready for customers to fill out before they leave the farm. You will mail these

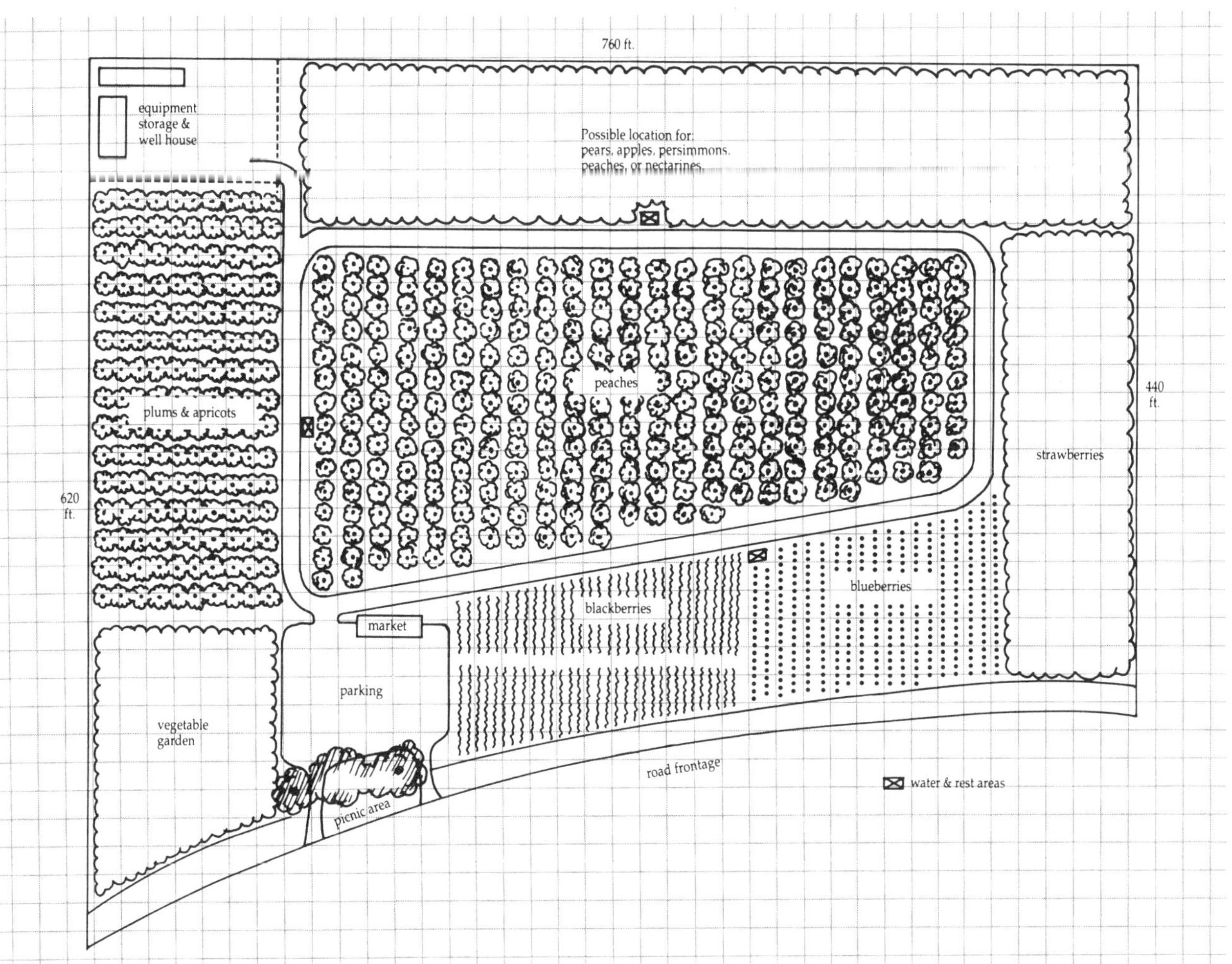

Possible plan for a 10-acre pick-your-own orchard.

out to them before next year's harvest begins and use them to develop a mailing list on a computer. If you expect to have fall crops, ask if they would like to fill out a separate card for a reminder about these crops.

- Make up a good map showing the way to the farm and print it on everything—business cards, reminder cards, stationery, T-shirts. The shirts may not need to include a map, but if they are printed with a striking design they can become another method of advertising your farm.
- Consider offering canning supplies (make sure they are competitively priced), processed goods (jelly, relish, hot sauce, and other condiments), crafts, and cookbooks. Most of all, be friendly and make your PYO a fun place to visit. People will return again and again if they remember your smiles and courtesy.
- Offer customers recipes that use the types of fruits and vegetables you grow. If your customers know how to make more than one or two dishes with your produce, they will buy larger quantities.

appendices

Sources for Fruit and Nut Catalogs, Supplies, and Information

It's frustrating to read about a luscious fruit and then be unable to locate a source for it. To some degree this is always going to be a problem; newly discovered varieties take a long time to get into catalogs.

Organizations like the North American Fruit Explorers (write them at Rt. 1, Box 94, Chapin, IL, 62628), who publish the quarterly *Pomona* can connect growers with other fruit enthusiasts who may be able to help them locate new, antique, and other hard-to-find varieties. The Southern Fruit Fellowship (address queries to David E. Ulmer, P.O. Box 14606, Santa Rosa, CA 95402) is a spinoff of the North American Fruit Explorers, who are dedicated to serving the interests of the southern grower. The California Rare Fruit Growers, Inc. (write them at The Fullerton Arboretum, California State University, Fullerton, CA, 92634) is also worth joining, particularly for growers who are interested in semitropical fruits. The Northern Nut Growers Association is also a helpful organization. Their interests aren't as limited as their name suggests and their publications are full of good propagation articles. To apply for membership contact: Northern Nut Growers Association, Kenneth Bauman, Treasurer, 9870 South Palmer Road, New Carlisle, OH 45344.

All of these organizations are open to anyone. All also offer publications and hold regular meetings. The Northern American Fruit Explorers (NAFEX) has an annual meeting, the Southern Fruit Fellowship meets twice a year, and the California group meets annually in addition to holding regional and local group meetings.

The following listing of nursery catalogs is a brief guide to sources for southern growers. However, be aware that there are many fine local nurseries that go to great extremes to make locally adapted fruit and nut trees available to their clientele, but that do not ship mail order. Always check local sources for the majority of your fruit tree needs whenever possible.

Adams Co. Nursery, Inc.
P.O. Box 108
Aspers, PA 17304
(717) 677-8105
Free catalog. Obviously this is a northern nursery, but also a source for rootstocks. Many of the fruit varieties they offer will grow in much of the South.

Ahrens Strawberry Nursery
Route 1
Huntingburg, IN 47542
Free catalog. Good-quality strawberry plants available in the fall (September to November). Before ordering check to see if plants are available from them in the fall.

Allen Co.
P.O. Box 1577
Salisbury, MD 21801
Free catalog. Primarily a source for strawberry plants, but like Ahrens they also offer other berry plants.

Alliance Nursery
Route 1, Box 433
Marianna, FL 32446
Free list. New mail-order source for southern fruit varieties. Includes many locally "discovered" varieties. Offers Duckworth strain of pawpaw.

Amberg's Nursery, Inc.
3164 Whitney Road
Stanley, NY 14561
(716) 526-5405
Free catalog. Features tools and supplies for vineyards and other crops that use trellises.

Anderson Die and Manufacturing
2425 Southeast Moores Street
Portland, OR 97222
(503) 654-5629
Free wholesale price list. Supplier of growing containers for air pruning.

Applesource
Tom Vorbeck
Route 1
Chapin, IL 62628
(217) 245-7589
Free catalog. This isn't a source for fruit trees, but rather a source for apples. Many of the varieties they offer are antique or new types. Ordering from this catalog is a great way to try fruit that you may be years away from producing yourself or that you may not be able to grow due to a high-chilling requirement. Order an Explorer pack and you'll get two apples in six varieties. They may be small and russeted—or even downright ugly—but chances are they will be tasty. Have friends over for a tasting party. If you like you can order pick-your-own variety boxes that have more than 80 varieties to choose from.

Bass Pecan Company
P.O. Box 42
Lumberton, MS 39455
(601) 796-2461
Free catalog. Long-time supplier of pecan trees for growers in the South.

Berry Country Farms
P.O. Box 657
Brownsboro, TX 75756
(903) 882-3550
Free list. Berry specialist, particularly the BaBa berry (raspberry).

Bob Wells Nursery
P.O. Box 606
Lindale, TX 75771
(903) 882-3550
Supplier of southern fruit varieties—especially stone fruits.

Burns Pecan Nursery
P.O. Box 362
Ballinger, TX 76821
Free list. Offers the new Pecan variety Pawnee and others.

C.D. Nursery
P.O. Box 137
Monticello, FL 32344
(904) 997-2988
Free list. Source for Elliott, Cape Fear, and Sumner pecan varieties.

C. & C. Nursery
100 North McKenzie Street
Foley, AL 36535
(205) 943-8662
Free list. Patent rights on the Jubilee pecan.

Chestnut Hill Nursery
Route 1, Box 341
Alachua, FL 32615
(904) 462-2820
Fax: (904) 462-4330
Free catalog. Primarily a source of Dunstan chestnuts. They also offer a selection of Asian persimmons.

Cockrell's Riverside Nursery
Route 2, Box 76
Goldthwaite, TX 76844
(915) 938-5575
Free catalog. Wide selection of pecan varieties, including Pawnee and Forkert. Also has a selection of fruit trees.

Cottle Nursery
Route 1 Box 6
Faison, NC 28341
(919) 267-4531
Free list. This is a strawberry plant nursery that can provide rooted tip cuttings for fall planting. Unrooted tip cuttings are cost effective because they can also be purchased and rooted by the grower (closer to home), which eliminates the high shipping costs for transporting rooted plantlets in flats. Plants produced this way are much like the bedding plant plugs that greenhouse producers use to grow annuals. They have been shown to grow vigorously in the fall, whereas larger plants that are dug bareroot require considerable care, including overhead sprinkler irrigation, to overcome transplant shock.

Cumberland Valley Nurseries, Inc.
P.O. Box 471
McMinnville, TN 37110
1-800-492-0022 (out-of-state)
(615) 668-4153 (in-state)
Free list. This nursery was established in 1902. It is a source for many peach, nectarine, and plum varieties.

Dellwood Nursery
905 West Peachtree Avenue
Foley, AL 36535
(205) 943-8698

Free list. Discovered and propagates the Surprise pecan.

Edible Landscaping
P.O. Box 77
Afton, VA 22920
(804) 361-9134
Free catalog. This is a fascinating catalog full of interesting and difficult-to-find fruits. For example, they are a good source for hardy kiwis (unfortunately, they don't like summers in the lower South), pawpaws, jujubes, Asian persimmons, citrus, raspberries, juneberries (Amelanchier), blueberries, figs, and mulberries.

Finch Blueberry Nursery
P.O. Box 699
Bailey, NC 27807
(919) 235-4664
Free catalog. Another specialist in southern blueberry varieties.

Florida's Vineyard Nursery
P.O. Box 300
Orange Lake, FL 32681
(904) 591-2525
Free catalog. Source for many southern fruits, but especially muscadine grapes.

Forestry Suppliers Inc.
P.O. Box 8397
Jackson, MS 39284-8397
1-800-647-5368
Fax: 1-800-543-4203
Supplier of pruning tools, spray equipment, safety clothing, etc.

Gempler's
P.O. Box 270
Mt. Horeb, WI 53572
1-800-382-8473
Fax: 608-437-5383
Free catalog. Supplier of tools, safety, and work clothing.

Hastings Seed and Nursery Co.
P.O. Box 115535
Atlanta, GA 30310
(404) 524-8861
Free catalog. Offers fruit and nut varieties and vegetable and flower seeds for the South.

Ison's Nursery and Vineyard
Route 1, Box 191
Brooks, GA 30205
(404) 599-6970
Free catalog. This catalog is the premier source for new muscadine varieties. Also offers other fruits and irrigation supplies.

J-M Trading Corp.
241 Frontage Road, Suite 47
Burr Ridge, IL 60521
(708) 655-3305
1-800-323-7638
Fax: (708) 655-0463
Supplier of hand tools—pruning shears, budding and grafting knives.

Just Fruits
Route 2, Box 4818
Crawfordville, FL 32327
(904) 926-5644
Free catalog. Large assortment of interesting fruits adapted to the lower South. New introductions from the University of Florida are often available as are old home varieties like the Golden Boy pear. They offer unusual fruits and nuts like the chestnut, avocado, banana, black walnut, thornless cactus, jujube, mayhaw, olive, pawpaw, pineapple guava, and pomegranate.

Lario Co.
P.O. Box 2084
Mobile, AL 36652
(205) 457-7661
Fax: (205) 452-7538
Free wholesale price list. Containers for production of air-pruned seedlings.

Lawson's Nursery
Route 1, Box 473 (294)
Yellow Creek Road
Ball Ground, GA 30107
(404) 893-2141
Free catalog. Specialist in unusual and antique apple varieties.

L. E. Cooke Co.
26333 Road 140
Visalia, CA 93277
(209) 732-9146
Free wholesale catalog. Growers of a number of low-chilling fruit varieties. Source for chip budding tape.

A. M. Leonard, Inc.
6665 Spiker Road
P.O. Box 816
Piqua, OH 45356
This company offers no fruit or nut plants, but is a source for many of the tools growers need—grafting knives, pruning equipment, budding tape, shovels, and others.

Lewis Strawberry Nursery, Inc.
P.O. Box 24
Rocky Point, NC 28457
Extensive listing of strawberry plants, including varieties for the South.

Louisiana Nursery
Route 7, Box 43
Opelousas, LA 70570
(318) 948-3696
(318) 942-6404
Offers the "Magnolias and other garden

aristocrats" catalog. Extensive nursery listings with several catalogs. Limited fruit and nut listings, but offers a few surprising choices like Gehron seedless native persimmon and the Mitchell pawpaw.

Mellinger's
2310 West South Range Road
North Lima, OH 44452-9731
(216) 549-9861
Fax: (216) 549-3716
Phone orders: 1-800-321-7444
Free catalog. Full-range nursery with some fruit and nut trees (most adapted to the North). Also has a good assortment of pruning and propagation tools and supplies.

Mize Pecan Company
12005 Eucalyptus
San Antonio, TX 78245
(512) 679-7165
Free list. Offers pecan graftwood (scions), plus a variety of grafting and pruning tools.

Mueller Supply Company, Inc.
301 West Avenue G
Midlothian, TX 76065
(214) 775-3412
Fax: (214) 775-6313
Phone orders: 1-800-272-9920
Supplier of steel products, such as siding and wire.

New York Fruit Testing Co-op.
P.O. Box 462
North Street
Geneva, NY 14456
(315) 787-2205
Free catalog. Source for rootstocks and new varieties, especially for the upper South.

Nolin River Nut Tree Nursery
797 Port Wooden Road
Upton, Kentucky 42784
(502) 369-8551
Offers a variety of English (Persian) Walnut varieties, one of the largest selections of improved black walnuts in the country, heartnuts, Northern pecan varieties, hicans, hickories, chestnuts, and American persimmon varieties.

North Star Gardens
2124 University Avenue
St. Paul, MN 55114-1838
(612) 433-5850
Fax: 612-227-0022
Free catalog. A northen nursery that offers a large assortment of raspberries, some of which are worth trying in southern gardens.

Oberhellmann, Inc.
Willow City, TX 78675
Free list. Offers fruit grower supplies—sprayers, pruners, loppers, bird-scare devises, trellises, and tying supplies.

Orange Heights Pecan Nursery
Route 2, Box 126-H
Hawthorne, FL 32640
(904) 468-1573
Free wholesale price list. Source for Elliott and Curtis pecan varieties.

Orchard Equipment and Supply Co.
Route 116
P.O. Box 540
Conway, MA 01341
(413) 369-4335
Free catalog. Features spraying, pruning, and processing equipment.

Oregon Exotics—Rare Fruit Nursery
1065 Messinger Road
Grants Pass, OR 97527
(503) 846-7578
Free catalog. A northern nursery, but they have an extensive listing of unusual citrus, a good selection of berries, Asian pears, persimmons, figs, pineapple guavas (Feijoa), and loquats.

Oregon Rootstock, Inc.
10906 Monitor-McKee Road NE
Woodburn, OR 97071
(503) 654-5629
Wholesale only, but worth knowing about if you plan to establish your own orchard by budding.

Owens Vineyard and Nursery
Georgia Highway 85
Gay, GA 30218
Free catalog. Specializes in muscadine grapes and blueberries.

Pacific Tree Farms
4301 Lynwood Drive
Chula Vista, CA 92010
(619) 422-2400
Catalog has an extensive list of tropical and semitropical fruits.

Papaya Tree Nursery
12422 El Oro Way
Granada Hills, CA 91344
(818) 363-3680
Free list. Another source of tropical and semitropical varieties.

Rainbow Star Nursery
2324 Southwest 36th Terrace
Gainesville, FL 32607
(904) 378-4681
Has standard fruits like apples, pears, and peaches, but is especially valuable for the many Asian persimmons.

Signal Education Aids
2314 Broadway
Denver, CO 80205
(303) 295-0479
(303) 296-1030
Free list. Supplier of Starling and other bird distress calls.

Simpson Nurseries
P.O. Box 160
Monticello, FL 32344
(904) 997-2516
Fax: (904) 997-2518
Phone orders: 1-800-874-3571
Free list. Features a good assortment of pecan varieties adapted to the Southeast including: Curtis, Elliot, Kernodle, Cape Fear, Forkert, Gloria Grande, Jackson, Melrose, Pawnee, and Sumner. Also a good selection of southern fruit varieties.

Southmeadow Fruit Gardens (Grootendorst)
Lakeside, MI 49116
(616) 469-2865
Source for rootstocks (especially small quantities) and antique apple varieties.

Sherwood's Greenhouses
P.O. Box 6
Sibley, LA 71073
(318) 377-3653
Send stamped envelope for list. Source for selected (budded) mayhaws, pears, jujubes and other fruits adapted to the South.

Stark Bro's Nurseries & Orchards Co
P.O. Box 10
Louisiana, MO 63353-0010
1-800-325-4180
Fax: (314) 754-5290
Free catalog. Offers many varieties of fruit, but not much for the lower South. One of the few nurseries to still work with interstems and multiple variety trees.

Sunset Vineyard and Nursery
Route 1, Box 535
Sunset, TX 76270
(817) 845-2821
Free list. Good selection of trellis supplies.

Sunsweet Berry & Fruit Nursery
Box D
Sumner, GA 31789
(912) 386-8400
Free catalog. Standard listing of southern fruits.

Treesearch Farms
7625 Alabonson Road
Houston, TX 77088
(713) 937-9811
Free list. Features fruit varieties adapted to the Gulf Coast.

Texas Pecan Nursery
P.O. Box 306
Chandler, TX 75758
(214) 849-6203
Free List. Offers mostly pecans and some fruit trees.

Womack's Nursery Co.
Route 1, Box 80
De Leon, TX 76444-9660
(817) 893-6497
Free catalog. Good selection of fruits, berries, and pecans. Propagates and tests many of Dr. Shreve's English walnut varieties. Also offers nursery and orchard tools.

Sources for Organic, Low-toxicity Pesticides, Traps, and Beneficial Insects

AgriSense
4230 West Swift Avenue
Fresno, CA 93722
(209) 276-4250

Alternatives
3439 East 86th Street
Suite 259
Indianapolis, IN 46240
(317) 823-0432

Arizona Biological Control
P.O. Box 4247 CRB
Tucson, AZ 85738
(602) 825-9785

Beneficial Bugs
P.O. Box 1627
Apopka, FL 32703-1627
(305) 886-2386

Beneficial Insectary
245 Oak Run Road
Oak Run, CA 96069
(916) 472-3715

Bio-Resources
1210 Birch Street
Santa Paula, CA 93060
(805) 525-0526

BioLogic
418 Briar Lane
Chambersburg, PA 17201
(717) 263-2789

Biotactics, Inc.
7765 Lakeside Drive
Riverside, CA 92509
(714) 685-7681

Burgess Seed & Plant Co.
Department 91
905 Four Season Road
Bloomington, IL 61701
(309) 663-9551

Burpee Seed Company
300 Park Avenue
Warminster, PA 18974
(215) 674-4900

California Green LaceWings
P.O. Box 2495
Merced, CA 95341
(209) 722-4985

Clyde Robins Seed Co.
3670 Enterprise Avenue
Hayward, CA 94545
(415) 785-0425

Fairfax Biological Laboratories, Inc.
Clinton Corners, NY 12514
(914) 266-3705

Farmers Seed & Nursery
Department 71
1706 Morrissey Drive
Bloomington, IL 61704
(309) 663-9551

Foothill Agricultural Research, Inc.
510 West Chase Drive
Corona, CA 91720
(714) 371-0120

Gardens Alive
(Natural Gardening Research Center)
Highway 48, P.O. Box 149
Sunman, IN 47041
(812) 623-3800

Gardener's Supply
128 Intervale Road
Burlington, VT 05401
(802) 863-1700

Gerhart's
Avon Belden Road
North Ridgeville, OH 44039
(216) 327-8056

Harmony Farm Supply
P.O. Box 451
Graton, CA 95444
(707) 823-9125

Henry Field Seed & Nursery Co.
407 Sycamore Street
Shenandoah, IA 51602
(605) 665-4451

Integrated Orchard Management
821 North Stevenson Street
Visalia, CA 93291
(209) 625-5199

Miller Nursery
5060 West Lake Road
Canandaiqua, NY 14424
(716) 396-2647

National Gypsy Moth Management Group
Road 1, Box 715
Landisburg, PA 17040
(717) 789-3434

National Pest Controls
8864 Little Creek Drive
Orangevale, CA 95662
(916) 726-0855

Nationwide Seed & Supply
4801 Fengenbush Lane
Louisville, KY 40228
(502) 499-0115

Nature's Control
P.O. Box 35
Medford, OR 97501
(503) 899-8318

Necessary Trading Co.
P.O. Box 603
New Castle, VA 24127
(703) 864-5103

Nemates
P.O. Box 758
San Leandro, CA 94577

OrCon, Inc.
5132 Venice Boulevard
Los Angeles, CA 90019
(213) 937-7444

Organic Pest Management
P.O. Box 55267
Seattle, WA 98155
(206) 367-0707

Peaceful Valley Farm Supply
11173 Peaceful Valley Road
Nevada City, CA 95959
(916) 265-3276

Pest Management Supply, Inc.
P.O. Box 938
Amherst, MA 01004
1-800-272-7672

Plant Sciences, Inc.
514 Calabasas Road
Watsonville, CA 95076
(408) 728-7771

Reuter Laboratories
P.O. Box 551648
Dallas, TX 75355-1648

Richard Owen Nursery
Department 36
2300 East Lincoln Street
Bloomington, IL 61701
(309) 663-9551

Rincon-Witona Insectaries, Inc.
P.O. Box 95
OakView, CA 93022
(805) 643-5407

Sespe Creek Insectary
1400 Grand Avenue
Fillmore, CA 93015
(805) 524-3565

Spalding Laboratories
760 Printz Road
Arroyo Grande, CA 93420
(805) 489-5946

Troy Hygro Systems
4096 CTHES
East Troy, WI 53120
(414) 642-5928

Unique Insect Control
5504 Sperry Drive
Citrus Heights, CA 95621
(916) 961-7945

West Coast Ladybug Sales
P.O. Box 903
Gridley, CA 95948
(916) 534-0840

Wilk, Kitayama, and Mead
9093 Troxel Road
Chico, CA 95928
(916) 895-8424

State Extension Horticulture Offices

Virtually every county or parish has an extension agent that can assist you with variety selection and specific information on fruit culture. Listed below are the addresses for the extension horticulture departments at the various land grant universities in the southern states.

Alabama

Extension Horticulture
Department
Auburn University
Auburn, AL 36849
(205) 826-4985

Arizona

Extension Horticulture
Department of
Plant Science
University of Arizona
Tucson, AZ 85721
(602) 621-1400

Arkansas

Extension Horticulture
316 Plant Science Building
University of Arkansas
Fayetteville, AR 72701
(501) 572-2603

California

Extension Horticulture
Department of Pomology
University of California
Davis, CA 95616
(916) 752-0124

Florida

Extension Horticulture
Fruit Crop Department
University of Florida
Gainesville, FL 32611
(904) 392-4711

Georgia

Extension Horticulture
University of Georgia
Athens, GA 30602
(404) 844-4000

Kentucky

Extension Horticulture
Agriculture Science
Center North
Room N-318
University of Kentucky
Lexington, KY 40546
(606) 257-5685

Louisiana

Extension Horticulture
Room 155 J.C. Miller
Horticulture Building
Louisiana State University
Baton Rouge, LA 70803
(504) 388-2222

Mississippi

Extension Horticulture
P.O. Box 5446
Mississippi, MS 39762
(601) 325-3935

New Mexico

Extension Horticulture
P.O. 38E
New Mexico State
University
Las Cruces, NM 88003
(505) 646-2921

North Carolina

Extension Horticulture
Department of Horticulture
Science
North Carolina State
University
Raleigh, NC 27695-7609
(919) 737-3322

Oklahoma

Extension Nut/Fruit
Oklahoma State University
Stillwater, OK 74078
(405) 624-8685

South Carolina

Extension Horticulture
161 P & A S Building
Clemson University
Clemson, SC 29634-0375
(803) 766-3412

Texas

Extension Horticulture
225 Horticulture/Forestry
Building
Texas A&M University
College Station, TX 77843
(409) 845-7341

Virginia

Extension Horticulture
Virginia Polytechnic
Institute
Blacksburg, VA 24061
(703) 961-6723

West Virginia

Extension Horticulture
2088 Agricultural Science
Building
P.O. Box 6108
West Virginia University
Morgantown, WV
26506-6108
(304) 293-4801

index

R

S

T

V

W

Y